The Benedictine Order in the United States

The Benedictine Order in the United States

An Interpretive History

Joel Rippinger, O.S.B.

THE LITURGICAL PRESS
COLLEGEVILLE, MINNESOTA

Cover photo courtesy New Melleray Abbey, Peosta, Iowa.
Cover design by David Manahan, O.S.B.

Library of Congress Cataloging-in-Publication Data

Rippinger, Joel, 1948–
    The Benedictine Order in the United States : an interpretive
history / Joel Rippinger.
        p.   cm.
    Includes bibliographical references and index.
    ISBN 0-8146-1817-0
    1. Benedictines—United States—History.   I. Title.
BX3008.R56 1990
271'.1073—dc20

90-44480
CIP

Contents

Acknowledgments

In writing this history of the Benedictine Order in the United States, I was assisted by many members of that same monastic family. Heading the list of persons deserving of acknowledgment are the monks of Marmion Abbey, Aurora, Illinois. For many years they have exhibited a typically Benedictine tolerance toward a confrere given to sometimes strange habits of historical research and writing. Special recognition must also be given to the monks of the Priorato de San José in Sololá, Guatemala, who provided me with the space and personal freedom to complete most of the writing of this history.

The final form of this volume owes much to four Benedictines who reviewed the history in manuscript form. Fathers Colman Barry, Terrence Kardong, Paschal Baumstein, and Sister Claire Lynch provided perceptive historical judgment, specific suggestions for improvements in style and content, and a useful critical perspective. I am deeply grateful for their contribution.

Any attempt to single out individual Benedictine archivists would run the risk of omission. Instead, I would prefer to underline the invaluable assistance of those too frequently overlooked Benedictine women and men in communities throughout North America whose generous sharing of time, written sources, and photos helped bring this enterprise to its completion. A substantial debt of gratitude is owed to those Benedictine authors whose histories of individual communities offered me a needed reference point and sense of direction.

Rather than affix a litany of names and Benedictine institutions that have contributed to the realization of this work, I will simply express my sincere thankfulness for the characteristically monastic response of humble and generous service that greeted my requests.

Various resources outside the Benedictine family significantly aided me in my research. Financial grants from the Cushwa Center for the Study of American Catholicism at the University of Notre Dame, as well as the staff of the archives of that University, afforded a setting and assistance that were most appreciated. Personnel at a number of European archives during the decade of the seventies—Propaganda Fide in Rome and the Ludwig-Missionsverein in Munich in particular—opened up windows of investigation essential to the first part of this history. I also need to cite the example and support of Monsignor John Tracy Ellis, who graciously directed my first foray into historical writing during the seventies and whose own model of historical scholarship through the years has served as an inspiration.

Among the anonymous acknowledgments that merit inclusion are the circle of friends who for so long have constituted a base of support for my interest in Benedictine history and spirituality. Their prayers and unflagging encouragement have done much to generate this present project and many others.

Two members of that network of friends, Michael and Karen Muzzy, offered generous amounts of time and labor in seeing the final manuscript through the word-processing stage. For their assistance I am most grateful.

Finally, I need to mention with deepest affection my parents and immediate family, who have nurtured my Benedictine vocation from its beginning and have contributed immeasurably to the completion of this work by their faithful example and unwavering support.

Preface

The impulse to chronicle the growth and development of religious communities and congregations in the life of the Church has been a trademark of the Benedictine Order for many centuries. From the Venerable Bede's landmark *Ecclesiastical History of the English People*, through the long succession of medieval chronicles and customaries, on to the commemorative community histories of our own time, countless monastic historians have documented and commented on the times in which they lived. The Benedictines who first came to America in the nineteenth century adapted and discarded many traits of European monasticism; but one characteristic they retained and nurtured was the desire to leave a record of their labors. That historical record can be discovered, albeit in uneven layers, in the archives and published histories of many Benedictine communities in the United States today. It is a record that has been the beneficiary of an array of accounts, ranging from that of the amateur compiler of daily activity to that of the professional historian. Most of that record, however, has been devoted to the description of individual communities or of particular monastic figures.[1] Helpful as these commemorative volumes and biographical works have been in delineating the historical record, they remain limited in their scope.

The larger task of producing a synthetic work that attempts to integrate the story of the broader experience of Benedictine men and women in the United States with the history of the American Catholic

Church awaits completion. It is a task in some ways comparable to that attempted by monastic historians of recent years who have studied the Benedictine Order in a more global perspective.[2] It is certainly one that can draw upon the new advances in American Catholic historiography and the previously mentioned histories of monastic communities in the United States. However, it seems evident that there is a need for a new interpretive framework in which such a history must be presented. Given the wide scope of such a project and the more difficult challenge of assessing facts rather than merely reporting them, it is understandable why historians might approach such an undertaking with more than a little wariness. In accepting such a challenge, however, one is fortified by the knowledge that his or her work may serve as a stimulus for other monastic historians.

The story of monastic life in the United States in the last century and a half appears as rich and variegated as the Benedictine tradition itself. It is to be expected, therefore, that there will be a diversity of interpretations in recounting and evaluating this story. The interpretive perspective I bring to this task is a decidedly personal one. Having been a member of an American monastic community for over two decades, I have sampled some of the variety of American Benedictine life through individual study, travel, and ministry. I have been fortunate in having been given the opportunity to peruse the primary sources of archival records. In a more informal fashion, I have attempted to listen to many monastic voices over the years as they communicated the history of the oral tradition. Nonetheless, I realize that I can provide only a partial history of the Benedictine Order in the United States. If this subjective perspective proves to be inadequate for the readers of this work, I ask their indulgence. I also hope that any oversights and shortcomings of analysis will be corrected by those who are able to bring their own expertise and experience to a history whose richness deserves renewed exposition and interpretation.

CHAPTER 1

European Roots

The first requisite for understanding the genesis and growth of Benedictine life in the United States is a comprehension of its close connections with European monastic tradition. In much the same way as the history of the American Catholic Church is inextricably linked to its European Catholic heritage, so is the history of Benedictinism in the "New World" linked to its roots in the "Old World."

There have been few periods in the history of European monasticism that have witnessed the type of transformation that took place in the course of the nineteenth century. At the beginning of that century an overwhelming tide of social and political change had reduced the number of active Benedictine houses to their lowest number in over a millennium. The French Revolution, the ensuing devastation of the Napoleonic Wars in Austria and Italy, the hostile reform governments that developed in Spain and Switzerland, the secularization effected by the princes of Germany—all contributed to a climate in which monastic life appeared as only a declining vestige of Europe's *ancien régime*.

In contrast to this nadir in the first decades of the century, we find a reformed, vigorous, and highly centralized monastic family spreading throughout the Western Hemisphere at the close of the century. What had transpired to bring about such a sweeping change? While acknowledging the effect of shifting political and intellectual

11

currents in Europe, one can still maintain that the changed scene was largely due to a handful of individuals who were founding and entering monastic houses and instilling these communities with a reforming zeal that was infectious.

Nineteenth-Century Reforms

In the vanguard of these reformers was Abbot Prosper Guéranger. As a diocesan priest, Guéranger had visited the ruins of the ancient abbey of Solesmes in France. After this experience he decided to found there a monastic community that would model itself after the medieval monastery of Cluny. In 1837 Pope Gregory XVI raised Solesmes to the rank of an abbey and named its founder as its first abbot. The monastery of Solesmes and the houses that it established as part of a new Benedictine congregation became models of monastic observance and liturgical expression for many like-minded reformers of the period.[1]

Among the many visitors to Solesmes were two other diocesan priests who were contemplating a similar return to a medieval model of monastic life. Maurus and Placid Wolter, blood brothers, had come to their decision during a stay at the abbey of St. Paul-Outside-the-Walls in Rome. After professing their vows as Benedictine monks in Rome in 1860, they returned to their home in Germany's Black Forest and established there the monastic community of Beuron in 1863. The Wolter brothers were supported in their enterprise by a distinguished array of patrons. Pope Pius IX, Princess Katherine of Hohenzollern, and the family of Desclée were among those who gave them spiritual and material backing. The abbey of Beuron soon began attracting many aspirants by its example of monastic observance and scholarship.[2] By the end of the century, monks from Beuron had spread throughout Europe, founding monasteries at Prague and Seckau in Eastern Europe, Maria Laach in Germany, Maredsous in Belgium, and Erdington in England.

While in Rome, the Wolters had encountered an Italian monk, Father Pietro Casaretto, who shared their desire for a return to primitive monastic observance. But Casaretto coupled this vision with one of a missionary form of monasticism that would spread throughout the world. One of the means by which he attempted to accomplish this was the erection of colleges in which monks would be prepared for missionary work. Casaretto saw his original college in Genoa expand to similar training schools in Subiaco and Rome.[3] In 1872 the reformed Italian Subiaco Congregation came into existence, and Casaretto was made abbot general. As superior of this new Congregation of Primitive Observance, he took the initiative in training and transporting monk-missionaries for service to a number of continents. The congregation eventually evolved into Italian, French, Spanish, and Anglo-Belgian branches and gained many monastic adherents to Casaretto's vision. Perhaps the most outstanding of these was a former parish priest from France, Father Jean-Baptiste Muard, who had become a monk at Subiaco in 1849. Originally having founded a society of diocesan missionaries, Muard was drawn to the same combination of a community life of strict observance and missionary activity once he learned more about the Benedictine Rule and way of life. He established an austere form of Benedictine monasticism at La Pierre-qui-Vire, a community that retained the missionary enthusiasm of its founder.[4]

Contemporaneously with Muard, a restored English Benedictine Congregation manifested a similar missionary impulse. Emanating from Downside Abbey in England, monks of this congregation promoted a monasticism that stressed both a return to spiritual sources and an active involvement in educational, parochial, and missionary work.[5] Such figures as Bishop William Ullathorne and Bishop Bede Polding became examples of this peculiarly English strain of monastic revival. Both were missionary bishops in Australia and built their monastic ideal on a return to the earliest expressions of missionary activity by the monks of the early Middle Ages.[6] It was an ideal eloquently related by Polding in an address to the general chapter of the English Benedictine Congregation in 1846:

> The mind naturally reverts to the period when men of God, the latchet of whose shoes we declare ourselves in all sincerity unworthy to touch, went forth from the Holy City at the bidding of Pope St. Gregory the Great, to the barbarous climes of Northern Europe, to establish

the first monastery of our Order in our native land. History has recorded how it spread and how under its meek influence numbers found repose and salvation; how it provided Pastors for our parishes, Bishops for the population of Episcopal Sees. We deem ourselves peculiarly favored by Almighty God, that we have been called upon to imitate the conduct of these heroic Apostles of England. . . .[7]

A similar missionary ideal evolved in the mind of a Swiss-born Beuronese monk, Abbot Andreas Amrhein. In 1884 he founded in Germany a Benedictine community whose exclusive purpose was foreign missionary work; this community was to evolve into the Congregation of St. Ottilien.[8] Amrhein's initial efforts in German East Africa eventually expanded to the reaches of Asia and North America. The sentiment that spurred his monastic vision is well summarized in a letter of another monastic missionary, Monsignor Gamboni, the apostle of Central Africa, who wrote in 1872 to Pietro Casaretto: "The holy Order that has civilized the Western world must also do its work in Central Africa. It is absolutely essential that you destine for it subjects who have grown up in the shadow of Sacro Speco, and who will then be able to give their spirit to the much-afflicted Negro world."[9] Such inspirational language reflected the relentless drive of the monastic revival in Europe as the nineteenth century came to a close.

The Components of Reform

What is one to make of the various streams that formed this monastic revival? A historian must first acknowledge the mixture of ideas and personalities that formed the missionary activity of the nineteenth century.[10] But then one must also ask whether these different strains of reform shared a common vision or emerged from a spiritual soil similar in its composition.

Certainly there were some common elements that were essential components of this reform. The nineteenth century was the apex of the romantic movement in European art, music, and literature; religion, too, could claim to be part of that movement. There are few better instances of monastic reflection of this than Montalembert's classic work, *Monks of the West*. In this perspective, the missionary heritage of the eighth and ninth centuries combined with the medieval liturgical ideal of Cluny to constitute a historic vision that gave rise to many of the ideas of the nineteenth century. As one contemporary historian has described it: "From Montalembert's *Monks of the West* (appearing in English for the first time in 1861) to Carlyle's *Past and Present*, the historical literature of the nineteenth century established the monastery as the antithesis of all the sordid side of industrial life and religious questioning."[11]

If one were to continue to capsulize the elements of this religious *Zeitgeist* as it appeared in Catholic Europe, one would have to mention the renewed forms of piety and a reassertion of papal authority. Either by calculation or coincidence, the monastic revival embraced both of these characteristics at its center.

The ecclesial vision of Solesmes and Beuron, the baroque and aristocratic background of so many Swiss, Austrian, and German communities, the political allegiance of Spanish and Italian monasteries, the entire European monastic tradition, which embodied so much of the aesthetical richness of the Church's past, were matched by a strict adherence to the teaching and authority of the papacy, particularly at a time under Pius IX when the papal office was undergoing insistent attack. This solidarity with Rome and the Holy Father was manifested almost without exception throughout the monastic order, and in turn helped to secure the Holy See's approbation of so much of the monastic missionary expansion.[12] The ultramontanist branch of the nineteenth-century European Church was epitomized in the abbatial style and theological mindset of such monastic figures as Guéranger and the Wolter brothers. This attitude showed its staying power even as it crossed the Atlantic Ocean; its strength is underscored in the words of Martin Marty, an abbot with a reputation as a maverick:

> So long as the Benedictines identified themselves with Rome, they fulfilled their mission; and if we are to achieve our destiny, we must again become fully one with the divine and infallible center. The demand of the present period is to ally ourselves completely to the life of the Church and to give up all decentralizing ideas and special in-

terests. Only Dupanloup and Döllinger can expect that this center
should gravitate toward us and accommodate itself to us.[13]

A highly centralized papal authority was not the only aspect of
Roman religiosity that found favor with the monastic order. The renewed tide of Marian piety that appeared in the nineteenth century
also used the monastic revival for its spread throughout Europe. It
does not appear accidental that many of the main centers of Marian
pilgrimage on the Continent were Benedictine monasteries: Montserrat (Spain), Altötting (Germany), Einsiedeln (Switzerland) and
Montevergine (Italy). Even as the different Benedictine communities integrated the various forms of this piety into their spiritual life,
they exported and popularized it for countless others in their pastoral and missionary labors.

The Missionary Thrust of Monastic Reform

The nineteenth century was also a period marked by a strong surge
of colonialism among the European powers. It is not overly difficult
to perceive the missionary thrust of Benedictine houses in these same
European countries—a religious expression of what some would describe as political imperialism, others a search for empire. The same
urge that drove countries to acquire colonies played a part in the missionary endeavors of European monasteries. Thus, monks from Metten and Einsiedeln sailed to America, Benedictines of Beuron to Brazil
and Latin America, French monks of La Pierre-qui-Vire to Africa,
and both Spanish and English Benedictines to the newly colonized
continent of Australia.[14]

This missionary momentum was sustained by the vividly written
Annales published by the Society for the Propagation of the Faith,
especially those that recounted the exploits and heroism of missionaries in North America. It was an initiative stimulated still more by
the fervent pleas of missionaries who made personal appearances and
mission appeals in European monasteries. Not all the itinerant missionaries won over their audiences. An early French missionary priest
to the United States, Father Stephen Badin, was turned down in his
request to have English Benedictine monks of the abbey of Douai

in England establish a monastic community in the backwoods of Kentucky.[15] Others had more success. A young priest named Father Peter Lemke, who had been among the first to recognize the needs of the German-speaking immigrants in Pennsylvania, decided to canvass religious communities in Germany.[16] In Munich he met Father Boniface Wimmer and offered him land in Pennsylvania. Wimmer, who would become the founder of the American Cassinese Congregation, arrived there in 1846. The famed missionary to the Plains Indians, the Belgian Jesuit Father Pierre De Smet, spoke at the Swiss abbey of Einsiedeln and elicited in a young monk named Martin Marty first thoughts of America and the need to bring a monastic presence to the Indians.[17]

Another indicator of the missionary spirit at work in nineteenth-century Europe was the emergence of immigrant aid societies that sought to assist missionary efforts with material support. The Ludwig-Missionsverein in Munich, the Leopoldine Stiftung in Vienna, and the Société pour la Propagation de la Foi in Lyons were institutional examples of how the Catholic Church in Europe was willing to support religious and educational efforts of missionaries, particularly those in the United States.[18] Alongside the growth of mission societies, there was an emergence of new missionary orders and an increase in the number of zealous missionaries willing to leave the convents and monasteries of Europe to minister to European immigrants throughout the world.[19]

The goal of planting monastic roots in North America was not entirely an altruistic one. King Ludwig I of Bavaria saw the restored Benedictine life of monasteries in Bavaria as a natural conduit for transmitting Germanic culture and language to German immigrants who had settled in the United States. In an even more pragmatic manner, the abbots of Einsiedeln and Engelberg, worried about the threatened closure of their communities by the Swiss state at the time of the Sonderbund War, looked to America as a possible political refuge for their monks. Similar motives were at work in countries where constitutional crackdowns against the Catholic Church threatened the continued existence of religious orders. Superiors of German monasteries were more willing to send missionaries overseas during the *Kulturkampf* in the 1870s, and the enforcement of the French laic laws led to the anomalous setting of ascetical French monks working on the Western frontier with American Indians.[20]

The missionary momentum of the nineteenth century did not rest exclusively with European abbeys. Benedictine superiors, particularly those of Germanic-speaking communities, were besieged by requests from bishops for personnel who could minister to the needs of the increasing number of immigrants settling in the United States.[21] Whether it was the Irish bishop Michael O'Connor of Pittsburgh, the Swiss bishop Martin Henni of Milwaukee, or the French bishop Maurice St. Palais of Vincennes, the requests of these prelates to Benedictine communities in Europe could be summarized in a common refrain: Send personnel to minister to the needs of the newly arrived immigrants, to provide them with schools for a Catholic education, to celebrate the sacraments and tend to their pastoral needs, to set up seminaries to train priests.

Immediate and pressing as this need appeared to be to the bishops of the fledgling American Catholic Church, and willing as many monks were to set sail from Europe as missionaries, not all abbots were eager to consent to such urgent requests. Wrote Father Josef Mueller, business manager of the Ludwig-Missionsverein, to Bishop Henni of Milwaukee in 1847: "If all the Benedictines in Europe who are so inclined could leave, half of them would emigrate; but the abbots are opposing this."[22]

One of the abbots who expressed such opposition was Gregory Scherr of the abbey of Metten in Bavaria. But he was confronted by a classmate and confrere whose determination to serve as a monk-missionary to America was not to be denied. It is with this monk-missionary, Boniface Wimmer, that the history of Benedictines in the United States begins.

CHAPTER 2

Boniface Wimmer and the Beginnings of American Benedictine Monasticism

In dealing with the history of Benedictines in the United States, we meet one person whose position, influence, and pervasive presence were dominant. The figure of Boniface Wimmer is one whose stamp remains imprinted upon the features of American Benedictine life more than a century after his departure from the scene.

A recent biography of Wimmer does justice to the oversized accomplishments of the man and the overriding influence he exerted on Benedictine life in the United States.[1] But the recounting of the saga of Wimmer's monastic and missionary odyssey bears reflection, for it sets the tone for most of the subsequent course of American Benedictine history.

Wimmer was a man whose life was a litany of contradictions. As a diocesan priest, he impulsively entered a Benedictine monastery. As a monk, he spent all but his novitiate on assignment outside the community during his fourteen years at Metten. While a lover of art, music, and European culture, he spent most of his years as a religious superior in the barely civilized regions of America's frontier. While a promoter of individual initiative and choice, he could ruthlessly squash the suggestions of any subordinate whose opinions were not in accord with his own.

In his early adult years as a monk at Metten and professor in Munich, Wimmer's colleagues derisively called him "Projecten-

Metten Abbey in Bavaria, founding house of St. Vincent Archabbey, Latrobe, Pennsylvania

Macher." He was indeed a man of many projects and plans, but during the years 1842 to 1846 those many projects were melded into one—becoming a missionary to America. Between the inception of this "project" and its accomplishment, however, there was a chasm that for most would have seemed unbridgeable.

By 1845 Wimmer had come to the conclusion that Metten's greatest contribution to the Catholic Church in the United States would not consist in establishing a house in Munich for the training of missionaries, but rather in founding an American Benedictine monastery. With that in mind, he personally petitioned the Propaganda Fide in 1845 for permission to leave Germany and to found such a monastery. In the summer of that same year Wimmer received replies from Rome and his own superior at Metten, Abbot Gregory Scherr. Both refused his request.[2]

20

For most persons, such refusals would have been more than enough to put a damper on any further missionary ambition. But Wimmer was already showing those personality traits that would later mark his missionary labors. With a resourcefulness and political acumen rare even in more seasoned members of the Church's hierarchy, he continued to plan for his American venture. He first won the good will of King Ludwig I and his court chaplain, Father Josef Mueller, thereby receiving assurance of funding for the project. He interceded with the papal nuncio to Bavaria, asking his help in securing approval of his plan from the Propaganda Fide. He went on a recruiting tour of southern Germany and by December 1845 had persuaded approximately twenty young men to accompany him. He had even

King Ludwig I
of Bavaria,
benefactor of
Boniface Wimmer
and the
American
Benedictines

taken the liberty to write to Peter Lemke in America, informing him
that he would be arriving in Pennsylvania by the autumn of 1846.
Wimmer went about all this activity knowing that he had not yet
won the approval of his abbot or Metten's monastic chapter for the
plan. His confreres at Metten, no doubt scandalized by the effron-
tery of the "Projecten-Macher," refused to give him permission to
found a monastery and gave only grudging approval to his plan to
go to America as a missionary. Wimmer responded with one of his
celebrated personal defenses, combining the single-mindedness and
the disdain for contrary opinions that would characterize his future
role:

> . . . if I cannot work [in America] as a Benedictine, I will go in an-
> other habit. . . . If you do not trust me to govern a monastery . . .
> then let another priest go with me. Something has to be done by us;
> of this I am firmly convinced. My way can be made more difficult,
> but it cannot be closed. I can be delayed and retarded, but not
> stopped. I can be persecuted with suspicion and distrust . . . but
> I will go my way because I freely believe that God wills it.[3]

The persistence, if not the eloquence, of Wimmer's crusading cry
seemed to move his abbot. For whatever combination of reasons,
by February 1846 Abbot Gregory Scherr had given his assent to Wimmer's plan.

The outline of that plan had already been given public prominence in an article Wimmer had written for the *Augsburger Postzeitung*
of November 8, 1845. In that article he consciously linked his efforts with those of Benedictine missionaries who had preceded him
a millennium earlier and described how "conditions in America today are like those of Europe 1000 years ago, when the Benedictine
Order attained its fullest development and effectiveness by its won-
derful adaptability and stability."[4]

Manifesting much more adaptability than stability, Wimmer set
out for the United States from Rotterdam on August 10, 1846. With
him were eighteen prospective candidates, fourteen so-called lay
brothers and four aspirants to the priesthood. Only one of them had
ever previously experienced life in a Benedictine monastery. In a
delightful irony, Wimmer, the monk whose Benedictine formation

had consisted of one year in the novitiate, took the opportunity of the six-week voyage to instruct his charges in the fundamentals of monastic life. The brand of monastic life taught by Wimmer as "truly Benedictine" was different than that considered "acceptable" by many European monasteries. As Wimmer expressed it in writing to his abbot:

> To the extent of my strength and influence, I shall never give in to the thought that Benedictines in the new world portray the sad role of isolation and egoistic seclusion that is now being enacted again in German monasticism. Many conflicting opinions must be reconciled. I have firm convictions and others will have to follow me.[5]

Wimmer displayed that "firm conviction" upon his arrival in Pennsylvania, when, frustrated upon discovering the poor condition of the land promised him by Peter Lemke in Carrolltown, Cambria County, he decided to accept the offer of Bishop Michael O'Connor of Pittsburgh for the parish of Mount Saint Vincent in Westmoreland County. Ironically, Wimmer's property was not far from where Archbishop John Carroll of Baltimore wanted to establish a monastery of English Benedictines and "good laborious lay brothers" in 1794.[6] It was there, in the fall of 1846, near the town of Latrobe, that Wimmer began implementing his plan of providing pastoral care and educational institutions for the German-speaking Catholics of the area. This plan included a decisive commitment to offer a monastic presence that preferred active service in behalf of the local community to contemplative isolation.

Within a year Wimmer was receiving reinforcements. Father Peter Lechner, a fellow Benedictine, brought over from Bavaria more than twenty candidates for the lay brotherhood as the nucleus of a work force. With these young recruits, the community of St. Vincent was assured of the rapid physical growth that Wimmer saw as vital to his monastery's effectiveness. Even in its beginnings, however, this growth was accompanied by discontent over the young superior's hard-charging manner of monastic life. It was a discontent reflected by Father Lechner and other less activist monks, and was to recur frequently at St. Vincent in its formative years.

Episcopal Confrontation

Wimmer's more immediate concerns were with another form of discontent that came from a higher source—the bishop of Pittsburgh himself. In the ensuing confrontation between these two figures, one can see the shape and force of Boniface Wimmer's leadership.

The conflict involved a number of issues: (1) the conditions for operating the seminary at St. Vincent; (2) the canonical exemption to which Wimmer believed he was entitled; (3) the operation of a brewery on monastic grounds; and (4) having St. Vincent raised to the status of an independent house, with Wimmer as superior.[7]

The dispute began after Wimmer had been at St. Vincent only a few months. Bishop O'Connor, in his position as Wimmer's ordinary, presented him with a contract stipulating, among other things, that Wimmer allow him to appoint the parish priests at St. Vincent, that the newly opened seminary be required to accept O'Connor's handpicked students, and that the Benedictines provide pastoral assistance for surrounding parishes and the local convent of the Sisters of Mercy.[8]

Wimmer, already accustomed to resisting episcopal pressure, stood firm and forced the bishop to ease the contract's conditions. O'Connor realized that he had run up against a man with powers of persuasion and persistence equal to his own. But St. Vincent's superior had gone too far when he allowed a brewery to be operated on community property. Once O'Connor received news of this, he spared no efforts in attacking the German monks and launching his own campaign to curb the independence of Wimmer:

> A superior of a Benedictine monastery here had the indulgence, if you please, to open a common public house or tavern of which he gave charge to a scape-grace of a nephew that he had who had robbed him of some money which he got for him from the Bavarian missionary society. . . . All I could say would not induce him to desist, until he saw that I refused to do anything towards confirming his monastery, a rescript authorizing me to do the same having arrived in the meantime. He then dropt the tavern and said he would go to Rome. . . . Instead of this he went to Germany and has been getting to the King of Bavaria and others, I suppose, to intercede to have

his monastery made an Abbey and thus set me in defiance. I hope that instead of a mitre and crozier he will get what he wants much more badly, a good lesson in the shameful manner in which he has acted, disregarding all I could say to him.[9]

The fact that O'Connor was Irish and Wimmer German, that the bishop of Pittsburgh was a strong temperance advocate and the Bavarian monk the son of a saloonkeeper was only part of the conflict. It was undoubtedly a confrontation between different languages and cultural viewpoints, but also an example of the opposing views of bishop and religious superior, similar in nature to the clashes between bishops and religious orders that were so much a part of this period of American Catholic history.

Even as Wimmer set out for Europe in 1851 to plead his case, O'Connor was writing to his own Benedictine contact in Rome, Abbot Bernard Smith, expressing his personal feeling about the matter:

> I am decidedly of the opinion that the Holy See would do a most useful if not necessary act by procuring a suitable person for superior from one of the good Benedictine monasteries in Germany, say Metten or Scheyern or Einsiedeln in Switzerland. Bishop Henni of Milwaukee gave me this opinion only a few days ago and told me that there are several excellent subjects in Einsiedeln who would be willing to come if their abbot permitted them. You would do us all an important piece of service if you would endeavor to work this for us.[10]

Such appeals to secure Wimmer's removal indicate how little the autonomy and freedom of religious houses in the United States meant at this time. What was uppermost in O'Connor's mind was maintaining exclusive authority in his diocese. He believed that this could only be assured by a clear affirmation of his authority in the face of Wimmer's independence. But despite O'Connor's constant stream of letters sent to Propaganda Fide from 1851 to 1857, either asking for Wimmer's removal or for the withholding of St. Vincent's exemption, he was rebuffed in his purpose.[11]

Meanwhile, far from backing down, Wimmer was in the process of brokering his own solution to the confrontation. In Germany he persuaded the members of the Ludwig-Missionsverein to bypass the bishop of Pittsburgh and distribute their aid directly to the German

parishes and religious communities of the diocese.[12] Through his con-
tacts in Rome, Wimmer lobbied for autonomous authority as a community with an independent superior. In his eyes, the question of
who was selected abbot was not as important as the question of freedom in the elective process. As he wrote to King Ludwig:

> It would be no penance for me if I did not become abbot. I never
> desired it, I never sought it. . . . If only they will treat the monas-
> tery well, I will be content. Otherwise, I would do what I threatened
> to do: I would leave the monastery and build a new one under a just
> bishop, one in which I could live my vocation in peace.[13]

It is difficult to ascertain what could have constituted "peace"
for Wimmer, but there is no doubt that he emerged as the clear winner
in the fray with O'Connor. A brief received from Rome in 1855 raised
St. Vincent to the rank of an exempt abbey and gave Wimmer the
title of abbot for a three-year term (his tenure actually lasted thirty-
three years). Having shown the perspicacity to close down the financially burdensome brewery, Wimmer also received Rome's support
when the Holy See stated that O'Connor could no longer withhold
dispensations for Benedictines who were ready to be ordained but
were not of canonical age. Further, the supervisory rights of O'Connor
as Ordinary were curtailed, and more self-determination was given
to the monastic community in the control of their seminary and in
their parish work.[14] The now "official" superior of America's first
Benedictine monastery was given clearance to initiate his program
of activity.

Voices of Internal Dissent

Even as Wimmer was overcoming the opposition of Bishop
O'Connor, he was forced to confront internal dissent within his community. The dissent, which was to become a constant refrain in the
first decades of American Benedictine life, arose from a fundamental
and ongoing tension that existed between two distinct groups of
monks at St. Vincent. The first group included those who wanted
a stricter monastic observance, enclosure, and a life of prayer and
study; the second group desired a more activist style of missionary

Abbot Boniface Wimmer, O.S.B., founder of the American Cassinese Benedictines

and pastoral work, as well as manual labor.[15] This division at St. Vincent was a variation of the underlying tension between the active and contemplative poles that monasteries have experienced in every age, but it took on particular intensity under Wimmer and would become the topic of much of the subsequent debate about the purpose and presence of Benedictines in the United States. The first monk to publicly take issue with Wimmer's activist strain of monasticism at St. Vincent was Peter Lechner, former prior of the abbey of Scheyern. He had come to the new American foundation in 1847 and was appointed novice master. Lechner soon voiced his opposition to Wimmer's policy of obligatory manual labor for all candidates; he felt that such work distracted them from their spiritual formation. As a concession, Wimmer allowed novices and clerics to be exempt from field work. But when Lechner continued to criticize his superior's views on monastic formation, Wimmer reacted in blunt fashion. He told Lechner to resign as novice master and assigned him to an outlying mission of the community. Wimmer explained his action in a letter to Lechner's former superior, Abbot Rupert Leiss of Scheyern: "Your Father Peter seems to believe that people can live from the air on five or ten acres of land. Therefore I sent him to St. Joseph's where he can learn that only God is able to create something out of nothing."[16]

But Lechner's was not the only dissident voice. Thaddeus Brunner, a priest who had recently arrived from Metten, wrote to his abbot in Germany not long after Lechner's departure, reiterating some of the same complaints Lechner had made. When Wimmer was confronted with Brunner's list of grievances, his response was to the point: Father Brunner could pack his bags and join Lechner near Carrolltown.[17]

A sizable "contemplative" contingent at St. Vincent did in fact pack their bags in 1849. Lechner, Father Andrew Zugtriegel, a cleric, four novices, and three lay brothers were granted permission to transfer to the Trappist abbey of Gethsemani in Kentucky. The rosy vision of contemplative monasticism that this band of monastic reformers carried to Kentucky did not last for long. After about a year of living within the spartan confines of this Trappist commu-

nity recently established by monks from France, the group returned
to St. Vincent and assumed a lower profile.

By 1862, however, a new wave of reform sentiment crested as
the second general chapter of the recently formed Cassinese Congregation of American Benedictines undertook discussion of nothing less than the "reformation of the Congregation." The reformers,
led by the prior of St. Vincent, Father Othmar Wirtz, and the novice master, Father Wendelin Mayer, pressed for a stricter monastic
regimen. The general chapter did mandate a stricter regulation of the
monastic cloister and called for a more assiduous practice of spiritual
duties, but the tension between the proponents of the active life and
those of the contemplative life remained.[18]

It was at the time of this chapter in Latrobe that a young monk
of St. Vincent, Paul Keck, began attracting attention among the
reforming element in the community. A former actor in Europe, Keck
entered St. Vincent in 1859. He had originally won the confidence
of Boniface Wimmer with his spiritual visions and personal devotions,
and he also exerted a strong influence on some of the reformers, particularly Wirtz and Mayer. Keck made a strategic blunder in confronting Wimmer shortly after the general chapter and insisting that
the abbot give him permission to be ordained and to make a new
monastic foundation on his own. Wimmer, who as a young monk
had never been slack in insisting on his resolution to make a new
foundation, denied Keck's request and in 1863 expelled him from
the monastery without consulting the St. Vincent chapter of monks.

In fact, Keck was a charlatan and monastic poseur of the first order.
Nonetheless, after his departure he was able to carry on his campaign
against Wimmer with the aid of Wirtz and Mayer. He decided to
go to Rome to defend himself. As so many others who opposed Wimmer were to learn, that was an ill-conceived tactic, for Wimmer had
fostered his own high-level friendships in the Eternal City. It all came
to a head in 1865 when Keck's case was dismissed and the demands
of Wirtz to be given permission to establish an independent, more
contemplative monastery in Minnesota were rejected.[19]

These protests within the St. Vincent community against Wimmer's monastic style coincided with criticism leveled against him in

European monastic circles. Father Placid Wolter in particular found much to lament in the overemphasis on the active life in Wimmer's monasteries. The Beuronese monk contrasted the liturgical life of what he considered the best European Benedictine communities with the lack of the same in the United States, insisting that the administration of schools and missions was work better left to the Jesuits and Redemptorists.[20]

Eventually the spirit of Europe's cloistered monks hailed by Wolter found its way to St. Vincent. The director of music for the Latrobe community, Father Ignatius Treug, when attempting to implement newer European methods of Gregorian chant (with Wimmer's permission), was frustrated by opposition from within the monastery. He then transferred his stability to Beuron in 1878. Another member of St. Vincent, Father James Zilliox, the novice master, also asked for a transfer to Beuron at the same time, but he was refused. That refusal came only after Wimmer had discovered in June 1879 that yet another contingent of the St. Vincent community was planning to leave for either the abbey of Gethsemani or Beuron because of the "unmonastic" climate promoted by Wimmer. What made the news of this plan most devastating for the abbot of St. Vincent was the discovery that its two masterminds were, once again, monks he had placed in the most important community posts: the prior, Father Andrew Hintenach, and the novice master, Father Zilliox. Wimmer's response was to send Zilliox to St. Mary's Priory in Newark.[21] But one of the other dissidents, Father Maurice Kaeder, persuaded Zilliox to join with him in sending a formal letter of protest to Rome in 1881, criticizing the abbot with the by now familiar litany of complaints about laxity of observance and non-enforcement of monastic enclosure.[22] Wimmer, at that time seventy-three years of age, defended himself with an assertive apologia for his method of monastic practice:

> My own prior looks to Beuron and thinks he can find there his paradise. However, I am quite sure that the monks of Beuron will lose all that their life stands for if they do not participate in the care of souls as priests or missionaries and enter into the instruction and de-

velopment of youth and older people. I am convinced that we must take interest in the missions as do the begging Orders and Congregations.[23]

What had in fact galvanized all these disparate groups was precisely Wimmer's program of "missionary monasticism" and its energetic spread from St. Vincent, a program and a story that require a separate accounting.

CHAPTER 3

The Monastic Vision of Boniface Wimmer and Its Realization

There is no doubt that a considerable amount of the criticism directed against Wimmer during his years as abbot was due to his personality and manner of governing. His headstrong character was coupled with a reluctance to take counsel with fellow community members before making a decision. Moreover, once his decision was made, there was no brooking his determination to see it through.

The reverse side of these personality traits is a clear reflection of the undeniable charism of leadership that Wimmer possessed. Because of the clear vision of monastic life that he projected and his single-mindedness in attaining it, he attracted many followers. Wimmer himself was quite revealing in this regard in a letter he wrote to the Ludwig-Missionsverein two years after his arrival in the United States:

> What I have tried to carry out, or rather to begin, perhaps with some boldness and daring, many others before me wanted to do. They, however, did not take the risk, because they either did not have the strength, or did not receive the call to undertake it. . . . The brethren have, without doubt, put great confidence in my sincerity, my good intentions, my prudence and foresight, and also in my calling, since they followed me blindly into a far distant land. Although I have not always been even-tempered, I did not let them see my difficulties, worries and anxieties . . . one cannot burden these simple laborers, at least not with great decision-making. It could happen that

with the loss of confidence, we would also lose their obedience and then the whole undertaking would be in danger.[1]

What Wimmer failed to fathom was that the blind obedience expected of his first "simple laborers" at St. Vincent could not be accepted in the same measure by mature monks accustomed to having some voice in community decisions. His rationale to justify the exercise of such authority invited much criticism of his commands. He compared himself to a general in the field of battle who, in an emergency situation, must have the power to act and not be forced to appeal to a council of war at a distant site for instructions.[2] It was clear, in Wimmer's judgment, that he was in the thick of battle throughout his years as abbot, and he was not predisposed to pause before entering the field of conflict. Even in his later years, when he became more aware of the many criticisms leveled against his use of authority, he was reluctant to let go of the reins. As he wrote to Alexius Edelbrock, his fellow abbot at St. John's Abbey in Minnesota: "Since I have become older, calmer and more experienced, I try to avoid making use of my power and yet, if it would become necessary, I would do it. . . . It is good if we are loved, but we should also be feared. Where there is no fear, there is no discipline either, and without discipline, there is no respect."[3]

It would be much too facile to dismiss these words as those of a monastic martinet who took delight in exercising authority for its own sake. For Wimmer, whatever authority or influence he had as abbot was to be used to further his vision of Benedictine life in the United States. And in much the same way as his personality and exercise of authority elicited reactions of both love and fear, Wimmer's vision of an ever-expanding Benedictine family in North America at once attracted and repelled members of his own monastic family.

A good summary of the philosophy that generated this vision is found in a letter Wimmer wrote to the directors of the Ludwig-Missionsverein in 1857:

Each abbey must become the mother of other abbeys: the mission spirit does not allow me to rest nor to stand still. . . . The Benedictine Order has awakened from its one hundred years of stability to mobility and to the realization that its standard should not be absent in the field where the price of victory is one-half of the world. Just last year we were only on this side of the Allegheny; today we stand with one foot on the west bank of the Mississippi in Minnesota, and with the other, on the west bank of the Missouri in Kansas. In a few years you may find us near the Rocky Mountains and a little later in California on the Pacific Ocean. It has to be. The stream of immigration moves ever westward and we must follow it. . . . One must strike while the iron is hot and the fervor must not be allowed to cool down.[4]

Even more striking than the florid language of this monastic expression of Manifest Destiny is how closely its design matched up with later historical reality.

It is also imperative to realize how quickly Wimmer, the idealistic "Projecten-Macher," could become the consummate pragmatist in promoting his vision. He did this with the same sort of raw energy that marked the American quest for the frontier. And if at times his unflagging energy outstripped prudent planning, he was sure that the Lord would provide. He expressed this spirit in a letter to Abbot Utto Lang of Metten: "Under the circumstances there is always more work. For us it is a time for growth, for development. I must take as many candidates as I have room for in order to be ready when necessity calls. . . . We feel the urge to expand, and that is the reason there is no rest. Something new is always turning up."[5]

The Daughter Foundations

That "urge to expand" soon gave rise to new monasteries founded by monks of St. Vincent. During the first decade of St. Vincent's existence, however, the task of constructing a monastery and seminary took precedence over missionary enterprises. Nonetheless, missions in the Pennsylvania towns of Carrolltown, Indiana, Butler, and St. Marys were established as monastic outposts of the abbey in Latrobe.

At the end of that first decade, in January 1856, Boniface Wimmer returned from an eleven-month stay in Europe, reinforced in his purpose by Rome's decision to make St. Vincent an abbey and to confer on Wimmer the title of abbot. In that same year he convened the community of St. Vincent for the first general chapter of the recently formed American Cassinese Congregation. Among the matters on the agenda were requests from the bishops of St. Louis, Dubuque, Milwaukee, and St. Paul for the establishment of Benedictine monasteries in their dioceses.[6]

The chapter decided to establish a new foundation in the diocese of St. Paul. Wimmer explained the reason for the choice: "The new foundation was necessary in many respects, although inconvenient from a financial viewpoint. The West really becomes our base of operations, since it has more Germans and fewer priests and because things are not yet fixed. . . . We have prepared [at St. Vincent] almost one hundred young men for the service of the Church and now we have brought our banner up to the Father of Waters, only about seventy miles from its source, to the extreme boundary of European civilization, where we will even encounter the Indians. . . ."[7] Wimmer's words and imagery are redolent of the missionary letters of his namesake, the missionary monk Boniface, who a millennium earlier had crossed the edge of civilization in northern Europe and there planted the seed of Christian faith and monastic culture.

The first monks from St. Vincent who arrived in Minnesota in 1856 did encounter American Indians, as well as bone-chilling cold, a grasshopper plague, and a shortage of food. Despite the disruption of the Civil War, a Sioux uprising in 1862, and endless wrangles over land claims (the community changed location four times in the first decade), the fledgling foundation of St. Cloud Priory grew steadily and, just ten years after coming to Minnesota, elected its first abbot, Father Rupert Seidenbusch. The formal name of the new abbey was changed to St. Louis on the Lake,[8] but it soon became known as St. John's Abbey. Within a century this pioneer community on the "boundary of civilization" would become the largest Benedictine monastery in the world, as well as a center of learning, liturgy, and dialogue for Benedictine houses throughout the United States.

One year after the founding of this monastery in Minnesota, Wimmer, responding to the repeated requests of Bishop James Bayley of Newark, New Jersey, established St. Mary's Priory in that city. De-

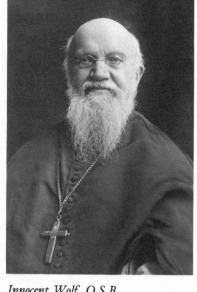

Rupert Seidenbusch, O.S.B.   *Innocent Wolf, O.S.B.*

spite the abbot's reservations about cities as an appropriate environment for monastic life, he recognized the immediate need of pastoral assistance for the German Catholics in that city. The Newark community faced its own "urban" frontier difficulties, as well as the sacrifice of many of its best members to other foundations of St. Vincent, but soon it too established itself as a permanent fixture on Wimmer's monastic map.

As if to compensate for his move to an Eastern city in 1857, Wimmer in that same year sent two monks to Kansas, where they were to secure the real estate claims made by the same Peter Lemke who had first invited Wimmer's monks to the United States. The abbey of St. Benedict in Atchison, Kansas, was a community of hardworking men, dedicated to their missionary task and determined to survive in the face of financial peril and uncertain leadership. Even if its monastic observance at times lacked a high standard, there were enough positive models to attract native vocations and to produce a cadre of zealous missionaries who were also observant monks. The mercurial direction the community experienced in its early years under

Peter Lemke, O.S.B.   *Augustine Wirth, O.S.B.*   *Oswald Moosmueller, O.S.B.*

Lemke and Prior Augustine Wirth eventually gave way to the stable leadership of two of Wimmer's prized pupils from St. Vincent, Fathers Oswald Moosmueller and Innocent Wolf.[9]

After these new ventures in Minnesota, New Jersey, and Kansas had been begun, Wimmer was chided for "going too fast" by some of his constant supply of critics. In response, he directed pointed words to the European source of this criticism: "If I were as timid as the directors of the Ludwig-Missionsverein wish me to be, I would now have no new foundations nor the old one so firmly established. Our motto must be: Forward, always forward."[10]

The pace of Wimmer's monastic expansion matched the compulsive and frenetic rush to open up the Western frontier. On the eve of the Civil War, Wimmer could point to new communities of Benedictines in Covington, Kentucky, and Galveston, Texas. He had also sent individual monks to Ontario, Canada; upstate New York; Erie, Pennsylvania; Richmond, Virginia; Chicago; and the Nebraska Territory. His efforts were marked by the same adventuresome and restless spirit that characterized nineteenth-century America. Wimmer himself offers a vivid description of that spirit and his own identification with it in a letter written to his patron, Ludwig I:

> In America everything is done on credit. . . . The whole American people often appears to me like a mass gambler: everyone gambles,

everyone takes risks as far as he can go; many thereby lose everything
and many succeed. . . . This spirit of reckless chance-taking, along
with such lack of concern for others, underlies the egoism that is so
noticeable in the American character and which may be called the key
to the tremendous and amazing advance in every area of the country. . . . Talent, energy and luck account for success in everything.[11]

What Wimmer may have lacked in talent and luck he more than
made up for in energy, an energy that fueled his own ''noticeable
egoism'' in enlarging his monastic family. Yet, this energy was accompanied by a resilient religious faith that led him to believe that
the God who had called him to enter upon this risky venture would
help him see it through to its successful completion.

Sowing Seed in the American South

While the Civil War brought a temporary halt to Wimmer's missionary drive, it also led him to take a more studied look at the American South. What he saw there was a poor, Protestant region, largely
devoid of Catholic priests. It was, in short, an area that promised
abundant fruit for those willing to sow a new monastic seed.

Before the Civil War, Wimmer had been willing to send monks
to select areas of the South to help German-speaking immigrants.
Father Alto Herman had been sent from St. Vincent to be prior of
a group of Benedictines called by Bishop John Odin to serve Ger-
man Catholics near San Antonio in 1859.[12] Not long after, the Civil
War and the great distance from St. Vincent created problems that
forced the monks to withdraw from Texas. In 1860, Father Leonard
Mayer had been asked to go to St. Mary's Church in Richmond,
Virginia, to assist the German-speaking Catholic community there.
But Richmond soon became the capital of the Confederacy, and
Mayer was cut off from all communication with St. Vincent through-
out the course of the war.[13]

In assessing possible sites for monastic settlement in the South
in this postbellum period, Wimmer eventually fixed on the state of
North Carolina. In 1875 Bishop James Gibbons asked him to found
a religious house and conduct a school on land in Gaston County.[14]
Wimmer seemed to prefer this site over several others then being con-

sidered for the reason that North Carolina had the least number of Catholics of all the states, and the site was located in one of the poorest dioceses in the country. The St. Vincent chapter concurred with Wimmer and accepted the North Carolina offer. Father Herman Wolfe of St. Vincent, pastor of St. Mary's Parish in Richmond, was named the first superior of the new community, which began its existence in April 1876.

The Benedictine Priory of Maryhelp, as the new foundation was designated by Wimmer, had a difficult beginning. Even though the abbot of St. Vincent supplied additional personnel from his community, there was little of positive note reported back to Latrobe from North Carolina. The farm was a failure, the school was a tenuous operation, and there was a chorus of complaints from the brothers and visiting missionaries concerning the superior. These complaints continued into 1878, when Wimmer assigned two American-born monks to Maryhelp and replaced Wolfe as superior with Father Placid Pilz, who remained in that capacity until 1886. In that same period the school had five different rectors, and by 1884 was reduced to twenty-three students. The farm continued its dismal performance. The only bright spot was the growth of two missions of Maryhelp at Richmond and Savannah.[15]

To improve the situation in North Carolina, Wimmer petitioned Rome to raise Maryhelp to the status of an abbey; he requested the same privilege for the community of St. Mary's, Newark. He received approval from Rome in January 1885. Wimmer immediately summoned the chapter at St. Vincent for an unprecedented dual election of abbots for the two houses. The election, held on February 11, brought some familiar figures to center stage. Father James Zilliox, one of the Beuronese burrs in Wimmer's side, was elected abbot of Newark on the second ballot of the morning chapter. In the afternoon Father Oswald Moosmueller, former prior of St. Benedict's Abbey in Atchison and Wimmer's trusted confidant, who had been given charge of the Savannah mission, was elected abbot of Maryhelp on the first ballot.[16]

Satisfied with both the results and the dispatch of the entire election, Wimmer telegraphed word of the chapter's decision to the absent Moosmueller and dismissed the chapter that same afternoon. Much to Wimmer's chagrin, Moosmueller telegraphed back that night, refusing to accept the office; no amount of arm-twisting by his abbot could persuade Moosmueller to accept the chapter's decision.

Wimmer's only alternative was to hold a second election. This was scheduled to be held at St. Vincent in July. In the interim, Wimmer had decided on his own favorite candidate: Father Leo Haid, a thirty-five-year-old protégé of the abbot, who had been involved in the operation of St. Vincent's schools for thirteen years. Despite Haid's protestations, he accepted his status as Wimmer's handpicked candidate and his subsequent election by the chapter as the new superior at Maryhelp.

As abbot, Haid proved to be less eager than his mentor to engage in large-scale missionary activity and more intent on fostering a regular and observant monastic life. Of invaluable assistance in promoting this monastic spirit at the North Carolina abbey was another monk from St. Vincent, Father Felix Hintemeyer, who was entrusted with major positions in the community and became an *eminence grise* for Haid during the next quarter century.

The new abbot also faced some practical problems in his new post. One of the most prickly ones arose at Savannah. The monastic community there had been established in 1874 by two monks of the Subiaco Congregation of the Primitive Observance who had worked with the black people on the Isle of Hope. When an epidemic of yellow fever forced them to leave Savannah, Abbot Wimmer agreed to take over the community, sending his most prominent trouble-shooter, Oswald Moosmueller, to be its first superior.[17] Soon Moosmueller was in charge of a parish in the city of Savannah, a chapel on the Isle of Hope, and an industrial school for black children on nearby Skidaway Island. By 1885 jurisdiction over the Savannah foundation had passed to Haid, but the personnel remained those appointed by Wimmer; moreover, Moosmueller insisted on maintaining his own independent administration of the community. During the next two years a struggle took place over who would direct the Savannah community. By the summer of 1887 it was clear that Leo Haid had

*Leo Haid, O.S.B.,
first abbot nullius
of Belmont Abbey
and bishop
of the vicariate
of North Carolina*

prevailed, and the entire mission was transferred from Moosmueller's control to that of Belmont Abbey.[18]

One other event that gave further prominence to Haid's role and that of the Benedictine Order in the South was the appointment of Belmont's abbot as bishop and vicar apostolic of North Carolina on December 7, 1887. It was an honor that vindicated the judgment of Boniface Wimmer about Haid's leadership abilities. But the next day Boniface Wimmer died at St. Vincent, "unaware that another of his sons had been promoted to the episcopal dignity."[19]

Before his death, however, Boniface Wimmer had offered his Florida mission to Leo Haid. This was not made official until the Belmont Abbey chapter registered its approval on October 10, 1883, with all the "bonus and onus" entailed in such a decision. The onus included some very questionable land transactions with a local official and an alleged moral scandal involving the mission's only Benedictine. But Haid had the perspicacity to place in charge of the mission a young monk, Father Charles Mohr, who singlehandedly set the mission's school on firm footing. Mohr was named conventual prior of the community in 1894, and became the first abbot of St. Leo Abbey in 1902.

41

The remaining Southern foundation of St. Bernard in Alabama was another striking testimony to Wimmer's power of will. In August 1875 the St. Vincent chapter met to decide whether or not to accept a request from Bishop Patrick Feehan of Nashville to establish a mission for the German settlers in Tennessee. The chapter rejected the offer.[20] Six months later, when Bishop John Quinlan of Mobile promised to give St. Vincent charge of the missions of Cullman Station and St. Florian in his diocese, Wimmer urged his monks to accept the offer because of the extreme financial and spiritual need of the German colony there, as well as "to help the poor bishops in that part of the country who have great concern for their neglected sheep, both white and black."[21] The persuasive voice of the abbot was once again effective.

Little progress was made, though, in establishing a permanent monastic foundation in Alabama in the years that followed. By November 1885 monks from St. Vincent served at parishes in Huntsville, Lauterdale County, and Tuscumbia, but the school at Tuscumbia was not prospering, and the poverty of the region was so endemic that Father Athanasius Hintenach counseled against supporting an independent abbey there.[22]

In April 1887 Wimmer was given an opportunity to surmount these obstacles. Bishop Jeremiah Sullivan of Mobile offered to turn over the parish of Cullman to the Benedictines. This parish was strongly German and had a Catholic population larger than that of the other Benedictine parishes in Alabama combined. Wimmer accepted the offer immediately and sent Father Andrew Hintenach (who within a year was to succeed Wimmer as abbot of St. Vincent) to take care of all mission activity in Alabama. He also sent Oswald Moosmueller from Savannah to the Cullman parish. That parish formed the nucleus of St. Bernard Abbey, which attained its independence in 1891.

The Legacy of Boniface Wimmer

By the time of Wimmer's death in 1887, the élan of his original vision and its practical realization were no longer in question. That the unfolding of that vision was marked by an inherent impulsiveness and an occasional failure should not detract from his overall achievement. In forty years of unflagging labor, Wimmer had created the institutional machinery and manpower to generate a sprawling network of monastic houses whose growth and missionary activity translated into a vital resource for the American Catholic Church. Moreover, the momentum of his program of monastic expansion was sustained throughout the whole American Cassinese Congregation after his death. New communities in Colorado (Holy Cross) and Washington (St. Martin) completed Wimmer's earlier vision of Benedictine settlements from the Rocky Mountains to the Pacific Ocean. Roots were also planted in the Midwest (St. Procopius, Cluny, and St. Bede in Illinois) and New England (St. Anselm in New Hampshire), and American Benedictines were working in the Bahama Islands before the end of the century.

Wimmer had not only realized the greater part of his plans to spread Benedictine monasticism, but from his original monastic family at St. Vincent he provided a generation of new leaders for the Church. Rupert Seidenbusch of St. John's, Innocent Wolf of St.Benedict's, James Zilliox and Hilary Pfraengle of St. Mary's, Leo Haid of Belmont, Benedict Menges of St. Bernard, Nepomucene Jaeger of St. Procopius, Vincent Huber of St. Bede, and Wimmer's two successors at St. Vincent, Andrew Hintenach and Leander Schnerr—all were abbots who had received their monastic formation under Wimmer at St. Vincent.

Even if one concedes that some of Wimmer's spiritual sons did not explicitly hold up his monastic ideal for emulation, they constituted a progeny that continued to pursue the patriarchal vision of the abbot-founder and first president of the American Cassinese Congregation. The shadow of Wimmer's presence loomed large over the landscape of American Benedictine life during its formative years, even as the legacy of its founder and charismatic leader lingered long after his death.

CHAPTER 4

The Swiss-Americans

St. Meinrad

The Swiss abbey of Einsiedeln, like many other Benedictine monasteries in Europe during the mid-nineteenth century, received a steady stream of requests to establish missionary foundations in the United States. One of those requests came from Bishop Maurice St. Palais of Vincennes, Indiana, who coupled his written request with a personal pilgrimage to the Swiss abbey. He was accompanied on this journey in 1852 by his diocesan chancellor, Father Joseph Kundek. Their goal was to persuade Einsiedeln's abbot, Henry Schmid, to send monks to their Indiana diocese. The timing of their trip was fortuitous, for when they arrived at Einsiedeln, the reading in the monastic refectory was being taken from Boniface Wimmer's accounts of missionary life in America as published in the *Annalen* of the Ludwig-Missionsverein.[1]

Just prior to the visit of the Bishop and his chancellor, the Swiss government had forced Einsiedeln to close its school in Bellinzona and seemed to harbor ideas of dissolving several Swiss monasteries as well. So it was not surprising that shortly after his conversations with the Vincennes representatives, Abbot Henry wrote to Propaganda Fide in Rome, asking for authorization to erect a Benedictine monastery in North America. Approval was given from Rome, and the monastic chapter of Einsiedeln voted their approval on November 19, 1852.[2]

Accordingly, two monks from Einsiedeln were sent to Indiana in 1853 to investigate Bishop St. Palais' offer. The two monks, Fathers Ulrich Christen and Bede O'Connor, stopped at St. Vincent to confer with Boniface Wimmer before heading down the Ohio River to Vincennes.[3] They were soon joined by two more Swiss monks, Father Eugene Schwerzmann of Engelberg Abbey and Father Jerome Bachmann, subprior of Einsiedeln, along with four lay companions. Land was purchased in Spencer County in the southwest part of Indiana. The pioneer spirit that animated the group is clearly expressed in a letter sent by Schwerzmann to his abbot:

> If America is a country where one must, as in Einsiedeln, pray to Mary from this vale of tears, the new world still has this advantage: here all is in growth and in bloom; there all has shriveled up and is dying. Here we have people experiencing the spring of new life while in Old Europe and especially in Switzerland the late autumn is past. . . . We are in a country where everyone is free to believe what he wants. Neither the government, nor custom, nor convenience forces anyone to any creed . . . this practiced spirit one finds in America corresponds to the spirit of our Church, for one can see that the power of truth does not have such a hard time here with prejudice. The only hindrance here is the emphasis on materialism. Mammon is the sole idol of America.[4]

In reality, the question of materialism was confronting the small community of monks in ways that Father Schwerzmann did not fully comprehend when he wrote this letter. This becomes apparent when the lament of financial difficulties appears in correspondence from other members of the community in 1854. Typical is a letter of Father Jerome Bachmann:

> For the founding of a Benedictine house we need loans which are necessary if we are to carry out our plans. Since we are sent out from Einsiedeln for this purpose and not, as [Precious Blood] Father Brunner and Boniface Wimmer, gone on our own, one must not hope so much on free will offering, for it is said: Einsiedeln will help you. If Einsiedeln is to have a house in America, it must help not only with its people but with money . . . .[5]

Although Abbot Schmid's initial plan had stressed a close tie with the motherhouse, he had mentioned nothing about a monetary subsidy.[6] In addition to having the community's land serve as a political refuge in case Einsiedeln were suppressed, Schmid had foreseen for the frontier community a limited apostolate of a small seminary and parish work that would not conflict with monastic duties. The four Benedictine priests who erected a small cabin at a place they called St. Meinrad and celebrated Mass there in March 1854 were aware of the expectations of the abbot of Einsiedeln. What they were not yet aware of was just how demanding their new venture would be. The harvest of the first year's crops was disappointing because of a drought. A gristmill and a sawmill purchased by the community were destroyed by fire. The missionary work of the priests was bringing in little money. When pressed by the bishop to do more parish work, Jerome Bachmann replied that he had come to America not to preach but to plow.[7]

Father Jerome's plowing did not last long. He was called back to Einsiedeln in late 1854 and reprimanded for his lack of effective stewardship.[8] He was replaced as superior by Father Athanasius Tschopp, who arrived at St. Meinrad in 1855 with a new companion from Einsiedeln, Father Chrysostom Foffa, and Father Jerome. Shortly after his arrival, however, Tschopp became seriously ill and had to return to Switzerland. To further aggravate the situation, there was infighting among the remaining monks over the administration of the community.

All this prompted Abbot Schmid to reevaluate Einsiedeln's commitment. In 1856 he contemplated a cutback in personnel, expressing his frustration at the "unbridgeable gulf" between the two continents that made the new foundation's progress so difficult.[9] By 1858 the abbot was seriously considering liquidating St. Meinrad and calling its monks back to their Swiss motherhouse, with their Indiana property being given over to Boniface Wimmer.[10]

The St. Meinrad community attempted to dissuade the abbot from this move, suggesting instead that a new superior be sent from Einsiedeln and stressing that the spiritual life of the many souls served by St. Meinrad's monks was in the balance.[11] As a last resort, some

Einsiedeln Abbey in Switzerland, founding house of St. Meinrad Archabbey, St. Meinrad, Indiana

of the Indiana monks were ready to follow the suggestion of their former superior, Athanasius Tschopp, and model themselves after Wimmer, in the sense of operating St. Meinrad completely independently of Einsiedeln and hoping that the needed financial help could be secured from the mission aid societies of Europe rather than from the motherhouse at Einsiedeln.[12]

By 1860 the St. Meinrad community, all too conscious of its precarious position, made an emotional plea to Einsiedeln's abbot for urgent assistance in revitalizing the mission foundation. In response, Abbot Schmid made a decision that was to radically alter the history of St. Meinrad: he sent two young priests to Indiana to determine the advisability of continuing the monastic house there. In selecting Fathers Martin Marty and Fintan Mundwiler for this task, Schmid chose the two men who, as superiors of St. Meinrad for the next forty years, were to determine that community's destiny in untold ways.

Martin Marty, O.S.B.

Fintan Mundwiler, O.S.B.

The original monastery (1854) of St. Meinrad

The extremity of St. Meinrad's problems in 1860 depended upon the perspective from which they were viewed. Writing to Abbot Schmid, Bishop St. Palais stated that the debt of St. Meinrad was only about ten percent of that of Boniface Wimmer and the value of the community's land could cover that cost. According to the bishop, all that was needed was a superior who could inspire confidence in the community and serve as a good administrator.[13]

The Marty Years

The hoped-for superior came in the person of a twenty-six-year-old monk who had been given instructions by his abbot to act as superior of the St. Meinrad community, even though he had been given no official rank. The monk in question, Father Martin Marty, was being groomed for an appointment to the important position of novice master and instructor of clerics at Einsiedeln by his abbot, and it was thought that a temporary test of responsibility would be a valuable experience.[14] The temporary was to become permanent in a most impressive fashion.

Arriving at the American foundation on September 28, 1860, Marty made a number of decisive moves. He reopened the monastic school and founded the town of St. Meinrad. The sale of lots attracted a Catholic population and greatly improved the community's potential for survival and subsequent growth.[15] He increased the productivity of the farm by introducing more efficient agricultural techniques, secured loans at lower interest rates from European sources, and began demanding exact financial statements from his priests in the missions.[16]

Marty's letters to Einsiedeln that first year reflect both the sober reality of the situation he faced and the infectious optimism he brought to it. Reporting to his abbot, he remarked: "What we perhaps never learned in Einsiedeln, we have a chance to experience here theoretically and practically concerning the vow of poverty, for we *are* poor, poorer than some of the Swiss beggars."[17] And in response to what he interpreted as the skeptical attitude of the motherhouse toward the American foundation, Marty wrote:

The letters from Einsiedeln show little hope in the future of St. Meinrad and there are many good reasons for this, but it seems to me that if the good God did not wish to preserve St. Meinrad and make use of it, He had plenty of chances to let it fail and there has been so much good done here, so much sacrificed, so much work accomplished, so much suffered, that the blessing of God will come, will support St. Meinrad, and slowly there will be progress and it will become, through obedience, what it should have been from the beginning.[18]

The difficulties of the Civil War notwithstanding, progress was made at St. Meinrad on all fronts, much of it due to the able direction and vision of Marty. In recognition of these accomplishments, Abbot Schmid in May 1865 conferred on him complete formal authority in spiritual and temporal matters at St. Meinrad. Once St. Meinrad attained its independence as an abbey five years later, the monastic capitulars also confirmed their confidence in Marty by casting thirteen of their fourteen ballots for him as abbot.[19]

All this was testimony not only to Marty's leadership abilities but also to his persuasive and vibrant personality. He was an incredibly gifted individual: a theologian, musician, linguist, and historian. He was at once an eloquent preacher who moved congregations as he traveled regularly to mission assignments; an accomplished organist who set a high standard of sacred music for his community; a devout monk whose affinity for the monastic life and its history edified his American confreres. In his capacity as theologian, he accompanied the bishop of Vincennes to the Provincial Synod of Cincinnati in 1861 and to the Second Plenary Council of Baltimore in 1866. As a teacher, he accepted a full load of classes at St. Meinrad's College and gave instructions on a regular basis to the young monks of the monastery. As a historian, he was a member of the United States Catholic Historical Society and wrote several volumes on the history of the Benedictine Order.[20] In all these roles, Marty was ever the individualist, showing a willingness to experiment and to pragmatically employ new methods even as he built upon the bedrock of his own revered monastic tradition.

Like his Cassinese counterpart, Boniface Wimmer, Marty was a man of sweeping vision and a natural lightning rod for criticism from those whose monastic model was different from his. A revealing look at the nature of that criticism can be seen in two significant steps the young abbot took.

Ever since he arrived at St. Meinrad, Marty had been keenly interested in the community's liturgical life. One of his primary purposes in establishing Catholic schools in the vicinity of the monastery was the "liturgical education" of the Catholic people in the region.[21] This same interest in the liturgy prompted him to study the community prayer at St. Meinrad and to consider the respective merits of the Roman and monastic breviaries. He came to the conclusion that the Roman breviary was better suited to the liturgical life of the monks at St. Meinrad and that it was also historically more suitable in affirming the character of the Divine Office in monastic tradition. Unfortunately, Marty had failed to consult with any other members of his community (to say nothing of superiors in Einsiedeln or Rome) before putting his decision to use the Roman breviary into effect on Easter Sunday, April 5, 1874.[22] The change precipitated a firestorm of dissent on several fronts. From within the monastic community at St. Meinrad, certain monks who had accused Marty of being self-willed and highhanded in his exercise of authority saw confirmation of this assessment in his decision. Father Caspar Seiler, a monk from Einsiedeln, happened to be visiting St. Meinrad just at this time and in a lengthy letter to his abbot in Switzerland voiced some of the reservations about Marty's authoritative role in the community:

> In his position as superior, Abbot Martin in general seems to me to be altogether too idealistic, all too ardently and with all his soul in pursuit of self-constituted ideals—yet with the best of intentions and heroic devotedness—instead of having due regard for the state of affairs at hand. This is obviously the reason why he has so little regard for things established, for customs, Statutes, Bishops, other monasteries and abbots, when there is a question of pursuing an idea the excellence of which he is convinced. This disregard manifests itself in conduct and judgment. . . . Instead of customs, traditions, statutes, considerate consultation and planning, there are just his pet ideas, which, however, apparently change according as he seems to recognize something better.[23]

Even before this letter reached Einsiedeln, Marty's decision to use the Roman Breviary had provoked consternation in monastic circles on the European continent. As in Wimmer's case, the main protests leveled against Marty came from Beuron. They were spearheaded by Placid Wolter, who, in the summer of 1875, sent out a circular letter roundly criticizing Marty's action. It was sent to monasteries across Europe, calling upon them to protest Abbot Marty's decision and to take action "in the face of bold attempts and accomplished facts of traditionless Americanism."[24]

In retrospect, one can see how this controversy, like Wimmer's brewery controversy, became a symbol of the discontent harbored by many over Marty's innovations and governing style. The influence that Wolter's circular letter had in Rome and Einsiedeln was considerable, and the Congregation of Rites eventually ordered Marty to restore the monastic breviary in August 1875.[25] The new abbot of Einsiedeln, Basil Oberholzer, saw to it that the decree was sent to Abbot Marty. Ever the obedient monk, Marty enforced the decree immediately. But he could not resist offering a defense of his actions and at the same time a stinging retort to his critics:

> There is too much phrase and not enough real understanding in all these arguments [of F. Placidus]; these men have always lived in plenty and convenience and have not been disciplined by the hard experience of practical life. They do not live upon the labor of their laybrothers as we do in this country; their brothers are only cohorts of these Rev. Gentlemen, who are the favorites of this and that princess or countess and draw from the treasuries of Counts and Barons. They are not to do the same work for the secular clergy of Germany as we must do for the clergy of this country; their life is more contemplative than active and the monastic breviary is not in their way. Of all Benedictines in Europe there are perhaps not ten sufficiently acquainted with the Roman Breviary and therefore they have no idea how much superior is it to the monastic one.[26]

Marty's explicit mention of the polarity of the active and contemplative aspects of the monastic life could aptly be associated with another volley of criticism that he was receiving at this time regarding his decision to have St. Meinrad actively undertake missionary work.

Marty's wholehearted involvement in the apostolate to American Indians will be treated elsewhere. Here it need only be said that this work, which he began in 1876 and continued until his resignation in 1880 (and beyond that as bishop), evoked considerable controversy among the members of his community. His absence from St. Meinrad for long periods of time and the demands he made of monastic personnel led to diverse manifestations of dissent. In the summer of 1877 all the priests of St. Meinrad, led by Fathers Isidore Hobi and Wolfgang Schlumpf, signed a letter urging Marty to come back home from the Indian missions in the Dakotas.[27] They objected not only to Marty's desire to accept an increasing number of pastoral tasks but also to the seemingly arbitrary way in which he took them on. Schlumpf captured the essence of the disagreement when he wrote:

> Up till now we have never had a chapter meeting nor any other deliberative conference to draw up legislation, or to come to a decision on a new mission project, such as took place when Einsiedeln was considering the new foundation at St. Meinrad. Here the entire arrangement depends wholly on the will of the abbot. Therefore, we are operating not according to the law, but only *praecepta,* precepts which cease at the death of the abbot.[28]

This dissent echoed some of the complaints emanating from St. Vincent against Wimmer and from St. John's against Abbot Alexius Edelbrock at this same time. What had become clear to members of the first Swiss-American monastic community was that Martin Marty the model European monk had been transformed into Martin Marty the American missionary, and St. Meinrad was to inherit Marty's missionary mantle.

Once Marty had been made bishop and left the community in 1880, there was considerable sentiment to withdraw missionary commitments at St. Meinrad. But Marty's successor as abbot, Fintan Mundwiler, was caught in the quicksand of apostolic activity that two decades of Marty's leadership had produced. Mundwiler presided over St. Meinrad's fortunes for the next seventeen years and did his best to consolidate Marty's missionary commitments, even as he tried to foster a more monastic spirit in the house. Although a classmate and great admirer of Marty, Mundwiler had a different outlook on the role of St. Meinrad as a monastic community. He expressed his feelings in a letter he wrote to Frowin Conrad, another classmate and fellow Benedictine superior, whose monastic ideal matched his own:

> By reason of the experience that we have made in the last years, my ardor to the colonies has cooled. I am of the opinion that we should not start one before we have grown strong within and without and have a sufficient number of proved and solid religious from which to select without harm to their own salvation and without detriment to the house; otherwise, the undertakings will not do well.[29]

The spiritual foundation of Mundwiler's misgivings about missionary activity will be touched on later, but there is no denying the fact that early in its history St. Meinrad experienced some of the same tension as Wimmer's foundations. That tension also accompanied the story of the other half of the Swiss monastic presence in the United States, centered at Conception Abbey in Missouri.

Engelberg's Missouri Foundation

The beginnings of Conception Abbey are considerably more complicated than those of St. Meinrad. They go back to the efforts of an earnest Irish-American missionary, Father James Power, to lure a religious community to minister to the needs of a colony he had established in western Missouri before the Civil War. Power's first appeal was to the Trappist monks of Mount Melleray, Ireland, who had just begun a new foundation at New Melleray, near Dubuque, Iowa. The chapter of the Irish motherhouse, which at one time had given serious consideration to transferring the entire community to America, turned down the proposal. Power next appealed to Boniface Wimmer, and in 1865 the St. Vincent chapter responded favorably to the request. But Bishop Peter Kenrick of St. Louis refused to give his permission. Finally in 1872 Power had a fellow Irishman, Bishop John Hogan, of the recently erected diocese of St. Joseph, Missouri, petition Martin Marty and the monks of St. Meinrad to come to Missouri.[30]

Above: "New Engelberg" Abbey, Conception, Missouri (1875). Below: Engelberg Abbey, Switzerland, founding house of Conception and Mount Angel Abbeys

Bishop Hogan's letter reached Marty only shortly after a period in which he had been in correspondence with Father Frowin Conrad, a monk of Engelberg Abbey and a former classmate of Marty's at Einsiedeln. They had broached the possibility of Engelberg establishing a monastic house in America. Marty had wanted Conrad to come to St. Meinrad to investigate possible sites, but Conrad's abbot at Engelberg, Anselm Villiger, had written Marty that Engelberg was not capable of such an undertaking. However, when Bishop Hogan's letter reached Marty, the latter suggested that Hogan send his request to Engelberg Abbey. By the time Hogan's letter reached Engelberg in late 1872, the political situation in Switzerland had deteriorated with respect to the state's tolerance of Benedictine monasteries, to the point that Abbot Villiger was thinking seriously of the need for a place of sanctuary outside the country if Engelberg were suppressed. So it was that Villiger presented Bishop Hogan's request to the monastic chapter; it was approved on January 7, 1873.[31]

As was the case with Einsiedeln's Abbot Henry Schmid in his selection of Martin Marty and Fintan Mundwiler, Abbot Anselm Villiger's choice of Fathers Frowin Conrad and Adelhelm Odermatt to be the founders of the American foundation was to become one of great consequence. For the next quarter century and beyond, these two widely different personalities were to be responsible for significant new growth of monastic life in the United States.

The two men left Engelberg on April 27, 1873, and before embarking on their ocean voyage spent some time at the monastery of Beuron. Conrad had visited there before and was a close friend of one of its founders, Placid Wolter. During this visit Abbot Maurus Wolter entrusted to Conrad a copy of the Beuronese liturgical *Ceremoniale*.[32] Little did Conrad realize then that before long this was to be used as prima facie evidence against him in accusations of disloyalty to Engelberg.

After arriving at New York in May 1873, the two Engelberg monks made the by now obligatory stop at St. Vincent, where they met with Boniface Wimmer. From there they traveled to St. Meinrad, where news of their arrival in the United States had just reached Marty. Once he had received confirmation of the Engelberg expedition, he sent his prior, Fintan Mundwiler, to St. Joseph, Missouri, to accept Bishop Hogan's offer. After some negotiation, Mundwiler selected a parcel of land forty miles from St. Joseph in Nodaway County called Conception.

For the next few months Conrad and Odermatt remained at St. Meinrad, talking at length with Marty about the problems of starting a new foundation. Building upon the chastening experience of Einsiedeln's American beginning, Conrad wrote to Engelberg, asking for permission to move to Conception and open a novitiate, assuring the abbot that he intended to make the new colony "a true daughter of Engelberg," a monastic community whose stability would counter the rapid pace of the American way of life.[33]

Villiger tentatively approved Conrad's plan to open a novitiate and at the same time revealed some of the different opinions in the Engelberg community with regard to making a monastic foundation in the United States:

> With regard to your request to open a novitiate this fall, some of our fathers are opposed; they insisted that the new monastery in America must be a second Engelberg and that it must be populated only with novices who have their training at Engelberg. The reason given for this is the fact that in the event that Engelberg should be suppressed and that we have to flee to America, we might feel fully at home there and might still have what exists for us here in Switzerland. I opposed this position with all my heart and I said: "No, we do not want a new Engelberg in America, but rather a new monastic community, fresh and vigorous in spirit, observance, and in manner of life." Novices trained at Engelberg who have become accustomed to our mildness and even our laxities would not fare well in America.[34]

At the same time, Conrad was sending assurance of his own to Engelberg: "Father Abbot, there is no cause for anyone to fear that this new house will become estranged from the motherhouse when its first members make their novitiate in the new monastery. Here we realize how much we owe to Engelberg and that without her help we would not be here."[35]

Having given his abbot assurances of faithfulness, Conrad began his monastic experiment in September 1873, when he moved into the parish house in Conception that Fintan Mundwiler had helped to build. Father Adelhelm was to reside at the parish house in nearby Maryville. Soon Conrad began receiving candidates for the monastic life, so many that some had to be sent to Maryville until the monastic enclosure at Conception was completed.[36]

Much is known about the monastic life at Conception in its infancy largely because of a journal that Conrad kept assiduously from his first days in America until shortly before his death a half-century later. It is an invaluable source for tracing Conception's history and reveals the monastic mindset of someone who was fully committed to forging a genuine Benedictine observance for his community. Conrad's monastic vision was different from the missionary model of Wimmer and Marty, but he did not feel bound to any one rigid form of monastic observance. He collected what he thought were the best elements of Benedictine tradition for his community. He also faced the same reality that his predecessors in America had faced: the heavy demand for monastic personnel in parishes and missions made an enclosed monastic life all but impossible. But before Conrad could fully confront the perennial problem of active and contemplative monasticism, he had to face another challenge, one that came from his own family and his own motherhouse.

In 1875 Father Ignatius Conrad, Frowin's brother and a monk of Einsiedeln Abbey, arrived at Conception to spend some time acquainting himself with the American foundation. Father Ignatius had spent two years at Beuron before entering Einsiedeln and had developed a dislike for the German abbey's monastic style every bit as deep as that held by Anselm Villiger. Observing his brother's predilection for implementing Beuronese practices at Conception, Ignatius Conrad recognized like-minded spirits in the Conception community who felt that this was a betrayal of the Swiss roots of the Missouri monastery. Perhaps the most virulent opponent of Conrad's Beuronese sympathies was Adelhelm Odermatt, who invited Ignatius Conrad to spend some time with him at his parish house in Maryville during the spring and summer of 1876. During that time the two engaged in a letter-writing campaign to Anselm Villiger, informing him of what they considered to be the deviant monastic practices of Prior Frowin Conrad.

The letters had a telling and immediate effect on the Engelberg abbot. His response came in the form of what Conception historian Father Edward Malone calls "the Bomb"—a lengthy letter dated November 8, 1876, excoriating Frowin Conrad for his adaptation of Beuronese customs and imposing a list of ultimatums on the Conception superior.[37]

The impact this letter had on Frowin Conrad was also immediate and is recorded in his journal:

> Today the heaviest trial since coming to this country came upon me. I received a letter from our Rt. Rev. Abbot in which he leveled accusations of ingratitude and disobedience against Engelberg because of my adaptation of Beuronese usages. . . . He desired under a threatening deposition that I should copy Engelberg in everything that could be done without endangering discipline such as hymns and psalms (which are to be said according to the usage of St. Gall). He also said that I should change the Beuron *Ceremoniale* with that of Engelberg and that . . . *culpa* and profession should be like that of Engelberg.[38]

To say that Conrad felt betrayed would be an understatement. His abbot had based his searing letter on one-sided reports without making a full investigation of what was taking place in Missouri. It is a testament to Frowin Conrad's monastic humility and obedience that he accepted the reprimand and immediately announced the stipulated changes in the Conception community. He did this without mentioning his own knowledge of the efforts of Fathers Ignatius and Adelhelm or the veiled threat in the abbot's letter to appoint Adelhelm Odermatt as superior of the community if Prior Frowin did not conform to Swiss usages.

Notwithstanding his steadfast submission, Conrad displayed some of the personal hurt that "the Bomb" from Engelberg had caused him in a letter sent to Villiger several months later:

> I took from Engelberg what I had received there and with it laid the foundation of this new edifice. If I have adapted some things from other monasteries, it is because I have considered them to be in harmony with the Holy Rule and our own local conditions. . . . Whenever I found something at another monastery which seemed to me to promote humility or charity, the glory of God or our common

prayer, I took this and would have continued to do so, had not your veto of November 8 intervened.[39]

But it was in his journal that Conrad finally gave a spiritual gilding to the whole affair, writing:

> I often sought in repeated letters to convince the Reverend Abbot [Villiger] of the way things really were here, as well as recalling to mind . . . his own words before I left Engelberg, supporting my decision to retain certain chant and ceremonies from Beuron. However God permitted that endeavors of this kind were interpreted as disobedience, which may have been the case. I do thank the abbot and my superiors from my heart for this trial which I no doubt have merited. I can see now that over the past year there were rumors which gave indication that the ax would fall. . . . May the Lord turn everything to our best if it be well for me that he do so.[40]

In point of fact, the Beuronese influence never did depart entirely from Conception. Conrad continued to correspond with Placid Wolter and to visit Beuron on his trips to Europe. The chant of the monastic choir and architecture of the abbey church later constructed under Conrad were stamped with the imprint of Beuron. The procedures for monastic profession and abbatial elections eventually reverted to Beuronese practice. When the time came to form a separate Swiss-American congregation in 1881, Abbots Frowin Conrad and Fintan Mundwiler of St. Meinrad were in accord that the statutes of the European Swiss Congregation needed to be modified by Beuronese customs.[41]

The discord between Engelberg and Conception in 1876 occasioned another split—this one between Conrad and Adelhelm Odermatt. Because of their different personalities and preferences for monastic models, the two had been at odds from the time they first came to Conception. At the time of the controversy over Conrad's adoption of Beuronese practices, Odermatt had indicated a desire to found at Maryville a new Engelberg, a priory directly dependent on the Swiss motherhouse.[42] By 1881, when Conception was ready to be given status as an abbey, the break between the two "founders" was complete as Odermatt was given permission by Anselm Villiger to make a new foundation in America.

Left: Frowin Conrad, O.S.B., first abbot of Conception Abbey. Right: Adelhelm Odermatt, O.S.B., first prior of Mount Angel Abbey

Frowin Conrad was named the first abbot of Conception on June 29, 1881, a position that he held without interruption for over forty years. In that time his community experienced remarkable growth. Benedictine sisters from Maria Rickenbach in Switzerland came to America and settled near Conception. A new monastery was constructed in 1881 and an impressive new basilica in 1891. The college at Conception grew in size, as did the number of vocations in the community. Parish commitments throughout Missouri and a number of Indian missions in the Dakotas were a test of Conrad's resolve to make Conception "a genuine Benedictine monastery." In ways beyond his knowing or planning, it was developing a solidly American identity, even as it absorbed the sound spiritual example and love for Benedictine tradition embodied by Conrad.

As all this was taking place, another strand of Swiss monasticism was beginning to take root many miles away, one that gave witness to the pluralism that Benedictines were presenting to nineteenth-century America.

Westward Expansion

The motives that prompted Adelhelm Odermatt to set out for the West in 1881 to found a monastery were multiple. His dissatisfaction with Beuronese practices in Missouri was only one reason for the journey. For Odermatt, it was also a question of experiencing a call to propagate the same missionary monasticism he had seen at work in the Cassinese houses of Boniface Wimmer. He even adverted to the evangelizing example of Wimmer's monasteries "in the East" in a letter he sent to Anselm Villiger in 1881, trying to persuade Engelberg to sponsor a similar undertaking in the American West.[43]

Odermatt's plan included nothing less than the establishment of a third congregation of Benedictine monks in the United States. The keystone of this congregation would be a mother abbey on the West Coast, serving as a spiritual center and place of training for candidates. From there a string of monasteries would be established whose purpose would be to help evangelize the states of California, Oregon, and Washington.[44]

Odermatt's vision was shared by Father Nicholas Frei, a young confrere from Conception who accompanied him on his trek westward. Like so many pioneers who had preceded them, the two monks were taken with the immense possibilities that lay open to them as they headed toward the Rocky Mountains and Pacific Ocean. Wrote Frei to his abbot at Engelberg: "Up to this time I have not encountered any more picturesque, rich and temperate area in America than this. A huge field of work is opened to us and opportunity is given to do whatever is possible."[45]

Some of the initial enthusiasm of the pioneer pair of monks was tempered when, upon investigating possible sites in Utah and Nevada, they found the obstacles of the Mormon population and the rugged terrain too formidable. But the West Coast held more promise. There they had been offered sites by Joseph Alemany, archbishop of San Francisco, in the Santa Iñez Valley and in Oregon by Archbishop Charles Seghers of Portland. The lure offered by the latter included a small colony of German settlers in the Willamette Valley. Seghers had also secured the services of Benedictine sisters from Minnesota to work at an Indian mission in his diocese and had made a formal request to the monks of St. John's Abbey in Minnesota to lend their assistance.[46] If that were not enough to persuade Odermatt, Segher's preferred site for the monastery was on a butte surrounded by German Catholic farm families and a countryside similar to that around Engelberg. Odermatt settled on this site at Fillmore, Oregon, as the preferred one on his visit there in November 1881.

Next, Odermatt had to sell his proposal to Engelberg. Traveling back to Switzerland, he gave a fulsome account of the advantages of the Fillmore site to the monastic community. Apparently the presentation was a convincing one, because the Engelberg chapter voted their approval for the new foundation on July 3, 1882. Odermatt immediately made plans to return to Oregon, sparing no effort to make his "New Engelberg" succeed. He took with him thirty trunks of supplies and forty young persons anxious to experience the wonders of the American West, including ten monks from Engelberg, Benedictine sisters, and a group of laborers. The reaction to their departure is captured in an entry of Anselm Villiger's journal:

> What upsets me even more than the cost of the expedition is the fact that the people selected for this trip include too many who are lacking maturity in their vocation. On this very point I made my comments known and I now have little optimism about this expedition because in my opinion those who are leaving lack the necessary experience.[47]

In the same month that Odermatt departed from Engelberg, September 1882, another abbot, Frowin Conrad, was expressing similar reservations about the new enterprise in his journal:

> It appears that there is great enthusiasm in Engelberg for the foundation in Oregon, where a "pure" second Engelberg is proposed. I can only hope that my fears are not warranted. It seems to me that they have been overly impulsive in beginning the foundation and have not considered all of the difficulties that accompany a new beginning. It is my opinion that they would have proceeded more securely if they had first decided to establish our own monastery of Conception on a firm foundation.[48]

The concerns of both abbots proved to be prophetic. During the ensuing decade, the zest for the project in Oregon subsided as Odermatt began making extensive land purchases and started a building program that included a monastery, church, school, and printing shop. Even though he wrote extensively to the mission aid societies of Europe for funds,[49] it was Engelberg that bore the brunt of the Oregon community's debt. The Swiss monastery had to draw upon its own reserves in order to loan money to Odermatt and so had to postpone its own building program for twenty years.[50] It was only Villiger's determined decision to sacrifice Engelberg's personnel and money that kept the Oregon community afloat in its early years. As Villiger wrote in his journal when opposition was directed toward him for deciding to send two newly ordained priests to what was now called Mount Angel Priory in 1887:

> For me it is infinitely painful for some time to have seen how little interest our capitulars have in the new foundation which they themselves decided to start in a common chapter vote. They want the end but not the means to the end. The new foundation, truly the worry and problem child of my old age, would have come to grief long ago had it not been for my ten-and-twentyfold decisive intervention on its behalf.[51]

The Mount Angel community came to grief in a completely unexpected way when, in May 1892, the monastery, church, and school were completely destroyed by fire. The heady dream of a string of monasteries along the West Coast had been snuffed out long before the ashes of that fire. But the indefatigable Odermatt would not let his dream of Mount Angel die. After the fire he stepped down as superior of the community to go on an extended fund-raising tour that would last seven years. By 1899, when he was reappointed prior, the debt was beginning to be paid off, a new monastery was being built, and the community was growing in numbers.

At this time several of the key actors in the drama of Engelberg's monastic odyssey in America came together once again. Abbot Anselm Villiger died in January 1901. His successor, Leodegar Scherr, soon sent letters to both the prior of Mount Angel, Adelhelm Oder-

First monastery of Mount Angel, with priory, seminary, and church (1889)

matt, and the abbot of Conception, Frowin Conrad. Conrad, in his position as president of the Swiss-American Congregation, was instructed to proceed to Mount Angel for a canonical visitation. He was to review the priory's monastic observance, check its financial condition, and supervise the election of a new prior.[52] Conrad dutifully fulfilled his mission and tactfully sidestepped any confrontation with his old nemesis Odermatt. The fact that the visitation resulted in a long list of recommendations for monastic observances that had been neglected under Odermatt and in the election of a new prior to replace him did bring a certain vindication to Conrad.[53]

The visitation also brought Mount Angel to the point where it was ready to stand on its own. In 1904 it was formally made an independent abbey of the Swiss-American Congregation.[54] And as the Oregon community of Odermatt's dream began to involve itself in

65

apostolates of education, publishing, parish work, and missionary work among the American Indians, its founder received his own recognition for a long life's labor by being named titular abbot of his community in 1916.

Swiss-American Benedictines in the South

If Mount Angel was a living memorial to the single-mindedness of Adelhelm Odermatt, another Swiss-American foundation, the community of New Subiaco, Arkansas, was one of the many legacies of the individualism of Martin Marty. Like Mount Angel, the Arkansas monastery had its origin in a small colony of German-speaking farmers. Upon returning to St. Meinrad from an extensive trip to the Indian missions of the Northern Plains in the summer of 1877, Marty was presented with a joint proposal from the Little Rock and Fort Smith Railroad and Bishop Edward Fitzgerald of Little Rock to provide pastoral care for a planned colony of German Catholics.[55] Projecting that this would take the form of a new monastic foundation, Marty submitted the offer, along with one from the state of Washington and one from Bishop Seghers of Portland, to the monastic chapter of St. Meinrad. The offers were discussed, but no definite commitment was given.[56] Part of the reluctance of the St. Meinrad community to accept the proposals could be attributed to the growing alarm over the commitment that Marty had already made to the Indian missions.

The chapter's sentiment had little effect, however, for by November 1877 Marty, on a return trip to the Indian missions, had come to an agreement with the German agent of the railroad company. The abbot and the railroad would select the land. The railroad would donate 640 acres for the monastery and 100 acres for a convent of Benedictine sisters, already promised by the Benedictine community in Ferdinand, Indiana. In return, the abbot agreed to build two churches and two schools for the spiritual needs of the German settlers.[57]

Marty then presented the contract as a *fait accompli* to his prior, Fintan Mundwiler. Mundwiler sent a monk from St. Meinrad, Isidore Hobi, to inspect the land; he returned to Indiana just before Christmas in 1877, speaking of the Arkansas site as ''a paradise fallen from heaven.''[58]

But the colony's first permanent Benedictine inhabitants, who arrived from St. Meinrad in March 1878, found little of earthly delight in the garden so glowingly described. Father Wolfgang Schlumpf and the two Benedictine brothers who accompanied him, Kaspar Hildesheim and Hilarin Benetz, labored that whole year in meeting the minimum stipulation of the contract with the Fort Smith railway company. They were successful in doing so largely because of Schlumpf's business acumen and remarkable capacity for work.

The ongoing problem at New Subiaco was more one of personnel than of the financial woes that had plagued earlier Swiss foundations. In its earliest years the community at Subiaco (then known as St. Benedict's Priory) seemed to attract a curious blend of itinerant Benedictine priests and eccentric lay brothers. Father Aegidius Hennemann of St. Boniface Abbey in Munich arrived in 1878 and discovered that he could not get along with Schlumpf. He left the community and purchased land of his own in southwestern Louisiana, with the intent of founding a new monastic community.[59] In 1879 Father Eugene Weibel, a monk of Maria Stein Abbey in Switzerland, came to Arkansas, and by the end of the year he had left New Subiaco and set up a mission center in the eastern part of Arkansas, where he later founded an Olivetan Benedictine community of sisters.[60] During the same year, the only remaining priest from St. Meinrad left the community, as did one of the original lay brothers.

As a crown to all these developments, at the end of 1879 word came that Marty had been named the new bishop of the Dakota Vicariate and an election of a new abbot would be held at St. Meinrad. By the time Fintan Mundwiler was elected abbot of St. Meinrad in February 1880, the two remaining lay brothers in Arkansas had left, as well as two of the sisters from Ferdinand. Schlumpf appealed to both Mundwiler and Abbot Basil Oberholzer of Einsiedeln for help. Abbot Fintan, in a reversal of his predecessor's high-handedness, asked the St. Meinrad chapter to accept responsibility for the Arkansas priory. At the same time, Mundwiler thought it imperative that the foundation of New Subiaco be given the full support of Einsiedeln. He wrote to Oberholzer: "I think it is good that as many as possible of the Einsiedeln Fathers should be together in Arkansas, but only those who get along with one another and can accept deprivation. Since the region there is small, everyone must go without usual conveniences and comforts and be prepared for sacrifice and burden."[61]

The Einsiedeln community was willing to accept the great "sacrifice and burden" of providing the Arkansas foundation with many new monks. Father Bonaventure Binzegger was sent from Einsiedeln in 1880 to be the new prior, replacing Schlumpf, who returned to St. Meinrad. But the problems of New Subiaco did not diminish with the addition of Swiss monks. A newly ordained priest, Father Vincent Wehrle, arrived from Einsiedeln in 1882 and soon challenged many of Binzegger's ideas. By 1883 Binzegger was forced out as prior, and his successor, Father Benedict Brunet, met the same fate. By early 1885 Schlumpf was back as prior, but the climate within the community was far from ideal. Wrote one observer, Father Matthew Sättele, of the clashes between personnel in the community:

> I believe there is a storm brewing. Father Vincent is disgusted here. He is a constant rebel, always causing unrest and dissatisfaction, and sulking at all orders and warnings of Abbot Fintan. Twice now Father Wolfgang had to report him to Abbot Fintan and to demand that he be removed. Abbot Fintan wanted to assign him to Little Rock, to Father Felix; but Father Vincent declared outright that he would not go—and with good reason; for Father Felix and Father Vincent would never get along any better than cat and mouse. Father Wolfgang no longer wants Father Vincent within reach of St. Benedict's, since he has not ceased to fill the novices and candidates with dissatisfaction, by not obeying the commands of Father Prior, and by being as cold as an iceberg to both of us.[62]

Such was the conflict of community life on the frontier. Not long after Sättele's report, Wehrle was reassigned to Devils Lake, North Dakota, from where he would carve his own distinct niche in American Benedictine history.

New Subiaco Abbey in Arkansas (1895)

Soon after Wehrle's departure the fortunes of the New Subiaco community did appear to turn around. In 1886 the community was made an independent priory and opened its own novitiate. In 1887 Einsiedeln sent over Father Gall d'Aujourd'hui, a charismatic and scholarly young monk, along with eight of his students—dubbed the "Eight Beatitudes"—all of whom eventually made profession to the New Subiaco foundation and gave it a stable core of young monks.[63] With a continuing flow of recruits from Einsiedeln, along with an influx of American vocations, the New Subiaco Priory was raised to the status of an abbey in 1891.[64] In 1892 Ignatius Conrad, the former fomenter of so much dissent against Conception Abbey's first abbot, was elected first abbot of New Subiaco. He selected Wolfgang Schlumpf as his prior and Gall d'Aujourd'hui as his novice master. These three monks from Einsiedeln constituted a ruling troika, testifying to the Swiss community's influence on the fortunes of New Subiaco.

The election of Ignatius Conrad was also a vote of approval for the missionary character of New Subiaco's monastic orientation. That missionary character came more from the practical exigencies facing the community than from any deliberate design on Conrad's part. As the new abbot wrote to his counterpart in Einsiedeln:

You express your astonishment that I conduct so many missions and
retreats and you wonder what the members of the monastery think
of it. I can understand why you raise the question, even with its im-
plication that I am living as a gyrovague. I have mentioned previously
what good Bishop Hogan told me on the day of my blessing as abbot: "I was vagabond bishop for years and you will continue as a vagabond abbot; you cannot have it any other way in mission territory."
It would certainly be more comfortable to stay at home with the
brothers rather than take up the work and exertion connected with
giving missions and retreats. But I must see that there is food on hand
to feed and provide for over seventy people, in addition to our pressing need for new and permanent buildings. Where else could I acquire money to take care of these things? Do you want me to make
debts as they did in Oregon and then write "papa" at the motherhouse asking: help me to pay off a great fraction of a million; I am
unable to liquidate the debt I have incurred.[65]

Leaving aside Ignatius Conrad's critical allusion to the debt owed
by Mount Angel, one can recognize in these words the same set of
practical demands that faced other frontier superiors in the nineteenth
century, forcing their communities to eke out a hardscrabble existence with a strong slant toward missionary and parish work. New
Subiaco was typical in its instinct for survival. In spite of devastating
fires, a predominantly Protestant population surrounding it, and a
perilous financial state, its educational and parish apostolates thrived.
It was even able to make its own foundation in Texas, fulfilling the
promise of Wimmer's pre-Civil War Benedictine presence.[66]

Part of the credit for this accomplishment must be ascribed to
the longevity of the abbots of these early communities. Ignatius Conrad was abbot at New Subiaco for thirty-three years. His brother
served as abbot of Conception Abbey even longer—from 1881 to
1923. These were matched by abbots in the American Cassinese Congregation. Competing with Wimmer's tenure of over four decades
as superior were Innocent Wolf and Leo Haid, both of whom served
as superior of their respective communities in Atchison and Belmont
for over thirty-five years.

St. Meinrad began another foundation in the South before the
nineteenth century came to a close. In 1890 monks from St. Mein-

rad came to Gessen, Louisiana, at the invitation of Archbishop Francis Janssens of New Orleans, to found a community that eventually moved to Covington and became St. Joseph's Abbey in 1903.[67] This community followed in the footsteps of the earlier Swiss foundations, concentrating on pastoral work with a local colony of Germans and an expanding educational apostolate. They were also following in the steps of Benedictine women who had come to Louisiana twenty years earlier. The story of those women needs to be presented in order to fully appreciate the American Benedictine contribution to the Catholic Church in the United States.

CHAPTER 5

Benedictine Women

Eichstätt and Its Foundations

Consecrated women were an integral part of the history of Benedictine life in the United States from its beginnings. If at times in the past the role and contributions of Benedictine women have been slighted, it needs to be affirmed that the efforts of several generations of communities of women have served as an essential component of the work of American Benedictines. In recent years the historical record has rightly given more recognition to their role, due in large part to the histories that have been written by members from their own ranks with access to carefully compiled community archives.[1] The account given here of the historical development and influence of communities of Benedictine women in America relies heavily on these works.

Like so many other Benedictine houses in Europe at the beginning of the nineteenth century, the convent of Benedictine sisters in the Bavarian town of Eichstätt was suppressed under the Napoleonic Secularization Act of 1806. Like its male counterpart of Metten in Bavaria, St. Walburga's Convent was restored by King Ludwig I. On a trip to Europe in the spring of 1851, Boniface Wimmer stopped at Eichstätt and petitioned its superior, Mother Eduarda Schnitzer, to send sisters to St. Marys, Pennsylvania, where monks from St. Vincent were providing for the needs of a small Catholic community.[2] Wimmer had for a long time wanted to bring Benedictine sisters to America, and the opportunity came when the School Sisters of Notre Dame withdrew from St. Marys in 1849. But before Wimmer could persuade the sisters to accompany him, he explained his plan for them to the Ludwig-Missionsverein in a letter to its president, Archbishop Karl Reisach of Munich:

> I am too much of a Benedictine to let this chance pass without transplanting the female branch of the Order into the New World. We have already had several candidates for such a convent who speak English well. Therefore, if I can get two more nuns and one lay sister to start religious life, we will soon have a community. I am firmly convinced that the old Orders, especially ours, if they come out of their seclusion and adapt themselves to modern demands, will have many advantages over modern society in so far as tradition, stability and discipline are concerned. They are modeled after monarchical principles of the Church and thus ought to have the same advantages as limited monarchies over Republics.[3]

Wimmer may have failed to see the irony in his advocacy of a monarchical religious structure, to be funded by a feudal-type Bavarian patron and transplanted to democratic America, but he did secure funding from the Ludwig-Missionsverein. Three sisters left Eichstätt for the United States in June 1852. Sister Benedicta Riepp, twenty-seven years of age and novice mistress at St. Walburga, was appointed superior. She was accompanied by Sister Walburga Dietrich and a lay sister, Maura Flieger. Upon their arrival in New York, they found no one to give them a formal welcome and had to proceed to St. Vincent on their own, arriving on July 8. There they were received by Wimmer and Bishop Michael O'Connor. Bishop O'Connor required, as a condition for the sisters' continued presence in his diocese, that their property be held in his name.[4]

In the autumn of that year the sisters began their proposed school at St. Marys, but conditions there fell far short of their expectations. Riepp's letters to King Ludwig I recount the gripping poverty of the children and their Benedictine teachers. Their difficulties were compounded by the primitive living conditions, the harsh climate, and the slowness of the sisters in learning English.[5] The description of the sisters' grim situation in Pennsylvania moved King Ludwig to send Riepp eight thousand florins. However, she never saw the money. It had been forwarded to Wimmer, and it was his judgment that the building program at St. Vincent should take priority over construction of a new convent for the sisters at St. Marys.[6]

The dispute fueled by Wimmer's action foreshadowed the controversy that would take place in succeeding years regarding jurisdiction over the sisters. Sister Benedicta was caught between her allegiance to St. Walburga's and Wimmer's claim to jurisdiction as ecclesiastical superior. In attempting to acquire a degree of independence from both (as in the case of her solicitation of funds from the Ludwig-Missionsverein), Riepp only exacerbated the situation, rankling not only Wimmer but some of the other community members at St. Walburga's and St. Marys as well. Wimmer's decision to open a novitiate at St. Marys in 1852 and his efforts to press the community to assert its independence from Eichstätt also drove a wedge between Riepp and her superior at St. Walburga's, creating a split that could only widen as Wimmer's maneuverings continued.

Wimmer did recognize the needs of the sisters, and he respected the work they were doing; but he was hurt when, after having the sisters establish their own novitiate, he heard criticism that emanated from Eichstätt about his arbitrary use of authority. To make clear who was the most authoritative interpreter of the priorities of Benedictine communities in America, Wimmer wrote to Gregory Scherr in 1853: ". . . the sisters in Eichstätt are fools if they expect to understand better what is needed in America than I do here in the place and on the spot."[7]

Despite this wrangling over the exercise of authority, candidates from both Bavaria and America continued to enter St. Marys. By December 1855 there were thirty-nine sisters. One of the Bavarian Benedictines who arrived that year was Sister Willibalda Scherbauer, who immediately sided with Riepp in the simmering conflict between her, Wimmer, and yet a third figure, Bishop Josue Young of Erie.

The beginnings of this conflict can be traced to Riepp's decision in 1856 to send four sisters to Erie at Bishop Young's request. Problems arose when Wimmer heard of the move. He immediately objected on several counts, particularly the sending of two novices with

St. Joseph's Convent, St. Marys, Pennsylvania (ca. 1865)

the group, young girls whom Wimmer judged were far from ready to teach or to live community life on their own. It was at this juncture that Wimmer first intimated his course of action "to end this feminine tyranny by deposing the Mother Superior [Riepp] and putting another in her place."[8]

The situation further worsened in 1856 because of a dispute over who was to serve as chaplain for the sisters at St. Marys. Father Benedict Haindl asked Boniface Wimmer to relieve him of his duties as chaplain for the sisters and transfer him back to St. Vincent. Wimmer did so, sending Father Rupert Seidenbusch in his place. Unfortunately, Seidenbusch had already developed a strained relationship with Riepp during his years as pastor of St. Marys Parish. The relationship did not improve when he was appointed chaplain of the convent and superior of the monks' priory at St. Marys. Seidenbusch had even more differences of opinion with the novice mistress, Sister Willibalda Scherbauer. Ultimately Wimmer forced the issue by calling a community meeting, at which both he and Seidenbusch were present, and confronting the sisters with an ultimatum: they could either follow Wimmer's recommendations or he would abandon all responsibility for their care. Not unexpectedly, the sisters agreed to follow Wimmer's recommendations.[9]

Developments took a more decisive turn in 1857. At that time Wimmer's new monastic community in Minnesota had asked St. Marys for volunteers to assist at their school in St. Cloud. A number of disgruntled sisters petitioned Wimmer to go to Minnesota. He gave his permission, on the condition that the sisters first undergo a period of instruction and preparation at St. Vincent's mission in Indiana, Pennsylvania. During this period a series of setbacks in the Minnesota community forced the sisters there to seek a delay in the departure of the St. Marys sisters. Wimmer reacted to this in June 1857 by transferring four sisters from the Indiana mission to teach in the school of St. Mary's Parish in Newark. While arranging for the sisters' transfer to Newark, Wimmer received perturbing news from Rupert Seidenbusch: Mother Benedicta (as she was then called by her sisters) and six other members of the community were leaving on their own for Erie and then on to Minnesota. The plan of Mother Benedicta, as it unfolded, was even more intricate. Having reached Erie, she dispatched seven sisters, under the leadership of Sister Willibalda Scherbauer, to St. Cloud. Mother Benedicta then left for Europe alone. She went first to Eichstätt, where she met with an unexpected rebuff from Mother Eduarda. Moreover, she was not allowed to leave the convent of her Bavarian motherhouse to present the case of the American sisters to Archbishop Carl August of Munich and King Ludwig.[10] Finally securing safe passage to Rome, she determined to settle there the question of the extent of Wimmer's authority, as well as her own. She did this by drawing up a bill of particulars against Wimmer. She presented her grievances to several influential German bishops and to Pope Pius IX.[11]

Upon hearing of Riepp's action, Wimmer acted with his accustomed determination, secure in the knowledge that he had his own influential circle of supporters in Rome. In November 1857 he wrote a lengthy letter refuting point by point the accusations Riepp had lodged against him.[12] He also announced to Father Demetrius di Marogna in Minnesota that the sisters who had fled there were to promise obedience to Abbot Wimmer as a condition for being cared for by the St. Cloud monks. Finally, Willibalda Scherbauer was to resign as superior and leave St. Cloud.[13]

By the end of 1857 it appeared that Wimmer had maintained his control. The superiors of his houses at St. Marys, Erie, Newark, and St. Cloud recognized the jurisdiction of the abbot of St. Vincent over the sisters' communities. In 1858 Wimmer gave a ready reply to the Propaganda Fide over the charges brought against him by Riepp. He also responded to the criticism from the Ludwig-Missionsverein with uncharacteristic meekness, admitting that he had made a mistake when, after receiving three thousand florins from King Ludwig intended for the St. Cloud convent in 1858, he had purchased land with it for the monks in St. Cloud.[14] Much more important from Wimmer's point of view was the recognition of his claim of authority over what he termed the irregular behavior of Benedicta Riepp.

Riepp's mission to Rome did not meet with the approval of all her sisters in America. In her own community of St. Marys, in a highly moralized assessment of the young superior's course of action, a chronicler wrote:

> Mother Benedicta undertook the foundation in Minnesota against the will of her higher ecclesiastical superiors and therefore all the sisters were not bound to obey this venture. Some had the courage to decide for St. Marys and remain where they had their vows. . . . God shows how the one [set of sisters going to Minnesota] triumphed in their pride and how the other set silently suffered their abandonment. He saw, too, in the future, and what it would bring to those who had left. Many trials and heavy storms of adversity waited upon those who expected to find happiness in the West. The severest lot of all fell upon Mother Benedicta. The deepest humiliation and blackest ingratitude was her portion. So it always happens when one places trust in human help. The sisters who remained in St. Marys fared much better.[15]

The denouement of the whole affair was bittersweet. Benedicta Riepp returned from Rome and spent her remaining years at the convent in St. Cloud, where she was reconciled with Abbot Wimmer.[16] In 1862, at the age of thirty-seven, she suffered the fate of so many of her sisters in frontier America—death from tuberculosis.[17]

Riepp's death closed out a first decade of development in the United States, a period during which Benedictine women entered into an all too familiar fray with their co-religionists, finding their

spiritual life and apostolic work controlled by authorities whose awareness of their peculiar heritage and spiritual tradition was frequently
inadequate. At the heart of that conflict there loomed a much larger
question regarding the canonical status of the American sisters. The
significance of that question and its ramifications for Benedictine sisters
in the United States require separate attention.

The Problem of Canonical Categories

Many of the tensions under which American Benedictine women
worked in the missionary climate of the United States were not much
different than those experienced by their male counterparts: the conflict between European and American culture, the demands of a new
language and the prospect of financial failure, the ongoing tension
between an enclosed life of prayer and pastoral duties, the pull between personal autonomy and episcopal control. What did show itself as a unique and extremely volatile issue for women of religious
orders in America, Benedictines included, was their status under canon
law and in particular their right to solemn vows. This question, at
once a theological and a historical one, has received much investigation in recent years.[18]

The discussion centers on the fact that European sisters who lived
in strict enclosure, such as the Benedictines, professed solemn vows.
Because of the mitigated enclosure necessitated by conditions in
America, the right of these women to make solemn vows in the
United States was called into question.

On March 21, 1857, nine Benedictine sisters of St. Joseph Convent, St. Marys, Pennsylvania, professed solemn vows. They were
received by Boniface Wimmer, who had been commissioned by the
bishop of Erie to do so.[19] They were the first and last solemn vows
made by Benedictine sisters in the United States during the nineteenth century.

Not long after Wimmer had witnessed these vows, he submitted
a series of proposals to Cardinal Alessandro Barnabo of the Propaganda
Fide, petitioning for the resolution of a number of questions dealing with American Benedictine sisters. They included: (1) recogniz-

St. Joseph's Convent, St. Marys, Pennsylvania (1965)

ing the three existing convents of sisters at St. Marys, Erie, and Newark
as priories; (2) incorporating these and subsequent foundations into
the American Cassinese Congregation of monks; (3) allowing all the
Benedictine sisters in the United States to come under the jurisdiction of the president of the American Cassinese Congregation (Wimmer); (4) allowing the sisters to take solemn vows, even though they
could not live in strict enclosure; (5) allowing the sisters to teach in
state-run schools; and (6) allowing the sisters to pray the Office of
the Blessed Virgin in place of the regular Benedictine Office.[20]

The proposals of Wimmer were handed over to the Congregation of Bishops and Religious. After more than a year of delibera-
tion, Wimmer received a reply. The response given by Cardinal
Barnabo was one of historic dimension, in that it determined the
mode of governance and manner of life of Benedictine sisters in America for the rest of the century. Two of Wimmer's crucial points were
rejected. The jurisdiction that he had so earnestly sought was denied; it was given instead to the bishops of the three dioceses in which
the convents were located. Also, the sisters would not be allowed
to take solemn vows, only simple ones.[21] Wimmer had suffered a
defeat and so had the sisters. The abbot's control over American

Benedictine women had been undercut. The sisters' failure to receive permission to make solemn vows and to join a central congregation deprived them of a monastic spirit and effective voice for the next half century.

Wimmer made subsequent efforts to convince Roman authorities of the need to preserve the privilege of solemn vows and organize the sisters into a single congregation. He claimed that he wanted for the sisters what he had already provided for his monks, namely, the status of a congregation with its own superior and common novitiate. Wimmer added the suggestion that the communities be divided into geographical provinces, a structure that would expedite transfers of sisters from house to house and evade the dangers of episcopal jurisdiction.[22] But the Congregation of Bishops rejected this petition as well, and Wimmer met with the same negative response when he attempted to put the question on the agenda of the American bishops at the Second Plenary Council of Baltimore in 1866.[23]

There ensued a long period during which Benedictine women in the United States found themselves living a largely apostolic life as communities of active sisters while still retaining hope of having the problem of canonical enclosure and their monastic identity redefined. They were assisted in their efforts by the Benedictine bishop of Leavenworth, Kansas, Louis Fink. In 1879 Fink petitioned Cardinal Giovanni Simeoni of the Propaganda Fide that the Benedictine sisters of the United States be governed by one constitution and form one congregation.[24] He then proceeded to invite the superiors of the women's Benedictine communities to meet and reach a consensus on the matter, a proposal that won the support of Boniface Wimmer. The meeting, originally scheduled for Covington, Kentucky, in the summer of 1879, had to be postponed because of a smallpox epidemic there. The superiors did meet in Chicago in July 1881 for the purpose of "adopting a uniform constitution and establishing a congregation among all communities."[25] But internal differences and a lack of planning slowed the completion of the process, as did foot-dragging on the part of Bishop Tobias Mullen of Erie. In 1880 Bishop Mullen had taken a stand against Fink's efforts in Rome to secure congregational status for the sisters, and he exerted his influence in squelching the petition.[26]

The project was revived in 1897 by Abbot Innocent Wolf of St. Benedict's Abbey in Atchison, who had the support of the abbot-president of the American Cassinese Congregation, Ernest Helmstetter of Newark. The completion of twenty years of lengthy transactions between the Holy See and American Benedictines coincided with the promulgation of the Code of Canon Law in 1917. The published Code reiterated the definition of Benedictine women as nuns with simple vows, while also preserving their distinct monastic identity by retaining the autonomy of the local superior. The upshot of the appearance of the new Code was that it gave a green light to the organization of a distinctively monastic type of congregation for the Benedictine women in the United States. With the support of Abbot Helmstetter and Abbot Primate Fidelis von Stotzingen, a commission appointed by Pope Benedict XV recommended in 1921 the formation of the Congregation of St. Scholastica. Pope Pius XI gave his approval the following year for a trial period of seven years for the communities constituting the congregation. The congregation's constitutions were approved in 1930.[27]

The way was now open for the formation of other congregations. The Congregation of St. Gertrude was approved in 1937, that of St. Benedict in 1956. The story of how these many communities matured, as well as the difficulties they faced from both bishops and abbots in asserting their own identity, requires a backward glance.

Expansion and the Burden of Authority

The impulse of Benedictine communities of sisters to expand soon after their arrival in America was one more legacy of Boniface Wimmer. It was the St. Vincent superior who induced Mother Scholastica Burkhardt of Erie to send three of her fifteen sisters to Covington, Kentucky, in 1859 to found a convent and school for girls.[28] Wimmer was also instrumental in the founding of women's communities in Newark and Elizabeth, New Jersey; Richmond, Virginia; and Chicago. His plan was to have the sisters provide support to the

Above: The community of St. Walburga, Covington, Kentucky (1916). Below: The community of Immaculate Conception Convent, Ferdinand, Indiana (ca. 1870)

Benedictine monks in their pastoral work. Thus it was no accident that most of the early convents were located near already established houses of monks in St. Cloud, Newark, Atchison, and Chicago. This pattern was followed by later Swiss-American houses as well, as the communities of women in Ferdinand, Indiana; Clyde, Missouri; and Mount Angel, Oregon, all settled near monasteries of Swiss monks.

Wimmer envisioned the sisters as missionaries, no less than his monks. In 1887 he sent women from Elizabeth, New Jersey, to a new Benedictine foundation in Ecuador after the bishop of Erie had refused to allow seven volunteers from St. Marys in Pennsylvania to serve there as missionaries.[29] The authoritarian vise formed by the bishop and the abbot left little room for the sisters' own initiative, and it is understandable why many women chafed under such limitations. However, lest history judge Wimmer too harshly as an oppressive patriarch, one should note what he wrote at the end of his life: "It should not be surprising that we monks should work along with the sisters as their leaders and protectors, according to our means; but without them, we could not accomplish much. Not to speak of their good example, they also bring a special blessing on our endeavors which is often tangible."[30]

At times that blessing seemed to be well disguised to the Benedictine women themselves. A case in point involved Bishop Mullen of Erie, already mentioned for refusing to endorse the formation of a congregation of Benedictine women. Even more indicative of his opposition to granting the sisters any autonomy were two elections over which he presided at St. Marys. In 1881 the community there overwhelmingly voted for Sister Theresa Vogel (18 votes) over Sister Isidora Pilz (5 votes) as prioress.[31] Ignoring the community's decision, Mullen appointed Sister Isidora as prioress. In a similar election held three years later, the voting results were the same and so was the appointment.[32]

Perhaps the most persistent example of episcopal as well as abbatial arbitrariness during the early years was that experienced by the Benedictine sisters in Minnesota. In 1868 Bishop Thomas Grace of St. Paul delegated authority over the Benedictine sisters in his diocese to the abbot of St. John's, Rupert Seidenbusch, who had been in conflict with Benedictine sisters when he was chaplain at St. Marys, Pennsylvania. Exercising his newly acquired authority, he summarily deposed Mother Willibalda Scherbauer as superior of St. Joseph Convent and announced the appointment of Sister Antonia Herman of Chicago as the new prioress. When Sister Antonia balked at Seidenbusch's requests for increased apostolic involvement on the part of the sisters, she was asked to resign. Bishop Grace then appointed Sister Aloysia Bath, who had been professed only two years, as prioress.[33] In the election of 1880 Abbot Alexius Edelbrock of St. John's presided. He insisted that the community elect Sister Scholastica Kerst as superior or the election would be invalid. To no one's great surprise, Sister Scholastica was elected.[34]

St. Joseph's sister community at Shakopee, Minnesota, did not fare much better. In 1876 Bishop Grace deposed the prioress and appointed Sister Gertrude Flynn as her replacement. But Mother Gertrude's desire to return to a more monastic observance did not sit well with the bishop, and in the election of 1879 he delegated authority to a local pastor known for his dislike of the community and its superior. Despite the fact that the Shakopee sisters decisively reelected Mother Gertrude, the pastor overturned the results and appointed another sister as superior, a choice ratified by Bishop Grace.[35] The sisters at Shakopee received an even greater shock the next year when Grace's successor, Bishop John Ireland, informed them that "the convent was suppressed" and they were to join St. Joseph's Convent or be dispensed from their vows.[36] The thirty sisters at Shakopee submitted to Ireland's dictate and moved to St. Joseph's Convent.

The sisters at St. Joseph's no doubt thought that things would take a turn for the better when they were freed from the authority of the archbishop of St. Paul and placed under the jurisdiction of Bishop Otto Zardetti of the new diocese of St. Cloud, erected in 1889. But they found in Bishop Zardetti's uncompromising orders an even greater test of their perseverance. By this time, however, the sisters had developed a type of resistance characterized by both ingenuity and affected ingenuousness. They showed the former in response to the bishop's intervention in their internal prayer life when they made two new foundations outside the boundaries of the St.

The laundry at St. Joseph's Convent, St. Marys, Pennsylvania

Cloud Diocese; they displayed the latter when, upon receiving an insistent demand from Zardetti that the community move their school from St. Joseph to St. Cloud, they feigned deafness.[37] Such historical documentation makes understandable the comment of a major interpretive study of American Benedictine women: "No place existed in the ecclesial consciousness of that time for the concept of development within a living tradition. . . . Conflicting self-understanding and expectations were thus woven into the fabric of American Benedictine women's history."[38]

During these difficult times the sisters could take comfort in the fact that they continued to grow in the number of new houses and new members. There is no challenging the indispensable role these women played in the education and pastoral care of the immigrants. Despite canonical conflicts and controversies, the services rendered by the first Benedictine communities of women equaled, and in some respects exceeded, those of the monks. They were much more numerous in the classrooms and offered unique witness in hospitals and orphanages. Even those who toiled in the domestic drudgery of laundry and kitchen maintained an independent and resolute faith in what they were about. Perhaps the best evidence of the solidity and effectiveness of that faith was the magnetic attraction that houses of Benedictine sisters had for young American women. The religious life of these early communities was both edifying and empowering, long before the latter word acquired its contemporary cachet. A sizable part of that attraction stemmed from a contingent of Benedictine sisters from Switzerland who were undergoing the same trials as the descendants of Eichstätt.

The Swiss Connection

The community of sisters at the convent of Maria Rickenbach in Switzerland was another outgrowth of the nineteenth-century monastic reform. Under the guidance of the monastery of Engelberg, a group of devout women settled at the shrine of Maria Rickenbach in 1857 and dedicated themselves to perpetual adoration of the Blessed Sacrament and the following of the Benedictine Rule.[39]

Their first spiritual mentor was the prior of Engelberg, Father Anselm Villiger. He drew up a set of statutes for the sisters based upon the Benedictine Rule and also arranged the community's horarium. When Villiger was elected abbot in 1866, he appointed Father Frowin Conrad chaplain of the convent. Ten years after its foundation the community of Maria Rickenbach had grown so much that new candidates had to be turned away for lack of room. So when Frowin Conrad wrote to Maria Rickenbach from America in 1873, asking for sisters to assist him at his new community of Conception, Mother Gertrude Leüpi was willing to give a favorable response.[40]

Five sisters arrived at Conception on September 5, 1874. Unfortunately, Frowin Conrad was not able to provide suitable accommodations for them, so they were temporarily housed in the parish church at nearby Maryville under the care of Adelhelm Odermatt. The sisters found themselves in a situation that must have given them pause. As members of a cloistered community, they were living in a ramshackle rectory with a priest. They were German-speaking sisters in the midst of an Irish Catholic community, unable to start a

Above: The convent of Maria Rickenbach, Switzerland. Below: The first convent of Benedictine sisters at Maryville, Missouri (1874)

school because they did not yet have a command of English. More-over, they were unable to fulfill their principal spiritual work of per-petual adoration.[41]

Despite these obstacles, the sisters persevered and found that ef-forts were being made to assist them. Abbot Martin Marty sent Sis-ter Rose Chapelle from the Benedictine convent in Ferdinand, Indiana, to teach the sisters English within a month of their arrival at Conception.[42] Not unlike Wimmer, Marty took an active interest in the welfare of the sisters and was not beyond exercising his author-ity. For example, he urged them to replace the German Office of St. Gertrude with the Latin Little Office of the Blessed Virgin be-cause of its more "ecclesial" character.[43] He also made suggestions as to their religious dress and the customs to be observed within the community.

Marty's intervention introduced the familiar situation of the sis-ters being placed between two different authorities on either side of the ocean. But in this case the authority on the European side was a male and the former spiritual director of the sisters. Once word of some of Marty's recommendations filtered back to Abbot Anselm Villiger, he wrote to Frowin Conrad, insisting that the sisters keep the Office of St. Gertrude, as well as the constitutions and traditions of Maria Rickenbach. He did not want Marty or other "outsiders" interfering in the sisters' religious life. He further requested that Sis-ter Anselma Ferber maintain authority in governing the convent, with a chaplain or confessor to be consulted only in matters of conscience.[44]

Frowin Conrad eased the situation by constructing a small con-vent building at Conception, to which three of the sisters transferred in December 1875. There, with Anselma Ferber as superior, they instituted a limited observance of perpetual adoration and opened a school. This move to Conception was to prove a decisive juncture in other ways as well. The three sisters at Conception agreed with their former chaplain and monastic mentor, Conrad, that an enclosed life of asceticism, prayer, and perpetual adoration was the best ex-pression of their charism. At the same time, the sisters who remained at St. Gertrude's Convent in Maryville were influenced by the mis-sionary orientation of Adelhelm Odermatt.

Gertrude Leüpi, O.S.B.,
superior of convents
at Maria Rickenbach,
Maryville, Missouri,
and
Yankton, South Dakota

The first official sign of this division came in 1880 when Gertrude Leüpi, having declined reelection as superior of Maria Rickenbach, asked to be sent to America. Anselm Villiger agreed to her wish, on the condition that she reside at Conception and from there serve as superior of both convents of sisters.[45]

By the time Leüpi arrived in late 1880, Adelhelm Odermatt was ready to leave Maryville for his new foundation at Mount Angel. She resisted his invitation to take part in his expedition to the West Coast. Then she received a request from Martin Marty to send some of her sisters to help him with his work among the American Indians in the Dakotas.[46] Leüpi's decision to send her sisters to the Dakotas marked a direction from which there was no turning back. They were soon involved not only in mission work with the American Indians but also in education and hospital care, all of which made their tradition of perpetual adoration extremely difficult to preserve. Thus it was that the group of sisters who left Maryville for Yankton, South Dakota, evolved into the Benedictine Congregation of St. Gertrude, and the community at Conception (Clyde) became the basis of the Benedictine Congregation of Perpetual Adoration.

Meanwhile, once Odermatt reached Mount Angel, he invited sisters from the Benedictine abbey of Sarnen in Switzerland to come to America. Partially because of their interest in mission work, partially because of their desire to find a political haven from the threatened closure of their house, they came to the United States in 1882, settling in Cottonwood, Idaho. Sisters from the Swiss convent of Melchtal followed the westward path and made a foundation in Sturgis, South Dakota, in 1889.

It is difficult to determine just how much initiative the sisters themselves exercised in moving to America. Most of the major decisions for the Swiss sisters were made by male authorities, but their monastic superiors tended to have more concern for the Benedictine spiritual tradition than some of the bishops and Cassinese abbots cited earlier.

As early as 1866, Martin Marty had indicated his openness to the founding of a contemplative house of Benedictine sisters near St. Meinrad.[47] The help he had given to the sisters of Maria Rickenbach after their arrival in America gave him a reputation as a caring pastor. Gertrude Leüpi called him a second St. Francis de Sales and wrote Anselm Villiger in appreciation of Marty's concern for them. Marty himself reflected his sensitivity to the sisters' needs in a letter to Frowin Conrad: "As to the sisters in Yankton, I must tell you that I do not urge them to take schools. . . . Your fears are mine and there are many cases by which they are justified. I shall be glad if you can persuade Mother Gertrude and Sister Odilia that a longer and more careful training in spiritual matters and in scholastic branches is absolutely required for the honor and welfare of the community."[48]

During his tenure as bishop in the Dakotas, however, Marty displayed an autocratic streak every bit as strong as Wimmer's. He determined the individual assignments of many sisters, ordered a change in their habit, and, in the case of the Yankton community, exiled their superior, Sister Xavier Fischlin, because of calumnious charges provided to him by dissidents in the community.[49]

Frowin Conrad, perhaps even better than Marty, filled the role of protector of the sisters. As the former chaplain of the Sisters of Perpetual Adoration, Conrad was zealous in his efforts to preserve their independence and Swiss statutes, and to promote their spiritual growth. This is revealed most clearly in a series of letters he addressed to Anselm Villiger:

> I tend to be stricter with regard to the enclosure for our sisters [at Clyde], so as to avoid their being controlled by some bishop and one day being joined with the other Benedictine Sisters under one Superior General.[50]

> It will be necessary to obtain the approval of the local ordinary for the taking of perpetual vows, since in this country the convents are entirely under the jurisdiction of the bishops. With time it might be advisable to obtain papal approval of the Statutes for the Clyde sisters in order to be more independent of the Bishop, so that no bishop can come and order our sisters to amalgamate with the others under one Superior General. During my stay at St. Vincent, some bishops spoke to me about such a plan, but I was able to change the conversation and have them refrain from talking about it. . . .[51]

> Regarding the sisters in Dakota, I share your opinion. We have to be very careful that the worldly spirit does not gain the upper hand. . . . I always stress that there be a careful selection and thorough training.[52]

Though he never formally joined Bishop Fink in his effort to win approval for establishing a single congregation for all Benedictine sisters in the United States, Conrad was certainly one with him in wanting to obtain a greater degree of independence for the sisters. For example, when he traveled to Rome in 1893 for the first congress of abbots, he brought with him a copy of the proposed constitutions for the Clyde sisters and gave it to the prefect of the Propaganda Fide, Cardinal Mieczislaw Ledechowski.[53] Conrad himself maintained his role as spiritual counselor and guide to both the Sisters of Perpetual Adoration at Clyde and Gertrude Leüpi's community in the Dakotas. At Clyde he invested novices, presided at professions and elections, appointed sisters to positions such as novice mistress, and conducted visitations for the sisters until 1910.

The community of sisters at Conception had moved to Clyde, Missouri, in 1882, while still under the leadership of Mother Anselma Ferber. After her death in the following year, a twenty-nine-year-old American sister, John Schrader, was elected superior. For the next thirty-seven years she shared with Frowin Conrad a long tenure, during which both the Conception and Clyde monastic communities grew and expanded.[54]

The Clyde sisters established foundations at Mount Angel, Oregon, in 1882 and Pocahontas, Arkansas, in 1888. Even though they did not receive final approval from Rome as a separate congregation until 1936, their identity as a group of monastic women dedicated to prayer and Eucharistic adoration was fixed, and the twentieth century saw them spread from Clyde to St. Louis and Kansas City, Oklahoma and Wyoming, Tucson and San Diego.

For all the growth and guidance that were the good fortune of the Swiss Benedictine sisters, they were not spared some of the same problems as those experienced by their German "cousins" with regard to the roughshod manner of some of their male superiors. When a Benedictine monk from the abbey of Maria Stein, Father Eugene Weibel, asked for a community of sisters to conduct schools in his mission territory in Arkansas, Frowin Conrad reluctantly consented, sending Sister Beatrice Renggli and a companion from Clyde to provide assistance. Arriving in Pocahontas in 1887, Renggli helped to found a school and was then elected the community's first superior. Before long, she found herself at loggerheads with Weibel on the matter of internal authority. With the approval of Bishop Edward Fitzgerald of Little Rock, Weibel deposed Renggli and replaced her with a much younger sister. Mother Beatrice (as the community called her for the rest of her life) silently accepted the order and took her regular place in the community.

In the same year (1892) that Renggli was deposed and forbidden to correspond with Frowin Conrad, Bishop Fitzgerald began accepting the vows of the novices.[55] As a means of acquiring even greater control, Weibel then arranged to have the sisters affiliated with the Olivetan Benedictine Congregation, a process that resulted in more changes in their constitutions from Conception. A crowning blow came in 1897 when Weibel called for a snap election for superior at Pocahontas, at which he presided. After an ingenious personal tabulation of absentee and other ballots, he announced that Sister Cecilia Huler would be the new superior. He then proceeded to move the convent from Pocahontas to Jonesboro.

American Indian sisters, Elbowoods, North Dakota (ca. 1890)

But Mother Beatrice was to have a last riposte. In 1898, when the community dedicated its new convent in Jonesboro, Arkansas, Weibel and Bishop Fitzgerald took their places at the head table for the banquet. The steak dinner was served by none other than Mother Beatrice, who, upon seeing her two distinguished guests, honored them with a fine plate of hash rather than a steak.[56]

Eugene Weibel was not the only Arkansas Benedictine who adhered to such paternalistic ways. Father Bonaventure Binzegger of New Subiaco Abbey, in a retreat he gave to Benedictine sisters, provided the following spiritual advice: "You must become like a scrub rag, one that can be thrown about and used at will; one that does not flinch even though it be stepped upon. Humility which abases you will make you true religious and genuine Benedictines."[57] Assuredly the bishops and chaplains of the sisters in Arkansas and elsewhere afforded them many opportunities to practice humility.

Even when the sisters were allowed to express their Benedictine identity, they sometimes evoked an angry response from certain priests and bishops. A missionary priest from South Dakota, Father Francis Craft, contended that Martin Marty and other Benedictines were crippling his attempts to start an order of American Indian sisters.[58]

93

Craft saw the conflict in terms of a wider battle taking place between two opposing groups in the American Catholic Church at the end of the nineteenth century—the Americanizers and the Conservatives. He capsulized his own reaction to the work of Benedictine monks in the Dakotas as follows:

> Now we hear from those in a position to know that it is the purpose of Benedictines and bishops to break up the Sisters and drive me out of the Church if we submit to their unjust and cruel demands or to drive us all out of the Church if we do not. . . . They will never forgive us our American blood and birth and our success in doing what they so long held cannot be done. . . . It is useless for the bishops to ask us to deal with the Benedictines. I have tried it in every way for the last ten years and know it to be useless, but we are willing to deal with the bishops. Here we are the only American Order of Sisters and the only ones to take up the progressive views of Leo XIII, the representatives of the theory that Rome in America is American. I learn that our worst enemies are the Benedictines of St. Meinrad's, somewhere in your State and of Conception, Missouri. The priests of these two houses have, we learn, been corresponding together and laying plans for a long time to destroy the American Sisters.[59]

Craft's suspicions that a conservative cabal of imperious monks was out to thwart any effort on the part of American sisters to assert their independence were overinflated. They also flew in the face of the reality that American convents of Benedictines were themselves in the process of being "Americanized."

Although American Benedictine sisters still made occasional trips to Europe to recruit new postulants and volunteers well into the twentieth century, American-born vocations were on the rise.[60] In 1879, 53 percent of the 452 Benedictine sisters in American convents had been born in the United States, although only one of the sixteen superiors had been born in America. By 1903 the native-born population had risen to 58 percent of the total of 1814 Benedictine sisters, and twelve of the twenty-two superiors had been born in the United States.[61] The background against which this growth took place was the swelling tide of immigration to the United States in the late nineteenth century and the experience of assimilation that accompanied it, an experience of which the American Benedictines were very much a part.

Chapter 6

Immigration and Assimilation

The history of the American Benedictines is inextricably linked to the history of immigrant America. This is readily seen when one realizes that the primary purpose of the Benedictines in coming to the United States was the pastoral care of the European immigrants. Not only did Benedictine communities attend to the spiritual and educational needs of the transplanted Europeans, but the immigrants themselves became the source for the growth of the majority of monastic communities in the United States. Their students filled the schools, their hard-earned money helped to construct monastic churches and cloisters, and their sons and daughters supplied monasteries and convents with an increasing number of new members. A confluence of historical forces made this collaboration between the immigrant Europeans and the Benedictine Order possible, and it merits elaboration.

Early Missionaries

The French Revolution, which had forced the closure of so many monastic houses in France, freed a number of monks to pursue pastoral and missionary labors among French Catholics in the United States. Father Peter Joseph Didier, a Benedictine of the Maurist Congregation, was granted faculties by the Propaganda Fide in 1790 to

95

do missionary work in an area along the Ohio River that had been settled by French families.[1] Father Charles Guny, a Benedictine from Cambrai, France, came to America in the company of the famed Belgian missionary Father Charles Nerinckx in 1804. He worked with French-speaking Catholics in Kentucky before joining a community of Trappists in 1807.[2] A Benedictine priest from Florence, Italy, Father Louis Leopold Moni, came to the United States in 1818 to work with French Catholics in New Orleans and southern Louisiana. He continued that work until 1842 and became the rector of St. Louis Cathedral in New Orleans.[3]

Not all the early Benedictine missionaries from Europe were welcomed for their contribution to the American Catholic Church or the faith of the immigrants. Father Andreas Smolnikar, a Slovenian parish priest who later entered the Austrian Benedictine abbey of St. Paul, is a case in point. On the basis of an apocalyptic vision he was purported to have received on February 7, 1835, he began to propound his own millennialist doctrine. He carried that vision to Boston in 1837, where he began to minister to a group of German-speaking Catholics who were under the jurisdiction of Bishop Benedict Fenwick. Within four months Smolnikar had excommunicated Bishop Fenwick and assumed a role as leader of his new apostolic church.[4]

The Germans

The German-speaking immigrants who attracted Smolnikar were just the beginning of a rising tide of Catholics from Germany who entered the United States in the years before the Civil War. Unlike many of the Irish who came to America in the same period, as well as the majority of the newer immigrants of southern and eastern Europe who came toward the end of the century, the German Catholics who crossed the Atlantic were not poverty-stricken. But if the schools and churches were to be built, if parish communities were to develop, substantial financial help was required. That help came in large part from immigrant aid societies such as the Ludwig-Missionsverein, the Leopoldinen Stiftung, and the St. Raphaelsverein.

All these societies, which had begun only in the course of the nineteenth century, provided a constant flow of money and personnel to help care for the immigrants' needs. Although the immigrants themselves were the primary beneficiaries of this assistance, the means by which it was distributed was most typically the religious community. The list of individual American Benedictine superiors, monks, and sisters who petitioned and received aid from these societies is far too long to enumerate.[5] But even if not all the requests were answered, the financial contribution of these societies to the German-speaking immigrants was a reliable and essential lifeline to the service provided by Benedictine communities.

Yet, the funds provided by the immigrant aid societies were only a part of a much larger plan whose scope is conveyed in Boniface Wimmer's initial vision of a medieval European model transplanted to America:

> All reports from America inform us that German immigrants are concentrating in places where churches have been erected, or where German-speaking priests have taken up their residence. This would be found to be the case even to a greater extent if there were a monastery somewhere with a good school attached. In a short time a large German population would be found near the monastery, just as was the case in the Middle Ages, when villages, towns and cities sprang up near Benedictine abbeys.[6]

In areas of predominantly German settlement, such as a Stearns County, Minnesota, or Spencer County, Indiana, the formative character of a monastic community in the nurturing process was unquestionable. It was at once a liturgical and educational center, dispenser of social and sacramental services, a cultural symbol of faith and the fatherland. Even in areas where there was originally a more mixed immigrant population, the impact of a Benedictine house on the ethnic complexion of the community was considerable. Wrote Martin Marty of St. Meinrad a few short years after his arrival: "The existence of our Benedictine mission house has been the principal incentive for a good number of Catholics to settle here and to build an island in the midst of the Protestant and English settlers in Indiana, in which the German element so dominates that almost exclusively the German language is heard.''[7] From this perspective, Benedictines saw themselves as evangelizers of a still overwhelmingly Protestant continent of North America. Some of their fellow immigrants held a similar view. Sarah Peter, a convert and German lay leader in the American Catholic Church, saw the Benedictines as constituting a means for converting Protestants. As she wrote to Abbot Bernard Smith in 1857: "Our Catholics seem to forget their duties toward unbelievers and to shut [themselves] up within themselves. It is my only hope that [by means of the religious houses] . . . Protestants will be won by the good example and conversation of our religious, and that conversions may follow.''[8]

However much the encouragement of evangelizing efforts to win over Protestant Americans fell within the accepted framework of interdenominational conduct in the last century, it was quite another step to advocate openly the driving out of natives and the creation of ethnic enclaves. Such seems to have been the intent of Abbot Anselm Villiger of Engelberg, who, after receiving word that a German-Catholic baron had purchased the town of Fillmore, Oregon, wrote in his diary: ''The future of Fillmore is decided. It will be a German-Catholic town, which is of prime importance for our foundation. The Protestants and Yankees will not hold out long among Catholics and will leave.''[9] Such property-grabbing and proselytizing were reminders that the era of ecumenism was still far off.

For the most part, the first Benedictines were occupied with ministering to members of their own Church. For both Catholic and Protestant German-speaking immigrants, the chief instrument whereby not only the faith but the language and culture were preserved was the school.[10] That link will be treated at greater length in a subsequent chapter. Here one may simply note that Benedictine communities were also effective in organizing devotional societies that attracted and involved the immigrants in a variety of parish activities. At a typical parish staffed by the monks of St. Meinrad, one could identify the Gesellschaft der heiligen Scholastika and the Marianische Gesellschaft for the women, the St. Joseph Verein for the men, the St. Aloysius Verein for the children, and numerous others.[11] At a similar German parish staffed by St. John's monks in Minne-

Monks of Mount Angel Abbey in Oregon at work in the abbey printing press (ca. 1910)

sota, there were the Bonifatius Verein, the Joseph Brüder, and the Benedictus Verein. These groups would hold fairs and festivals to raise money for the parish, functions not unlike those of countless other Catholic parishes, but these societies also had the purpose of promoting German culture and spared no effort in doing so.[12]

The press was also an essential organ of maintaining contact with the immigrants. In 1867 Benedictine priests of Assumption Parish in St. Paul, Minnesota, launched the German-language newspaper *Der Wanderer* for the purpose of keeping alive and enhancing the traditions of the Catholic faith and the German fatherland.[13] By 1889 St. John's Abbey had its own printing press and was publishing material in both German and English. St. Meinrad was known for publishing *St. Meinrads-Raben* and the German monthly magazine *St. Benedikts-Panier*.[14] Mount Angel had the largest private printing press on the West Coast at the turn of the century and published the popular *St. Joseph Blatt* and *Der Armen Seelen Freund*.

The Germans were not the only ones to benefit from the Benedictine press in the United States. In Chicago, at the end of the nineteenth century, Benedictines were publishing the daily *Narod*, the

weekly *Katolik,* an agricultural bi-weekly, and numerous catechetical materials as products of St. Procopius Press in service to the Czech
Catholic community.[15] The American Indians had the *Indian Advocate,* a quarterly publication of the monks of Sacred Heart Abbey
in Oklahoma that appeared from 1893 to 1910.[16]

The growing diversity of Benedictine publishers signaled a changed
cultural context from that encountered by the founding generation
of American Benedictines. For the first few decades of their presence
in the United States, the history of American Benedictines was unquestionably tied to the German-speaking immigrants. It was a presence that was in turn strengthened by the widespread settlement of
Germans in some of the rural areas developed by Benedictine communities, the immigrants' high regard for the Catholic schools run
by the Benedictines, and the affinity German Catholics felt for the
European monastic tradition.[17] By the last few decades of the nineteenth century, however, new immigrant groups began arriving from
Europe and called upon Benedictine houses for help. In giving closer
scrutiny to the story of one of these groups, the Czech Catholics,
we may provide the reader with a surer sense of the progress and the
obstacles experienced by all of them.

The New Immigration

In the 1870s the first Czechs, or Bohemians, began arriving in
the United States in significant numbers. The Czechs, like the Germans before them, were farmers. Over half of the foreign-born Czechs
in the United States in 1900 were engaged in agriculture.[18] They also
had a higher level of education than Slovaks, Lithuanians, or Ukrain-
ians, as well as a higher percentage of skilled workers.[19]

One of the first states in which Czechs settled was Nebraska. By
1876 there were at least five thousand Catholic Czechs in the vicariate of Bishop James O'Connor, and he had only one priest to serve
their needs. Desperate for pastoral assistance, the bishop wrote two
letters to his friend Boniface Wimmer in the fall of 1876. In them
he asked for aid from St. Vincent's in caring for "the Germans, Bohemians and Poles" in his jurisdiction.[20]

In April 1877 Wimmer received the consent of the chapter at St. Vincent's to answer Bishop O'Connor's plea. In the summer of that same year he sent to Omaha Father Wenceslaus Kocarnik, a Bohemian-born monk of St. Vincent who had been ordained just three years. For the next seven years Kocarnik labored in the city and country parishes of eastern Nebraska, attempting to serve the massive needs of his fellow Czechs and to establish a monastic foundation. But the combination of cruel winters, conflicts with Czech parishioners, and the seeming unwillingness on the part of St. Vincent to send more monks rendered his efforts ineffectual.

In March 1884 Father Wenceslaus traveled from Nebraska to St. Procopius Parish in Chicago, where, with his former Czech classmate from St. Vincent, Father Nepomucene Jaeger, he conducted a parish mission. This became the occasion for the pastor of St. Procopius, diocesan priest Father William Coka, to propose an idea: Jaeger would leave his Czech parish in Allegheny, Pennsylvania, and take Coka's place in Chicago. Coka would become pastor of the Allegheny parish and, most importantly, Chicago rather than Nebraska would be the location for a new Czech monastery.[21] Wimmer sealed the arrangement by agreeing to Coka's terms, and after receiving permission from Bishop Patrick Feehan of Chicago to take over St. Procopius Parish, he appointed Nepomucene Jaeger as pastor and Fathers Wenceslaus and Sigismund Siger as his assistants.

So it was that in 1885 Wimmer had taken another decisive step in his program of missionary monasticism. The abbot who had once considered cities unsuitable for Benedictine monasteries had now set roots in the second largest city in the country. There were an estimated fifty thousand Czechs in Chicago and an estimated twenty thousand in St. Procopius Parish alone, both of which numbers were to nearly double after the first decade of Benedictine presence there.[22]

In light of such numbers, Wimmer was enthusiastic about the prospects for growth. He made plans for a convent of Benedictine sisters at St. Procopius under the leadership of Sister Nepomucene Jaeger, the sister of Father Nepomucene.[23] In 1886 a tract of land was purchased for the construction of a new monastery and rectory, and a new school was opened. Wimmer sent two new monks from

St. Vincent to the priory—Father Idelphonse Wittman and a theology student named Procopius Neuzil, who was to become the foundation's third abbot. In 1887 St. Procopius was made an independent priory and in 1894 an abbey, with Jaeger as the first abbot.

The impact of the community in its early years was immediate and particularly evident in three areas that served as a paradigm for Benedictine influence upon the immigrants: publishing, education, and parochial assistance. The biggest challenge to Czech Catholics in America at this time was the powerful voice of the largely non-Catholic group of Czech "freethinkers." A mixture of rationalist, socialist, and atheistic ideologies, the freethinkers used an array of magazines, newspapers, and stump-speakers to propagate their anti-Catholic views. Beginning in 1889, the Benedictines of St. Procopius published their own Catholic defense by starting the Benedictine Bohemian Press. In the next thirty years, under the leadership of Fathers Procopius Neuzil and Valentine Kohlbeck, the press reached the height of its influence, publishing both daily and weekly newspapers, a monthly magazine of spiritual reading, devotional leaflets, hymnals, and a Czech grammar. The "press war" it carried on with the freethinkers was at times bitter and fanatical, but the publications of the Benedictine Press did help to assure that the Czech Catholics in Chicago would remain loyal to their faith.[24]

The apostolate of the press complemented the continuing work of pastoral care. The formation of the new Czech parish of St. Vitus in 1888 was a sign of the rapidly expanding community of Chicago's Czechs. In the following year St. Procopius launched its parish missions throughout the country, a program that touched the lives of thousands of rural Czech Catholics. Having purchased a tract of rural land west of Chicago at the turn of the century, the monastic community built there a convent for Benedictine sisters, an orphanage, and farm. This site was later to become the home for the monastery itself and its schools. The monks also moved westward with the immigrants, accepting responsibility for a new Czech parish in Berwyn, Illinois. St. Procopius also initiated a colonizing project in northern Wisconsin, a "New Bohemia," but it never achieved the success of the Chicago-based projects for Czech immigrants.[25]

In all this expansion the Czech Benedictines were intent upon broadening and strengthening their educational apostolate. The high school that they had founded in Chicago in 1887 was moved to the suburban Lisle site in 1901. Upper-level courses were introduced and St. Procopius College evolved. When the abbey itself was moved to Lisle in 1916, the monks opened a seminary to train Czech and Slovak students for the priesthood.

Just how much Czech Catholics in Chicago and elsewhere relied upon the Benedictine monks and sisters who ministered to them is difficult to ascertain, but the flourishing monastic community of St. Procopius was one more sign of how the religious and ethnic values of monks and immigrants often helped to support one another.

The community of St. Procopius also helped to underwrite the Benedictine "ethnic-urban" experiment with the Slovak community of Cleveland. Among the students at St. Procopius Seminary in the 1920s were two Slovak aspirants to the priesthood, Gregory Vaniscak and Stanislaus Gmuca. In 1925 the dream of these two young men to found a Benedictine Slovak community was realized when the chapter of St. Procopius Abbey authorized the establishment of an independent priory in Cleveland.[26] The Cleveland community committed itself to staffing a school and providing pastoral help for Slovak Catholic immigrants. Stanislaus Gmuca became the first abbot of St. Andrew's Abbey in 1934.

America's major cities were not the only areas where Benedictines ministered to the new immigrants. The Colorado foundation of the American Cassinese Congregation, originally situated in the Boulder County area in the 1880s, later moved to Pueblo, Colorado, because of the pastoral need to serve the Czech, Polish, Slavic, and Germanic settlers in that area.[27] At the same time, Swiss monks in North Dakota were caring for the needs of a new wave of German-Russian farmers who had come to the northern Great Plains.

Americanization and the Americanist Crisis

In the midst of their ministry to the immigrants, the Benedictines became involved with a great deal of internal ethnic conflict.

The history of the American Catholic Church has been characterized in large part by the tension between contending immigrant
groups, and the American Benedictines were very much a part of that
history.

A representative example of how Benedictines dealt with this conflict can be seen in the story of Martin Marty, whose Swiss nationality lent itself to brokering many an ethnic impasse. The delicacy of
Marty's task was reflected in a letter he wrote to one of the first Irish
priests of St. Meinrad, who was sent to join a German and a Czech
priest at a mission in the Dakotas:

> I should be very sorry to see any national animosity between the people
> and if it exists among the priests, it cannot help but pass on sooner
> or later over to the laity. You are now three priests each of a different
> origin; but I still hope and pray that Catholic charity may prevail and
> that faults, which national feeling begets, may be overshadowed and
> pardoned by those who feel grieved by the first impression.[28]

Earlier in his career at St. Meinrad, Marty had to handle the resentment of the French clergy of the diocese of Vincennes over the "Ger-
manization" of southern Indiana[29] and the language and practices
of non-Germans. This antagonism was nowhere more clearly played
out than in the differences displayed between Irish and German
Catholic immigrants.

Marty repeatedly stressed that the Irish contribution to the American Catholic Church was an impressive and noteworthy one, adding
that there was no need to see it as a cause for rivalry. He was especially sensitive to this issue during his later years as bishop. In 1880
he was appointed by the Irish Catholic Colonization Association to
serve on a committee for finding desirable tracts of land in the West.[30]
At the Third Plenary Council of Baltimore in 1884, Marty inserted
a decree that catechetical instruction be given in English, even if the
child used another language.[31] And at a congress of German Catholics held in Cincinnati in September 1888, Marty proposed that
English-speaking Catholics of the United States be invited to organize
congresses similar to those of German-speaking Catholics in order
to "preserve the desirable characteristics and culture."[32]

Alexius Edelbrock, O.S.B.,
second abbot
of St. John's Abbey,
Collegeville, Minnesota

Boniface Wimmer displayed some of this same sensitivity when in 1873 he attempted to establish a separate monastery for Irish Catholics who wanted to enter Benedictine communities of the Cassinese Congregation. Three priest-monks from the abbeys of St. Vincent, St. John's, and St. Benedict's became the pioneer monks of St. Malachy's Priory in Creston, Iowa. Wimmer's motives, however, had as much to do with missionary expansion as with monastic harmony. As he wrote to the Abbot Alexius Edelbrock of St. John's: "They will aid in spreading the Order in America, Canada and Ireland and after a few years bring salvation to many Irish."[33] The monks of Creston did assist for a time in "saving souls" in eastern Iowa, but the community died the same year as its founder, Boniface Wimmer, in 1887.

Abbot Alexius Edelbrock was another example of a Benedictine superior who allowed a certain latitude for the Americanization of German ways. Responding to a query of the Irish editor of the archdiocesan newspaper, Abbot Alexius acknowledged both his respect for American institutions and his conviction that the German Catholics had a right to worship in the language of their choice: "Though

a German by birth I have lived in this country since a child and ad-
mire and love its institutions. The question of nationality should not
enter into God's Church. Unquestionably Catholics should have every
opportunity to practice their religion in their own language . . . .
there is no widespread ill feeling between Catholics on account of
national differences and priests and religious are respected by all ir-
respective of where they were born.''[34]

Despite the best intentions of Edelbrock and others, the Benedictines often found themselves in the midst of pastoral assignments
where their German identity set them at odds with other religious,
bishops, and laity. This conflict was part of a much larger problem
in the American Catholic Church that was coming to a crisis point
at the end of the nineteenth century: the so-called Americanism controversy. In brief, the controversy pitted, on one side, German Catholics who felt compelled to preserve their language and their cultural
heritage, insisting on the right to have schools in which the German
tongue was used and churches in which they could hear pastors preach
and give instructions in German; on the other side was a contingent
of prelates and leading figures in the American Catholic Church (who
happened to be identified with the Irish element) who felt that the
European immigrants should be Americanized, which meant learning the English language and adapting to or absorbing the political
and cultural freedoms of the United States.

Given the fact that German continued to be spoken in most of
the Benedictine houses in the United States in the second half of
the nineteenth century,[35] and that many of the German immigrants
sent their children to Benedictine schools so that they could maintain a living link with the German language and culture, it is no surprise as to where most American Benedictines stood on the
Americanism question. Although most of the superiors of Benedictine communities stayed on the sidelines and reserved comment during the public debate on the Americanist question during the last
two decades of the nineteenth century, there were some inevitable
clashes. In 1884, at the Third Plenary Council of Baltimore, Bishop
John Keane, an Americanizer, led an attempt to ban American
Benedictines from making any liquor except Mass wine. It appeared

to many to be a repeat of the brewery controversy between O'Connor and Wimmer of earlier years. But Keane had the firm backing of other members of the hierarchy, including Bishop John Ireland of St. Paul. The move was finally defeated after a debate that featured the rebuttal of Keane's position by Benedictine Bishop Rupert Seidenbusch of the Vicariate of Northern Minnesota.[36]

However it was not Keane but John Ireland who loomed as the most formidable opponent of the American Benedictines during this period. At the same plenary council of 1884, Ireland teamed with Bishop John Spalding of Peoria to pass legislation that would prohibit any religious order from receiving a deed or title to any parish or church property. It was also Ireland who expelled the Benedictine sisters from Shakopee, Minnesota, exerted pressure on Rupert Seidenbusch to step down as bishop of his vicariate, and headed a visitation of St. John's Abbey that led to the resignation of Abbot Alexius Edelbrock.[37]

The forced resignation of Edelbrock was especially painful for the abbot of the Collegeville community, who had prided himself on the cordial relations that had previously existed between the two prelates.[38] Edelbrock's reaction to Ireland's tactics was capsulized in a candid comment he made to Abbot Bernard Smith: "It's plain that the Bishop of St. Paul acts too high-handed [ly]. Religious have in his eye apparently no rights which he needs to respect; his will is law."[39]

Although Ireland himself had professed admiration for monastic life and manifested much less antipathy toward Benedictines than toward the Jesuits, the "German question" served to put matters in a different light. This was particularly evident in the area of Catholic education, where Ireland's own ideas were provoking a great deal of controversy. His famous "Faribault Plan," by which he proposed to have Catholic school children in Minnesota take classes in state-sponsored schools, shocked many who operated Catholic educational institutions. The opinion of Isidore Hobi, a priest of St. Meinrad Archabbey, is indicative of the resentment aroused by Ireland's plan among Benedictines. At the height of the controversy in 1893, Hobi wrote:

Archbishop Ireland of St. Paul, the leader of the church liberals in
America and an outspoken critic of both Germans and Religious, came
out in favor of state schools while giving a speech at the convention
of our national educational society. Among other things he made the
remarkable statement: "As a solution to the difficulty I would mix
the regular state-school with the religion of the majority of the children of the country, even though this religion might be Protestant."
His speech stirred up a general resentment among the bishops, priests
and catholics and disturbed many. . . . Much could be said here of
the evil consequences caused by Archbishop Ireland's activity. The
Lord knows how many complaints from bishops, priests and laity were
sent to Rome until finally he was called to Rome. Those who know
Rome said that his talking ability and his money would work wonders.
They spoke rightly. Coming home he telegraphed: "I have conquered
in spite of the Germans and the Jesuits."[40]

Hobi also castigated Archbishop Denis O'Connell, rector of the North
American College in Rome, and Archbishop Francesco Satolli, who
had recently arrived as papal delegate to the United States, for their
support of the "frivolous propositions on the school question" of
Ireland.

Even some of the more reticent Benedictine superiors were aroused
by Ireland's school plan. Abbot Fintan Mundwiler of St. Meinrad
expressed his views about the controversy in a straightforward letter
to Einsiedeln:

Our American school difficulties will not go away. The liberal party
of Archbishop Ireland does not rest, and works for the spread of liber-
alism in regard to making the parish schools state schools and in soften-
ing the laws against secret societies, etc. One would be happy if Satolli,
who seems to be under the influence of the liberal party, would be
called back. The good bishops feel hindered and hesitate to come out
against the liberal priests because they fear to come in contact with
Satolli, who gladly gives ear to liberals.[41]

Six years after Mundwiler's letter, the incendiary character of the
public and private exchange on the education issue had cooled.
Ireland's school plan had self-destructed, Americanizers such as Keane
and O'Connell had lost their positions of influence at the Catholic
University and the North American College in Rome, and the now

Cardinal Satolli had done an about-face and aligned himself with the conservative element in the American Catholic Church.

For all the polemical fires fanned by the Americanist controversy and the ethnic rivalry among Catholic immigrants, these issues did not come close to matching the impassioned rhetorical and practical problems posed for American Benedictines by Protestant America, problems exacerbated by the perplexing question of political allegiance. Like the immigrants, the Benedictines were confronted for several generations with the challenge of assimilation from non-Catholic America and secular society.

Anti-Catholicism

The challenge immediately presented itself to the first Benedictines who came to the United States in the form of the renewed outbreak of nativism that had erupted in America prior to the Civil War. Nativist sentiment against the European immigrants in this period took many forms, but possibly the best known and insistent was that of its political arm, the Know-Nothing Party. Boniface Wimmer, not one known to refrain from commenting on those he considered to be in opposition to his beliefs, assessed the situation of the Know-Nothings in Pennsylvania at the time their power was cresting in 1854: "Our newest political sect, the Know-Nothings, would like to eat us, skin and hair, but it does not go so easily. The pressure on them is as it was on the Egyptians; they see us grow but they cannot stop us."[42]

But Wimmer's dismissal of the Know-Nothings with a scriptural allusion could not diffuse the reality that other Benedictines were facing at the same time. In 1854 Benedictine Father Nicholas Balleis asked to be relieved of his post as pastor of St. Mary's Parish, Newark, after his church had been sacked by a group of Know-Nothings.[43] In 1855 a member of the Know-Nothing Party was elected regional school superintendent in the district in which Benedictine sisters had just established their academy at St. Marys, Pennsylvania. When the superintendent demanded that the sisters submit to a personal examination by him or have their state aid withdrawn, Benedicta Riepp

resisted the order. But she later expressed her fear in a letter to Archbishop Reisach of Munich: "This is a serious matter, especially here
in a free country that we Catholics, and in particular we sisters, should
have to submit to examination by such a man who is a member of
an organization considered to be the worst in the whole world, and
what is most sad is that this society has the upper hand in this country and many of its members are at the top in all matters of the
state."[44]

Exaggerated as Mother Benedicta's description of the actual influence of the Know-Nothings and their malevolence may have been,
the climate of apprehension and religious paranoia it reflected was
a direct result of the desire of Benedictine communities to make their
abbeys and convents secure bastions of the Catholic faith, "far from
the infectious example of another faith or of unbelievers."[45]

But even as their religious faith and tolerance were being tested,
the Benedictines faced the test of political loyalty produced by the
crisis of the Civil War. Once again, some of the hard choices they
faced were described in a typically subjective fashion by Boniface Wimmer. Styling himself as political pundit, he wrote in 1856:

> These recent days have been a time of great excitement in our land
> on account of the coming presidential election. The whole nation di-
> vides itself into three parties: the Democrats, or true republicans, who
> take the Union and the Constitution seriously; the (pseudo) Repub-
> licans, who wanted our northern states to succeed at the expense of
> the southern states and at the cost of a bloody civil war, and who
> are enemies of the Catholic Church, including revolutionaries of '48
> and all kinds of political fanatics; and the American or Know-Nothing
> Party who regard Catholics and all immigrants with the same ha-
> tred. . . . We Catholics are all on the side of the Democrats, as were
> many of the Germans who were formerly Protestants.[46]

Wimmer's characterization of political reality in the United States
at the time of the 1856 presidential election may have lacked accu-
racy, but his leanings toward the Democratic Party were of a piece
with those of both his fellow Catholics and Benedictines, even though
most religious superiors did not go to the lengths he did in giving
voting directives to his community on election day.

Another genuine problem occasioned by the Civil War was the matter of Benedictine monks being subject to the draft. After four of his lay brothers had been drafted into the Union Army, Wimmer himself went to Washington to meet with President Lincoln and obtain their release. Aided by the intervention of Archbishop Kenrick of Philadelphia, Wimmer secured an agreement with the War Department that the monks of St. Vincent and all Benedictines in the Union states would be exempt from military service for the remainder of the war.[47]

The situation was different at St. Meinrad, where monks were drafted to serve in the Union army, as well as in federal positions such as postmaster.[48] For the monks of St. Meinrad, however, this had the positive effect of dispelling suspicions that the German community was sympathetic to the Southern side.

There were genuine Southern sympathizers at St. Vincent who created some problems for Wimmer. A monk he had sent to St. Mary's Parish in Richmond before the war, Father Herman Wolfe, spent three years as an officer in the Confederate army.[49] Another St. Vincent monk, Father Emmeran Bliemel, served as a Confederate army chaplain and was killed in action.[50]

Although Benedictine sisters were not subject to the draft and were too far removed from population centers in the North to provide the hospital care performed by many other American sisters during the war, Wimmer in 1863 did ask the Benedictines of St. Marys Convent to "pray for the averting of the calamity." The calamity in question was not, as one might conjecture, the defeat that threatened the Union troops at Gettysburg or even prolongation of the conflict; the diary of the sister who recorded Wimmer's words mentions that the "prayers were successful" in that no more monks of St. Vincent were drafted.[51]

After the Civil War, Benedictine houses in different parts of the United States were confronted with the new problems of assimilation. The communities founded in heavily Protestant areas of the South were marked by a Catholic and European subculture that clashed with that of their non-Catholic neighbors. The oral histories of such communities as Belmont in North Carolina, St. Bernard

Abbey in Alabama, and New Subiaco Abbey in Arkansas are steeped in stories of ethnic discrimination and religious misunderstanding, with prejudice and proselytism abounding on both sides. In this respect, too, the Benedictines were at one with the times, exuding the air of an embattled and emerging minority in a country that still preened itself on its Protestant heritage.

Benedictine women remained especially vulnerable to overt religious discrimination. Some of the exploitive nativist literature of the pre-Civil War period, for example *The Awful Disclosures of Maria Monk*, had centered on lurid tales of convent life and scandalous activity "within the walls." That these writings retained a remarkable resiliency in the popular mind is substantiated by the frequent references in community histories to expressions of anti-Catholic behavior directed toward sisters.

In 1868 a group of sisters traveling from the Benedictine convent in Chicago to Minnesota were required to exchange their religious habits for Shaker dress so as to disguise their religious identity.[52] Several years later, after sisters in Duluth, Minnesota, had opened a school and hospital, the resurgent nativism of the American Protective Association forced the Benedictines to stay off the streets because of physical intimidation they received from A.P.A. members.[53] Sometimes the religious prejudice showed itself in a more legitimate political guise. In 1894 the state of Pennsylvania passed a law banning anyone wearing a religious habit from teaching in a public school and stating that no religious could be permanently certified as a teacher. At St. Marys Convent, where the Benedictines had taught in the town's schools for over forty years, the legislation created considerable consternation. The people of St. Marys helped to bring about an amendment of the certification ban, but the prohibition of the religious habit remained on the books.[54]

Other Benedictines saw a calculated connection between nativist groups and legislative measures that were taken against Catholic schools. Isidore Hobi, a monk of St. Meinrad, gave a provocative, if partisan, description of the situation in 1893, when the power of the A.P.A. was at its peak:

In Europe because of the close relation between Church and State politics has some significance for the Church, but here, because of separation of Church and State, the politics should not have anything to do with us. That would be the case if the rights of the Church, State and private persons were precisely defined. But that is not the case. You know the tendencies and the activity of the secret societies in Europe and how this power injured the activity of the Church in Latin America. The efforts of these societies can be seen here too. To achieve this purpose, they try to get control of the education of the youth in schools. This is achieved by laws forcing Catholic children to attend the godless state schools. . . . For several years an attempt was made in Indiana to force children to attend public schools, but it was prevented by legislators to whom Catholic priests made the matter clear. But it is certain that the Masons and the APA will work against the Church as long as God permits.[55]

Another traditional line of attack against Benedictines was that taken by temperance advocates. Recasting some of the same arguments used earlier by Catholic bishops such as Michael O'Connor and John Keane, nativist tracts picked up the familiar refrain of the evils of drink and debauched religious. One of these, written by a Reverend George Zurcher of Buffalo and published in 1898 under the title *Monks and Their Decline*, castigated Benedictines in general and St. Vincent Archabbey in particular for their refusal to conform to pleas for temperance on the part of the American Catholic hierarchy, claiming: "The monk priests are largely to blame that the temperance laws of the Catholic Church in America [sic] are not observed in so many sections of the country."[56] Zurcher petulantly transcribed O.S.B. as "the Order of Sacred Brewers," contrasting the German monks with the more upstanding examples of temperance among other Catholic groups.

Assimilation

Nativist attacks made more agonizing the already difficult balancing act of preserving monastic values derived from European tradition while pragmatically adapting to American culture. How difficult this process of assimilation was can be seen in the case of Martin Marty. As abbot and bishop, Marty readily adopted American practices and traditions when he felt that they served the good of the faithful. He encouraged miners in the Dakotas to join a union at a time when such organizations were condemned as secret societies by the Church.[57] He served in important government posts and was the only Catholic on the Board of Regents for Indian Affairs. He was quick to praise the American government as one "under which the Church is free and untrammeled in her divine work and wears the diadem of justice when almost every European power may be branded as the foe of the Church."[58] Yet Marty also advised monastic confreres to ignore executive orders from Washington because of liberty of conscience.[59] He roundly condemned the Bureau of Indian Affairs for its bias against Catholics and its promotion of Protestant denominations. He hailed the heroism he saw on the American frontier even as he nostalgically turned to the traditions of his mother abbey of Einsiedeln at times when the alien forces of the frontier weighed him down. It is also striking that Marty's years in America coincided with the crucial time span in which that assimilation process took place—the second half of the nineteenth century.

With the advent of the new century, the pressures to assimilate had slackened. Pope Leo XIII's encyclical *Testem Benevolentiae* rendered mute the "heresy" of Americanism, even as a gradual Americanization of life within Benedictine houses took place. Native-born vocations were increasing, and monastic communities were no longer dependent upon Europe for their personnel. The provincial nationalism of the Catholic immigrants was giving way to a mix of patriotic approval of America as a world power and growing acceptance of ethnic diversity. This was reflected in the person of Father Chrysostom Schreiner of St. John's Abbey. Rushing to Florida from the Benedictine mission in the Bahamas at the start of the Spanish-American War, he volunteered as a chaplain for Teddy Roosevelt's Rough Riders.[60] The change was witnessed on a wider scale in the increasing diversification of monastic houses and the slow erosion of the monolith of German monastic culture.

At the turn of the century, the election of John Kennedy to the presidency was still in the distant future. Benedictines still had to face the anti-German backlash of World War I, the Ku Klux Klan, and the demands of still newer immigrant groups to whom they would be called to minister. But they had emerged from the nineteenth-century crucible of immigrant assimilation into a twentieth-century American Catholic Church in which they had become a positive and increasingly influential force.

CHAPTER 7

Education

The endeavor of the Benedictine Order most crucial in touching the lives of the immigrants and expediting their entry into American society was that of education. Initially this work entailed preserving a European heritage of language and culture, while at the same time passing on an age-old inheritance of faith that was closely tied to the monastic tradition. From the start, there was little controversy over the notion of making this work a central concern of the Benedictine mission to America, and more than a century of experience has shown how much that educational enterprise has evolved.

The Monastic School

The earliest aspirations of Benedictines who came to the United States included a desire to establish schools alongside their monastic communities. These were not to be just places of learning and a means of preserving the Catholic faith, but truly monastic schools that would provide vocations to the priesthood and monastic life. Seminary schools that would transmit the monastic spirit and provide Benedictine vocations to serve the surrounding immigrant community were at the heart of the original vision of St. Vincent and St. Meinrad.[1]

An obvious help to the Benedictines in establishing their educational apostolate was the affinity that had always existed between the

German people and the school. More than any other single ethnic group in the United States, the German-Americans saw the school as the keystone of their faith community. To build the school first and the church afterward was a common rule of thumb that conveyed their priorities. This also fit conveniently into a more ancient tradition of monastic education that the Catholic Church over many centuries had come to expect of Benedictines. One of the monks of the St. Meinrad community, Father Chrysostom Foffa, expressed this expectation in emphatic form when he wrote:

> A school without a monastery is an institute foreign to our Order and estranges the faculty from it—even though such schools may have existed and still exist; nor would such a school fully attain its purpose; on the one hand, the pupils would not receive that education of mind, heart and character that they would receive in the monastic atmosphere; the Benedictines, on the other hand, engaged in school work outside the monastery would become ever more estranged from their nature and purpose. There can be no question of a monastery without a school.[2]

The indispensable place of a school alongside a new monastery recurs frequently in the correspondence of American Benedictine founders. Adelhelm Odermatt claimed that "if we cannot win Catholic youth with Catholic schools, our mission will ultimately fail."[3] Martin Marty insisted that the first priority of his monks should be the catechetical instruction and Catholic education of children.[4] For the Benedictine women as well, the work of teaching was one of the few givens they could count on when they came to America.[5] But the monastic school of European Benedictines would have to undergo alteration if it were to adapt to its new environment. Whether one speaks of the *Stiftsschule* of the Swiss abbeys or the *Gymnasium* of the German houses, the European model was that of a school in which the students would receive a classical education and follow a schedule patterned after that of the monastery. This concept was not easily adaptable to the immigrants' way of life on the American frontier. Flexibility of schedule as well as in pedagogical methods was required. Those methods were perhaps best summarized by Boniface Wimmer, who declared that his purpose was to teach students "first what is necessary, then what is useful, and finally what is beautiful and will contribute to their refinement."[6]

The word "college," as understood in educational circles today, denotes something far different from the first Benedictine schools. The typical Benedictine college of the nineteenth century enrolled students from the age of ten to twenty, some taking commercial or trade courses, others taking a more traditional liberal arts curriculum or pursuing studies for the priesthood.

Teaching and Scholarship

One of the problems of the early Benedictine colleges was that the teachers often were sorely in need of education themselves. Not only did many of the first monks and sisters lack linguistic skills, but they had little or no professional preparation to prepare them for the classroom. One is at times led to wonder if the relative success of these schools was something that happened in spite of or because of their lack of professional expertise. The historian of one community might hold the answer to that question in the assessment he gives of St. Benedict's College at Atchison in 1877 with regard to the Benedictine faculty:

> None had received more than a skimpy education, but the best of them were so successful at educating themselves for the rest of their lives that they were fine teachers. . . . Short on education, without extraordinary ability, they had only their own willingness to work unbelievably hard, confident that they were doing God's work.[7]

But "God's work" for the Atchison monks and many other Benedictines of the period included numerous duties outside the classroom. A regular round of pastoral ministry for the priests and a full range of domestic duties for the sisters would often fill up the free time outside of school hours, to say nothing of the tension such duties could cause in regard to their spiritual responsibilities. The teaching duties of some members were more survival tests than specialized disciplines. To take only one example, for the school year 1888–89 Father Urban Fischer of Mount Angel was assigned to teach philosophy, Hebrew, Greek, astronomy, chemistry, botany, geology, phys-

The monastic band of Sacred Heart Abbey, Oklahoma (1898)

Damian Lavery, O.S.B., director of St. Benedict College, Atchison, Kansas, and the college bus (1920)

ics, geography, typing, and shorthand.[8] Even in this earlier age when Renaissance men were more likely to be found in monasteries, it is difficult to imagine how such a demanding class load could benefit pupil or teacher.

Given the exigencies of missionary work and the chronic shortages of personnel, one is struck by the amount of intellectual work and graduate study that did take place. Boniface Wimmer sent his young monks to what he considered the "best" schools: to Rome for theology and philosophy, to England for hermeneutics and Hebrew, to Munich for art and music, to Georgetown for science, and to Innsbruck for dogmatic theology.[9] St. Vincent also had an impressive corps of monk-scholars. Typical of these was Father Oswald Moosmueller. Throughout his years as prior at St. Vincent and superior at communities in Atchison, Savannah, and Wetaug, Illinois, Moosmueller found time to write books on the Benedictines in North America before Columbus and a biography of Boniface Wimmer, as well as to publish a German historical monthly (for two years) and a monthly German journal translated from the Latin lives of the saints (for six years).[10] He also served as superior of the house of studies established in Rome by Boniface Wimmer, another idea of the St. Vincent archabbot that proved to be ahead of its time.

Another monk who combined missionary work with scholarship was Martin Marty of St. Meinrad. During his time as abbot, he acquired a printing press and authored books dealing with subjects as varied as the history of the United States, the history of the Benedictine Order, two volumes on the Ordinary of the Mass for the laity, an English translation of the Benedictine Rule, and biographies of Bishops John Purcell of Cincinnati and John Henni of Milwaukee.[11] As bishop, Marty was known as a leading advocate of Catholic higher education in the United States and was a member of the committee that founded the Catholic University in Washington, D.C.[12]

The Problem of Language and Culture

Most Benedictines in the nineteenth century, however, were not college professors or monastic scholars. This was the period when the elementary school in the Catholic parish was proposed as the antidote to the "Protestant" or public school. The Catholic elementary school was also the chief instrument by which American Catholics dealt with the need to impart religious instruction to the increasing number of immigrant children. And since women of religious orders constituted the indispensable corps of personnel who staffed the parochial schools throughout the United States, countless Benedictine sisters devoted themselves to the task of teaching in Benedictine parishes and missions. The sisters had brought this educational apostolate with them from the community of Eichstätt and had given it top priority from the start of their work in America.[13] Although the sisters were well aware that the physical conditions of the classroom and the professional qualifications of their teachers were not the best, they could point with pride to students who had absorbed not only the fundamentals of the faith but also enough monastic tradition so that a sizable number could be counted on to become members of Benedictine houses.[14]

One other essential value imparted to those students who attended parochial schools run by Benedictines throughout the nineteenth century was the German language and culture. In attempting to maintain this ethnic identity, the Benedictines found themselves part of the previously mentioned controversy in the American Catholic Church between those who wanted to see immigrant children assimilate the values of American political and social institutions and those who insisted upon their right to preserve their religious and cultural heritage through separate parishes and schools.

A series of events in the Americanist dispute of the 1880s brought the two sides into confrontation. In 1882 the German clergy in the United States joined with German-American laity in organizing themselves into a national assembly (*Katholikentag*) and a German-American society of priests. In 1886 a German priest from Milwaukee, Father Peter Abbelen, presented a petition to Rome asking that equal rights be given to German Catholics and protesting what he saw as the forced Americanization advocated by Irish clergy and bishops. In 1891 a German Catholic layperson, Peter Paul Cahensly, personally presented to Pope Leo XIII the Lucerne Memorial. This statement argued, among other things, for religious instruction in German and separate parochial schools for each nationality. The Americanizers, led by Archbishop Ireland, were quick to retaliate and persuaded the Pope to declare that Cahensly's proposals were "neither opportune nor necessary."[15]

When it became obvious that Cahensly's memorial would not receive a response from the Vatican, some Benedictine superiors, after remaining silent for so long on the "German question," spoke out in response to what they saw as the impolitic intervention of Archbishop Ireland. In 1892, when the St. Paul archbishop was visiting Rome, Bishop Leo Haid of Belmont wrote to Abbot Bernard Smith, his curial procurator, requesting that "our school system remain intact despite the Archbishop's efforts."[16] Before the first Congress of Benedictine Abbots in Rome in 1893, Bishop Louis Fink was reported as expressing the wish that "the abbots will accomplish something good at Rome and give the true story of our school troubles which were conjured up by the devil through the assistance of churchmen in America."[17] There was little doubt that the churchmen in question were the Americanizers in the hierarchy.

The Professionalization of Benedictine Education

After 1893 the influence of the Americanizers in Rome and the United States was on the wane. At the same time, Benedictine educational institutions in the United States were losing some of their ethnic parochialism, and there was an impetus for more professionalism and specialization in preparing students for higher education.

This was in part a reaction to what had prevailed during the first half-century of Benedictine work in the field of education in the United States, when the school was considered little more than an adjunct to the monastery. While the schools did foster moral and religious development, they were often woefully short of sound faculty and a comprehensive curriculum. The overriding moral purpose of the first Benedictine schools is stated in the catalogue of St. Benedict's College, Atchison, for 1874–75: "To cultivate the heart, to form and cherish good habits, to prevent evil ones, in fine, to exercise a truly parental care over the morals of the pupils, no less than over their intellectual and physical development, are paramount duties, kept constantly and sacredly in view by the [Benedictine] Fathers.''[18]

This emphasis on character development and moral virtue prompted some educators to question the academic standards that resulted. As Father Leo Huebscher wrote of Benedictine educational efforts in the 1880s: ''Our colleges, I am sorry to say, do not compare favorably with the Jesuits' because they are much smaller. Either we have forgotten how to educate or we have not enough of worldly spirit in our schools to have them patronized by the grandées.''[19] In truth, there were few ''grandées'' who patronized Benedictine schools at this time, but Huebscher's criticism did lead to some changes in thinking.

An example of that change is seen in a proposal made by Father Vincent Huber of St. Bede's Priory, Peru, Illinois, in a letter he wrote to Archabbot Leander Schnerr of St. Vincent in 1899. His proposal was to have all the Benedictine colleges in the United States organized and unified, a process that could be initiated with an organizational meeting.[20] The meeting took place at St. John's Abbey in August 1899. One of its results was a consensus that classical studies should continue to be the basic component of courses in colleges of the Cassinese Congregation, as opposed to the popular commercial course of studies. A year later, in a meeting at St. Vincent Archabbey, representatives of nine Benedictine colleges fixed the cycle of the commercial courses for four years and the classical course for eight. This meant that the seminary program would consist of four years of high school and four years of philosophy or liberal arts.[21]

A similar move toward centralization was taking place in the Swiss Congregation. Frowin Conrad, who at one time had held firmly to the traditional concept of a monastic school, wrote in his journal in 1902:

> It is my growing conviction that more attention and effort should be given to our college program so that it may acquire a higher status. For this reason I appointed Father Athanasius to draw up a plan of studies for the upcoming school year when we will open our new building. I will also send Father Paul to Chicago to attend the Con-

*Peter Engel, O.S.B.,
fourth abbot
of St. John's Abbey,
Collegeville, Minnesota*

gress of the Catholic colleges of the U.S. to be held there July 9 &
10. In addition I will have the college incorporated in the association
which has been in existence now for three or four years.[22]

Other monastic superiors were changing their method of preparation of personnel even more radically, sending monks to major
American universities for graduate studies and research. In the vanguard of this effort was Abbot Peter Engel of St. John's Abbey at
Collegeville, Minnesota. In 1898 he sent Father Anselm Ortmann
to take graduate courses in physics at Johns Hopkins University, the
first time that an American monk attended a secular American graduate school. Other monks of St. John's were sent to Columbia and
the University of Minnesota.[23] Engel did not neglect Catholic university centers, but in addition to sending his monks to such traditional schools as the University of Notre Dame and the Catholic
University in Washington, he arranged for members of the Collegeville
community to study at European universities and monastic centers
in Rome, Paris, Munich, and Maria Laach, a practice that his successor, Abbot Alcuin Deutsch, continued.[24]

Before the First World War, St. Procopius Abbey in Lisle, Illinois, had eight members of its community studying at the University of Illinois. Once canon law created conditions too difficult for them to continue this practice, a summer program for teachers was begun at St. Procopius in 1921 and 1922, with the hope that other American Benedictine instructors would attend classes in their specialized fields of study.[25] During this same postwar period Abbot Valentine Kohlbeck of St. Procopius sent his monks to obtain doctorates at the Universities of Chicago and Illinois, as well as to Prague, Czechoslovakia.[26]

Another significant event that took place immediately after the First World War was a meeting at St. Vincent Archabbey to organize the National Benedictine Educational Association, the first national Benedictine organization for members of both the Cassinese and Swiss Congregations. It had as its general purpose to increase excellence in American Catholic education in general and American Benedictine education in particular.[27] From 1919 to 1942 this organization met in regular convention, and its proceedings were published in its *Bulletin*.[28] During the twenties and thirties there was an upsurge of interest in affiliating with national accreditation organizations, such as the North Central Association.

This was also a period during which Benedictine women developed a more diversified educational apostolate, taking on new responsibilities in secondary education. They opened colleges at St. Joseph and Duluth, Minnesota; Atchison, Kansas; Bismarck, North Dakota; and Yankton, South Dakota, and provided more opportunities in graduate education for the members of their communities. In fact, Benedictine women's communities intensified their commitment to the educational apostolate throughout the first half of the twentieth century. Of the sixty-eight missions staffed by sisters of St. Benedict's Convent in Minnesota from 1900 to 1950, fifty-two were devoted to schools.[29]

This diversification extended to the educational work of Benedictine monks. Preparatory high schools attracted many of the men's communities in the twentieth century. Eight Cassinese houses began operating such schools,[30] as did four monasteries of the Swiss-

St. Benedict's Convent, St. Joseph, Minnesota (ca. 1940)

St. Scholastica Priory, Duluth, Minnesota

Mount St. Scholastica Priory, Atchison, Kansas

Annunciation Priory, Bismarck, North Dakota (1970)

Sacred Heart Priory, Yankton, South Dakota

American Congregation.[31] Added to these were three preparatory schools started by houses of the English Benedictine Congregation and one established by the Hungarian Congregation,[32] two European congregations that arrived in the United States with the new century.

Especially characteristic of the educational efforts of both the Cassinese and Swiss houses during the twentieth century was the maintenance of seminary programs. Theological seminaries at St. Vincent and St. John's grew in size and diversity, even as other Cassinese communities such as St. Procopius were forced to discontinue their program. The apostolate of seminary education appeared even stronger in the Swiss-American Congregation, with major seminaries at St. Joseph's Abbey, St. Benedict, Louisiana; Conception Abbey, Conception, Missouri; Mount Angel Abbey, St. Benedict, Oregon; Westminster Abbey, Mission City, British Columbia; and St. Meinrad Archabbey, St. Meinrad, Indiana. St. Meinrad's major and minor seminaries in particular maintained a program of priestly formation that produced several generations of American priests.

As American Benedictines continued their geographical growth in the twentieth century, they carried their educational tradition with them. In Latin America, Benedictine schools were founded in Mexico (Tepeyac), Puerto Rico (San Juan), Guatemala (Sololá), and Colombia (Bogotá). Benedictine monks could be found working with minority groups in inner-city schools (Newark and Cleveland), as well as conducting high schools in America's hinterland (Elkhorn, Nebraska, and Peru, Illinois). The spectrum of Benedictine educational institutions ranged from military academies (Richmond, Virginia; Savannah, Georgia; and Aurora, Illinois) to headquarters for Pax Christi (Erie, Pennsylvania).

This changing complexion of the Benedictine educational apostolate was part of the transformation taking place in the Catholic population of the United States. Numerous sociologists of the post-Vatican II Church have charted this change, showing how the sons and daughters of immigrants who had sought admission to the elementary schools and monastic-style "colleges" of the nineteenth century were, by the second half of the twentieth century, transformed into an upwardly mobile stratum of American society whose socio-economic ranking and educational aspirations were at the highest levels. A new network of Benedictine educational institutions reflected this: specialized college and theological seminaries, coeducational colleges and prep schools, adult and community education centers. The last-mentioned were particularly evident in those communities that needed to convert classroom space of traditional Catholic schools that had closed during the period of educational transition in the 1960s and 1970s. Another obvious reflection of the changing nature of Catholic education was the increasing number of monastic men and women who had acquired graduate degrees.

Benedictines could also join a segment of their fellow American Catholics in claiming to have gone beyond an era of anti-intellectualism and of having achieved a certain respectability in areas of academic accomplishment. After World War II there was a renewed interest in areas of monastic scholarship as well. The organization of the American Benedictine Academy (1948) and the appearance of the scholarly journal *The American Benedictine Review* (1950) were matched by an increased membership of Benedictines in professional societies and specialized academic disciplines.

At the end of the twentieth century, education is no longer as common a component of the community apostolate as it was a century earlier. A considerable number of Benedictine schools have been forced to close their doors. Nonetheless, the connection of monastic communities with education is still a transparent fixture of Benedictine life. It is a heritage that continues to be part of the process of transformation in a pluralistic American Church and society.

CHAPTER 8

The Mission to the American Indians and Blacks

In their work as educators, missionaries, liturgists, farmers, and builders, American Benedictines drew from a European experience analogous to what they encountered in the United States. But there was one work they undertook for which there was no precedent: the mission to the American Indians and the blacks. This was not a work originally anticipated by Benedictine superiors of American houses, but one they accepted early on and one they tried to perform to the best of their ability. Like the struggle of the people served by this mission, the story is filled more with setbacks and failures than successes. Yet it deserves a privileged place in the history of the American Benedictine experience.

The Apostolate to the American Indians

The one person who may be considered the initiator and greatest promoter of the mission to the American Indians was Martin Marty of St. Meinrad Abbey. Already as a student and young priest in Switzerland, he had met the famed Belgian Indian missionary Father Pierre De Smet and had read of the work of other missionaries, such as Fathers Frederic Baraga and Samuel Mazzuchelli, who had worked among the American Indians. During his years as superior of St. Meinrad, from 1861 until well into the decade of the seventies, Marty was too preoccupied with the task of guiding his monastic community to fulfill his earlier yearning for work in the Indian missions.

In 1874, however, the Bureau of Catholic Indian Missions was established, with the express intent of meeting the spiritual and educational needs of the many Indian tribes that had been relocated by the government in the American West. The head of the bureau, Father John Baptist Brouillet, was searching desperately for missionaries and religious orders that would be willing to give themselves to this new missionary work. So it was that in the spring of 1876 Marty decided to make a brief visit to the Sioux reservation of Standing Rock in the Dakota Territory for the purpose of investigating the possibility of sending missionaries from his community at St. Meinrad to staff the reservation. Marty's visit was an emotionally moving one. Many Indian chiefs who had been baptized by De Smet came to him, expressing their joy that another "black robe" had arrived to minister to them.[1] Marty gave provisional consent to Brouillet after the visit, saying that he would be willing to take charge of the Standing Rock reservation, provided he could be assured of making a monastic foundation there.[2]

Marty's plan for this foundation was a fusion of monastic and missionary elements that harked back to the Benedictine model of the Middle Ages. He described his dream to the Bureau of Catholic Indian Missions:

> We need men, priests and brothers . . .and in order to get, train and sustain them we ought to have on a favorable spot in the Dakota country a Benedictine monastery on the same dimensions as the Abbeys erected one thousand years ago in the wilderness and among the barbarous nations of Europe. Such a house of God will not only secure the divine blessing, but it will also be a center of life and action, a retreat for bodily and spiritual restoration; and for the surrounding population of previously untutored savages this house will exhibit a bright and social aspect, where they will learn how to work and pray, how to cultivate their soil and their souls. In no distant future the Sons of St. Benedict shall thus see themselves surrounded by a double family, the monastic and rustic community, both united by faith, labor and common prayer.[3]

Marty's vision incorporated elements of the Jesuit *reducciones* of Latin America, of Father Junipero Serra's California missions, and of the feudal reality of medieval monasticism, a vision that Marty was tireless in pursuing.

During the next several years Marty made a series of visits to the Dakota Territory, during which he learned firsthand of the betrayal of the Indians by the United States government. He had occasion to personally attempt an overture of peace with Sitting Bull and other Sioux who had declared themselves at war with any citizen of the United States.[4] Throughout this period Marty was enlisting his fellow monks at St. Meinrad and the Benedictine sisters of the nearby convent at Ferdinand to help him in his missionary work with the Indians. He also sought the support of Einsiedeln Abbey, grandiloquently stating to Abbot Basil Oberholzer: "to us the work is given, at the entrance to the American alps, to build wooden chapels and schools as once was done at Böllingen in the Black Forest."[5]

But Marty's histrionic rhetoric did not meet with complete acceptance by his own community of St. Meinrad nor by his ordinary, the bishop of Vincennes. Among the reasons for this was the fact that Marty had not consulted with the monastic chapter when making his original response to go to the Dakotas, nor did he consult when he began appointing community members to serve in the missions. The majority of the St. Meinrad chapter, along with Bishop Maurice St. Palais, believed that the missionaries were more needed in southern Indiana.

In 1877 Father Eberhard Stadler led a group of monks at St. Meinrad in signing a petition that urged Marty to return to his abbey and forgo further involvement with the Indian missions. Stadler detailed his reasons for the petition in a letter he wrote to the abbot of Einsiedeln:

> Until now it has not remained unknown how Einsiedeln has been taken in for the Indian missions. I wish that one would with foresight pass them up. The matter is not in order. The abbot has no mission from Rome for this. The bishop [of Vincennes] is against it. The situation at St. Meinrad is doubtful if Abbot Martin does not return

at once. Almost unanimously a petition was made to Father Abbot that he come back [from the missions] at once.[6]

Another member of the St. Meinrad community, Father Wolfgang Schlumpf, added his own reasons for the petition:

> In April, 1877, orders arrived from the Dakotas that two fathers, two lay brothers, and four sisters should come there. Those that were to go prepared for the trip, and we were anxiously awaiting for the arrival of the Rt. Rev. Bishop [St. Palais], who had been called to ordain one of the priests who was to go to the mission. . . . Soon after the Bishop stopped on his way to Ferdinand at St. Meinrad and told F. Eberhard that he as bishop was the superior of the sisters and would not let them go to the Dakotas. He believed the abbot should use his monks for activities in the diocese.[7]

Despite such protests, Marty held firm. Bishop St. Palais' death in 1877 eased his worries somewhat. He did return to St. Meinrad, but he used his time there to give instructions in the Sioux language to the monks and sisters destined for the Dakota mission. He also learned of his appointment as vicar for the Indian missions, and during the next two years his responsibilities for the Indian missions multiplied as the time devoted to his abbatial duties dwindled.

The growing tension between Marty's dual commitments was finally lessened in 1879 when he was named vicar apostolic of the Dakota Territory. He promptly resigned as abbot in December 1879, before his episcopal consecration. Thus the budding antipathy on the part of some monks of St. Meinrad toward Marty's seeming neglect of the monastery was cut short.

The new bishop's greatest need was still to staff the missions under his vast jurisdiction of over 150,000 square miles. He looked instinctively to his fellow Swiss Benedictines. Mention has already been made of Marty's visit in 1881 to the convent of sisters at Maryville, Missouri, and his success in securing Mother Gertrude Leüpi's assistance. He also persuaded his two classmates and superiors at St. Meinrad and Conception, Fintan Mundwiler and Frowin Conrad, to send monks from their communities to assist him in his work. The flow of men from these two Benedictine houses over the following decades was as much a testament to Marty's personal appeal as to any priority assigned to the Indian missions by those who were sent.

Marty's search for personnel went beyond monasteries in the United States. He even traveled to Europe, where he recruited Swiss Benedictine sisters of Melchtal and Presentation sisters from Ireland to come to the Dakota Territory.[8] But Marty's prized recruit was a young socialite from Philadelphia named Katharine Drexel, whom he had met during a visit to the East Coast in 1885. That first visit resulted in the first of many financial gifts given to Marty's missionary endeavors by Drexel. It also seemed to plant the seed of her own call to found a religious order specifically oriented to the care of American Indians and blacks.[9] The extent of Marty's influence on the decision of Drexel to found the Sisters of the Blessed Sacrament is poignantly portrayed in the following letter:

> It was due, I think, to these visits of Bishop Marty that as a young girl I became interested in the Indian Missions. . . . He told me of his experience among the Indians of Standing Rock and how as a missionary he was leading these pagans to a knowledge and love of God. The accounts of his missionary expeditions, his desire to establish schools for these people, his own sacrificing and untiring labors on their behalf, thrilled my soul with a desire to reach out to these people, and I believe that to Bishop Marty's visits I may partially ascribe the missionary vocation which God in His mercy has vouchsafed to me, and I also believe that had I not met Bishop Marty my whole future career might have been entirely different.

> With characteristic humility, of himself he rarely spoke; but he was ever the apostle making known his work, his plans for the spiritual and temporal uplift of the Indian, and it was his mission work which appealed, since he ever kept his own personality in the background.[10]

Doubtless Katharine Drexel's efforts in subsequent years to help finance the monks of St. John's Abbey in their labors among the Indians of northern Minnesota and the monks of Belmont Abbey in their missionary work among blacks, as well as her personal encouragement of St. Vincent College in Latrobe to provide instruction for Indian missionaries, were extensions of her initial regard for Marty.

As bishop, Marty was less successful in attracting missionary priests for his work. As in the case of other missionary bishops of that time, Marty's pressing need for priests sometimes prompted him to accept "renegades" from religious orders and other refugees from remote dioceses who caused more harm than spiritual help.[11] Part of this was attributable to Brouillet's practice of sending Marty priests cast off by bishops in the Eastern United States, but part of it was also due to Marty's naiveté in expecting that all his brother priests would have the same saintly character and spiritual zeal for the missions that he had.[12]

Throughout his years in the Indian missions, Marty received recognition for his efforts from the American Catholic Church. In 1884 the Third Plenary Council of Baltimore appointed him to serve on the Committee for the Welfare of Negroes and Indians. In 1885 he was named by the government as the only Catholic member of the Board of Regents on Indian Affairs. In 1891 he was chosen to be president of the Bureau of Catholic Indian Missions. He was also an unofficial lobbyist for the interests of Indians before Congress.[13] Marty needed these positions of influence in dealing with the government policy of apportioning "contract" schools among religious denominations and in confronting the problem of the growing lack of government funding for Catholic schools on the Indian reservations.[14]

In 1889 Marty was named bishop of Sioux Falls, South Dakota. As a result of this change, his wide-ranging missionary expeditions among the Indians were curtailed, and he became increasingly involved with the administrative concerns of his diocese. But this did not prevent him from organizing annual Catholic Indian congresses and pressing forward to the goal of establishing a Benedictine monastery in the Dakotas. Even after his appointment as bishop of St. Cloud, Minnesota, in 1895, Marty maintained that "he would never give up the care of his Indian missions in the Dakotas and would continue the work he had begun there."[15]

When Marty died in 1896, the record of his activity was a mixed one. He had paved the way for Jesuits, Franciscans, and members of other religious orders to assist him in founding schools and missions in the Dakotas and Great Plains. He had persuaded monks of St. Meinrad and Conception Abbeys and Benedictine sisters from several convents to staff mission schools. Marty could be regarded as the indirect founder of St. Mary's Abbey (in Devils Lake and Richardton, North Dakota) by virtue of bringing that community's founder, Vincent Wehrle, to North Dakota. His summer congresses for the Indians have survived to the present day in the form of the annual Tekakwitha Conference of North American Indians.

While one can question some of the methods used by Marty to evangelize the American Indians and criticize his condescending use of language in discussing their indigenous culture, he was no different than his contemporaries on this score. One cannot dispute the fact that the percentage of Catholics among the Sioux of the Dakotas was higher than among any other comparable group of American Indians at the time of Marty's death. Nor can one easily dismiss the impression made by the blackrobe who was remembered as a friend to the tribes of the Great Plains long after he had left the scene of his missionary endeavors.

Marty was far from being alone in promoting involvement of the American Benedictines with the Indian missions. One of the first monks to have felt the lure of Marty's vision was Rupert Seidenbusch of St. John's Abbey, who had been named Vicar Apostolic of Northern Minnesota in 1875, shortly after Marty's initial trip to the Dakotas. In 1877 Seidenbusch suggested that his successor as abbot of St. John's, Alexius Edelbrock, have members of the Collegeville community serve as missionaries to the Chippewas, who constituted the majority of the population of the bishop's far-flung wilderness vicariate.[16] Although Boniface Wimmer lent his full support to this project,[17] some of the monks at St. John's expressed the same concerns that had been voiced by monks of St. Meinrad about new commitments to pastoral work among the Indians. But Edelbrock, like Marty, was ready to justify the project by pointing to historical examples of medieval monks converting the pagan tribes of northern Europe. He also pointed to the work of the St. Ottilien Congregation in East Africa and that of Benedictine bishops Polding and Salvado with the

Bernard Strassmeier, O.S.B., with altar boys at Fort Yates Indian Reservation (1919)

Benedictine sisters and students of Fort Yates Government Indian School (ca. 1890)

Aborigines in Australia, as well as Marty's mission to the Sioux. Edelbrock was not content with pointing to historical parallels; he traveled widely, visiting Indian reservations and showing an intense interest in the formation and recruitment of the monks he appointed to work there.[18]

The consequence of Edelbrock's commitment was that the St. John's Benedictines took over the White Earth Reservation and later added the Red Lake Reservation. Benedictine sisters from the nearby convent of St. Benedict in St. Joseph assisted them in this missionary activity, as did substantial financial contributions from Katharine Drexel. At Collegeville itself, there was an industrial school for Indians that operated between 1886 and 1896 under the sponsorship of the Bureau of Catholic Indian Affairs.[19]

While the two major congregations of American Benedictine monks and a considerable number of Benedictine sisters began their commitment to the American Indians, a French Benedictine priest, Father Isidore Robot, was named prefect apostolic of the Indian Territory of the Western United States in 1876. Robot was traveling as a lone missionary priest at the time, so his prefecture was committed to the care of the Benedictine monks of the French province of the Congregation of the Primitive Observance, of which he was a member.[20]

Financially dependent upon friends from the Bureau of Catholic Indian Missions and various missionary aid societies, Robot established Sacred Heart Mission in Oklahoma in 1877. Recruits for the mission monastery came from France, and as the novitiate opened that year, so did a "contract" government school for the Potawatomi.[21] After having started this new monastic community, Robot proudly wrote to the patriarch of the American Benedictines: "You may believe that we feel very happy following in the steps of Abbot Wimmer and his numerous and noble family, and our principal desire is to consecrate our lives and talents to the spiritual welfare of our neighbor, whatever may be his color, origin, or degradation, without neglecting the accomplishment of our monastic duties."[22]

As prefect of an ecclesiastical jurisdiction about one third the size of France and superior of a French-speaking community attempting

Sacred Heart Monastery in Oklahoma (ca. 1890)

to adapt itself to the rigors of the American frontier, Robot had to neglect many monastic customs. Due in no small part to his excessive workload, he died ten years after the foundation of his monastery, in 1887, the same year in which Boniface Wimmer died. By that time he had constructed, in addition to his monastery and its schools, four separate churches and twenty mission stations. After his death the Sacred Heart community of Benedictines continued Robot's apostolate to the Indians, and the founding abbot's legacy was passed on to the American Cassinese Congregation in 1924, when the community was transferred to Shawnee, Oklahoma.

Benedictine interest in the Indian missions was not limited to the nation's interior. On the West Coast, Mount Angel Abbey established Tillamook Mission in the Willamette Valley of Oregon and a school for Indian children on Vancouver Island in British Columbia.[23] The monks were assisted in this work by Benedictine sisters from Queen of Angels Convent in Mount Angel.[24]

The impetus for the apostolate among the Indians of the Northwest had come from the two men first responsible for bringing Benedictines there—Bishop John Seghers and Adelhelm Odermatt. In 1881, at the request of Seghers, Benedictine sisters from St. Joseph, Minnesota, came to Grande Ronde, Oregon. There they staffed the

Indian reservation for one year. When the sisters left Grande Ronde in 1882, Odermatt, then superior at Mount Angel Abbey, invited Benedictine sisters from Maryville, Missouri, and Sarnen, Switzerland, to replace them. His reasons for doing so captured much of the bold missionary spirit of that period: "To us is given the task of civilizing and converting this half-wild Indian tribe while the 'Protestant' government of the United States withdraws more and more from their welfare."[25]

Not all Benedictine monasteries were able to sustain the work of "civilizing and converting" the Indians. St. Vincent Archabbey failed in its attempt to establish a mission school for Indians in Banning, California, in 1888, and another one in New Mexico in 1890. St. Vincent's abbot at the time, Andrew Hintenach, responded to a request of Martin Marty for monks to assist in the Dakota Indian missions by saying that he could spare no men for the Indian missions of other communities when his own monastery could not staff its few commitments.

The personnel problem to which Hintenach pointed became even more pronounced in later years. That makes all the more remarkable the example of perseverance displayed by Benedictine monks and sisters in committing their entire lives to a missionary work whose difficulty was apparent to all and whose immediate benefits were not always readily detectable. It is clear that the same social problems that confronted the early Benedictine Indian missionaries remain today, as does the ongoing debate over missionary method and the mode of enculturation of American Indian rituals and customs.[26] But it is also clear that the constant commitment of several monastic communities to care for the American Indians over the course of a century left a lasting imprint. It also seems appropriate that Martin Marty's dream of a monastery in the Dakotas exclusively devoted to the American Indians was at least partially fulfilled when his community of St. Meinrad started the foundation of Blue Cloud Abbey at Marvin, South Dakota, in 1950, with a continuing apostolate to the Sioux.

The Mission to Black Americans

Running parallel with the ministry to the American Indians was a decided if less concentrated effort to assist the black population of the United States. The neglect of the blacks by the American Catholic Church is one of the less impressive marks of its history. In this respect, too, the American Benedictines were not unlike their fellow Catholic clergymen who looked upon the black American in much the same way as they viewed the American Indian—with a mixture of condescension, disdain, and apprehension.[27] This attitude is manifested in a statement made by Father Isidore Hobi, who in turn reflected the barely veiled racism of the southern Indiana monastic milieu in which he found himself: "One who knows the colored can understand why they were once treated with blows. Now they are not only free but are placed with whites. Where one had his choice he would take a naked Indian over a clothed colored."[28] Not all American Benedictines shared Hobi's prejudiced perspective. Nonetheless, the black was generally seen as someone similar to the American Indian: a person who came from an alien culture that had little or no religion and needed to be evangelized. For Benedictines, the best means of accomplishing this task was through the school.

This was certainly a principal reason why Boniface Wimmer agreed to take over a monastic foundation at Savannah, Georgia, in 1877 at the invitation of Bishop William Gross.[29] By this time Wimmer had come to recognize the need for the Church to minister to "those entirely neglected Negroes."[30] His views had changed since he first came to America. Some of that change can be seen in a letter he wrote after the close of the Civil War to a one-time defender of slavery, Bishop Patrick Lynch of Charleston, South Carolina:

> My opinion is that the Negro must, as matters are now, stand the competition with the white laborer willing or unwilling and learn to swim or perish in the stream alongside the whites, rather than in a separate colony. I have no antipathy against them; I was always against the war and abolition because I thought they are not capable of enjoying full liberty; but since they are free now, they must learn to act as free men.[31]

This was obviously a reason for Wimmer's subsequent sponsorship of an industrial school for black children on Skidaway Island in Georgia. His intention was to help the blacks learn to be free, but behind that altruistic motive was the obligation to "convert the pagan" much more than a desire to correct injustice or improve the economic plight of the freed slaves. The same priority dominated the planning of Bishop Louis Fink, a spiritual son of Wimmer's. His decision to build schools and churches for the "poor Negroes" who migrated to his Leavenworth diocese after the Civil War was based more on a desire to effect religious conversion than on consideration of the material needs of the freed slaves.[32]

One must also consider the inherent limitations of any programs of social assistance offered to the blacks by religious communities in the Reconstruction period. Benedictines in the South were faced with widespread hostility on the part of the local white population whenever they gave any indication of wanting to raise the educational or social level of the freed slaves. The school on Skidaway Island was forced to close largely because of the animosity of the local population. The monastic communities in Belmont, North Carolina, and St. Leo, Florida, met with opposition when they tried to admit blacks into their monasteries. Leo Haid of Belmont was compelled to ask St. Vincent Archabbey to accept a black candidate for the brotherhood because, as he said, "I know he will not be received by the Chapter as the feeling among the southerners is very strong against 'social inequality'— and I don't see how we can swim against the storm."[33] A few years later, in 1893, as his community was constructing a new abbey church, Haid wrote to Katharine Drexel about his reasons for wanting space provided for possible black worshipers:

> The moral effect on the Catholics in North Carolina especially, and in other Southern States, would be a great gain. If the Benedictines at the Abbey and in Charlotte break down the ugly prejudice against colored people—it would go far to enable the Bishop to insist on building all future Churches large enough to make decent room for the colored people. . . . There is no use in butting the head against the hard wall of prejudice—but we may climb over the wall or go around it slowly.[34]

The wall of prejudice also stretched westward. Both monks and sisters in Arkansas did their best to cope with racist objections to their educational efforts. After the Benedictine sisters in Pocahontas opened a school for black students in 1888, they received a stream of threatening letters saying that the school would be burned to the ground if allowed to continue. The sisters continued to operate the school and it was not harmed.[35] But by 1896 there were state laws in Arkansas that abolished all integrated schooling and pressured the monks at New Subiaco to discontinue their practice of accepting black students.[36]

It was only well into the twentieth century that the American Benedictines were to make real strides in their work with blacks. In 1948 St. John's Abbey founded St. Maur's Priory in South Union, Kentucky, for the express purpose of developing an interracial community. The design behind this foundation involved elements of Boniface Wimmer's original notion of "converting the colored through monastic schools," Booker T. Washington's "bootstrap" program at Tuskegee Institute, and Jesuit Father John LaFarge's ideal of an interracial religious community rooted in a theology of the Mystical Body.[37] The result was a racially integrated monastic community that occupied the site of an earlier community of American Shakers and a major seminary specifically oriented to educating blacks for the priesthood.[38]

Only two years earlier, in 1946, the monks of St. John's Abbey had established St. Augustine of Canterbury Monastery in the Bahamas. After a half century of largely missionary work among the native black population there, they were now able to provide a preparatory school for black students and candidates for the monastic life.

On the eve of the United States Supreme Court's decision on school integration in Brown vs. Board of Education in 1954, Benedictine schools in Louisiana and Alabama had already opened their doors to blacks, and even as that landmark decision was being enforced in Little Rock, Arkansas, Catholics in that state could point to the integrated New Subiaco Academy as a model of racial harmony.[39]

A monk of St. Joseph Abbey, St. Benedict, Louisiana, working among blacks

Sister Cheryl Nesbit, O.S.B., of St. Scholastica Priory, Fort Smith, Arkansas, working with elderly blacks (1974)

David Palmatier, O.S.B., visiting an Indian village in the western highlands of Guatemala (1970)

Students at the minor seminary of San José, Sololá, Guatemala

During the race riots in the summers of the late 1960s, Benedictine communities in Cleveland and Newark maintained their presence in the ghetto areas of these cities and won acclaim for the quality of graduates produced by their inner-city schools. Individual Benedictines joined the protesters against segregation at Selma and Birmingham in Alabama. Blacks no longer felt apprehensive about entering Benedictine communities, and the black Catholics of the United States looked for leadership and scholarship in such Benedictines as Fathers Boniface Hardin and Cyprian Davis.[40]

The assistance that American Benedictines gave to blacks and American Indians, like that of the American Catholic Church in general, was not always given for the purest of motives, nor was it always consistent with the real needs of the people. Yet, it did touch these minorities in important ways at a time when few other representatives of the Catholic Church were willing to show interest. The fact that substantial numbers of Benedictines are still serving the blacks and American Indians is testimony to the staying power of their commitment.

CHAPTER 9

A Social System Unraveled: The Monastic Conversi

While blacks and American Indians were relegated to second-class citizenship for most of the history of the United States, the Benedictine Order, in both its masculine and feminine branches, maintained a class system imported from Europe. It involved a group of persons called *conversi*: lay brothers and lay sisters, whose position in the monastic houses of American Benedictines was a source of controversy and cultural difference. The consequences of such a monastic class system are part of the living history of the Benedictine family.

The role of lay brothers and lay sisters was developed in European monasteries over several centuries. They performed the manual work of the monastic community; they were not given the privilege of professing solemn vows nor of having voting rights in chapter; they were not required to participate in the full common prayer of the monastic Office; and they usually wore distinctive dress and had separate living accommodations.[1] When the lay brothers and sisters came to the United States, they adopted some unique social characteristics of American monastic life.

The Lay Brothers

If there is one aspect of American Benedictine life that characterized its pioneer monks, it was the recruitment of large numbers of lay brothers. As was the case with so many other precedents estab-

147

lished by American Benedictines, this one was derived from the monastic vision of Boniface Wimmer. Although Wimmer's home abbey of Metten had only three lay brothers in 1846, he selected sixteen aspiring lay brothers to accompany him on his first trip to Pennsylvania that same year. It seems that Wimmer followed the practice of the late Middle Ages of admitting significant numbers of lay brothers to do the necessary manual labor, leaving the priests and clerics free for liturgical and missionary pursuits.

One European custom that Wimmer did not find to his liking was the absence of lay brothers at the Divine Office. He had originally planned to have the lay brothers attend all the Hours of the Office together with the clerical members of the community.[2] But after a short experience of monastic life in the wilds of Westmoreland County, the young superior began to realize that the most practicable horarium would be one that allowed the lay brothers to follow a separate schedule, freed from the obligation to pray the entire Office. Practicality took priority over piety, and the reason given was that the brothers did not know Latin. Behind that explanation, however, was the understanding that a schedule of manual work required large blocks of uninterrupted time in the morning and afternoon. Wimmer had also been quick to assess the changed conditions of community life in America. With a large farm and a need for shops and mills to make the abbey as self-sufficient as possible, there was no substitute for lay brothers.

In 1849 Wimmer caused dissension in his community when he reneged on a promise to let several brothers take solemn vows.[3] He justified his action by explaining that the community had not yet received any canonical recognition. In 1852, when St. Vincent did receive canonical status as a priory, all the lay brothers pronounced solemn vows, but they were not allowed to participate in the discussions and decisions of the monastic chapter. As might have been expected, this contradictory situation engendered even more opposition.

In April 1861 Brother Joseph Sailer, one of the original group of monks who had accompanied Wimmer to America, wrote out a list of grievances against Abbot Boniface and forwarded it to Pope

Pius IX.[4] The principal complaint was that Wimmer had gone back on a series of promises he had made to the lay brothers when they first left Europe in 1846. Instead of being granted equal privileges and full incorporation into the community, they were, said Sailer, overworked and mistreated, without a real voice in the affairs of the monastery.

Brother Joseph's critical salvo moved the Propaganda Fide to ask for a special visitation to investigate the charges. Bishop Michael Domenec of Pittsburgh arrived at St. Vincent in September 1861 for the visitation, and after hearing some of the same complaints from other lay brothers in the community, he wrote to the Propaganda Fide, suggesting that in the future, brothers should make only simple vows.[5]

As if Bishop Domenec's response was not rebuke enough to Sailer, Wimmer convoked the St. Vincent chapter the following month to debate the matter—without any of the brothers present. It came as no surprise that the chapter failed to find grounds for the grievances of the brothers and communicated this to Propaganda Fide. The climax of the whole affair was that Wimmer refused any further requests of brothers to make solemn vows, a decision later reinforced by an official decree from Rome in 1866.[6]

It would be unfair, however, to think that Wimmer was unappreciative of the brothers' work at St. Vincent. In a letter to the Propaganda Fide in June 1855, he gave a detailed account of the lay-brother system and asked that words of commendation be given to individual brothers.[7] In a letter to Martin Marty in 1861, Wimmer acknowledged how vital the brothers had been during the founding period at Latrobe:

> I could not have founded the monastery without the Brothers and most likely you couldn't either. For it requires from the very outset a regular order of the day. . . . Two or three priests busy with care of souls or teaching do not constitute a monastery because they cannot hold to the daily order. If several Brothers are present, it will be all right. . . . Some of my Fathers do not like the idea of having so many Brothers around. I notice that those who think and act this way are always such as have no love for strict order.[8]

For Marty's own monastery of St. Meinrad, Abbot Henry Schmid of Einsiedeln had written down precise provisions for the admission of lay brothers and had anticipated Wimmer's conditions by requiring them to enter the Indiana house only with simple vows and insisting that they restrict their duties to manual work.[9]

The lay brothers of St. Meinrad, like the brothers of other houses, followed a separate schedule of work and prayer. In the early years of St. Meinrad's existence, the brothers prayed the Little Office of the Blessed Virgin in German apart from the rest of the community; but even their daily prayer schedule was dictated by the demands of labor. This led to such anomalous practices as gathering in choir at 1:30 P.M. and praying in succession the rosary, the litany of the Blessed Virgin, Vespers, and Compline. The brothers would return to choir at 7:30 P.M. for Matins and Lauds.[10]

In 1872 Marty attempted to reverse the strict separation of clerical and lay members in his community. He decided to establish a joint novitiate for clerics and brothers, insisting that brothers be given equal rank with the priest-monks and take part in the monastery's Latin Office. The title "Brother" was to be used for all members of the community, as opposed to the title "Father" or "Frater" for priests and clerics respectively.[11]

It is noteworthy that Marty launched the experiment for reasons having to do more with pragmatic needs than theoretical conviction. He wrote:

> The mixing of brothers and fraters was not planned but was a necessary result of our poverty. We could hardly do it otherwise. We had only one room, only one person as instructor and novice master. Here too we must live from our work and manual labor pays much better than mental work. What we receive from the schools and missions is not enough for us. The Brothers are not our servants but our breadwinners and when the number of Fathers increases, we cannot use all of them in the school and on the missions and yet everyone whose age and health permits earns his bread. The Brothers must work so that the Fraters can study; at harvest time the work is so pressing that all must help. In America work is not demeaning and it should not be so with us . . . . all our Fathers and Fraters share in the field work and no one feels uncomfortable with this change. The Brothers are

also lifted up spiritually and if we wish the faithful in the world to share in the liturgy, we dare not deny it to our own people. For America is a republic where one person is as good as the other and it cannot hurt the most learned if they practice the 6th and 7th degrees of humility.[12]

Marty's action upset the traditionalists in the community, however. Isidore Hobi protested in a letter to his superior in Einsiedeln:

Here the brothers and fraters are mixed, without any distinction, in choir and in the study hall and separated from the professed fraters and brothers. In most cases one can guess that this one will be a brother and this one a frater by reason of the program of studies undertaken by the fraters, but this is not always the case. The result has been that we do not get any more "ordinary candidates." I myself (along with many other of the fathers) would never have entered under such conditions. . . . Is there between the brothers and fraters such similarity that both may be called and treated as brothers? They stand together in choir without distinction (but according to seniority) with the difference that only the brothers who can read Latin pray the entire Office. . . . Fraters and brothers go to Holy Communion as one and sit together at table; in chapter they say *culpa* together, the brothers speaking German. Both have the same dormitory and study hall desks. The sad results of this system are now visible and become clearer with each succeeding day. The pride and intemperance of the brothers is beyond description. . . . We have ground enough to ask for a visitation as the only means to save our community. All of the fathers want the old order of Einsiedeln to be imitated here. It is generally believed that Father Abbot [Marty] is disappointed. . . . It would be good if Abbot Boniface [Wimmer] or another would be delegated by Rome and given power. Then there would be no difficulty, since it would be regarded as a mortal sin to talk or act against an order from Rome.[13]

There obviously had to be reaction to the experiment that balanced the extreme impressions recorded by Marty and Hobi. Such was provided by Marty's prior and classmate, Fintan Mundwiler, who wrote the following assessment:

When the new arrangement was first proposed it was said that the brothers were too uncultured, the discipline would suffer, and those more cultured persons who might want to enter would be dissuaded. Formerly we heard the complaint that we wished to hold the brother down, to make them servants and the fraters gentlemen, and so many considered those who wanted to become brothers to be "dumb" and many were ridiculed and turned away from the monastery. And yet working brothers were necessary here, for without them one cannot have an economy that supports the monastery, where the land must be cultivated and all things made from scratch. So we decided to make the brothers' vocation more honorable and to give them a better education and formation. An effort was also made to improve the church music and the choir by having everyone take part in them, singing the Vespers psalms and hymns and learning the Gregorian Chant. It was said that if the laity could learn them, why not also the brothers, and if our Benedictine Sisters can pray and sing in Latin, why not the brothers? The fraters and brothers have become more equal as a result. The fraters are pleased with this, for during vacation they go with the brothers to work in the fields. In fact, the whole affair was going very well until last year when Father Isidore raised some questions about whether such a sharing was against church law. . . .[14]

Just a few months after Mundwiler's words were written, the experiment ended. The reason given was that too much time was required for the brothers to learn Latin and for the fraters to shoulder part of the manual work. But Father Isidore's critical comments reflected how real the threat posed by such integration was to the community's social fabric, at least from the perspective of a sizable number of priests.

Some of the same sentiment surfaced in other monasteries in response to the experiment at St. Meinrad. At Conception Abbey, Frowin Conrad reacted to news of Marty's action in emphatic terms: "To give Brothers full rank under the conditions here is presently impossible and even in this country is rather daring."[15] In a more sardonic vein, one of the lay brothers of St. Benedict's Abbey in Atchison wrote in his notes: "Monks and lay brothers, we assert, are one body with regard to the future life, but while on earth they are distinct, disenfranchised so to speak."[16]

A subconscious sense of superiority was most pronounced in the priests of Benedictine communities and is clearly displayed in some of their correspondence. Wolfgang Schlumpf, first superior of the community at New Subiaco, Arkansas, was upset at the money being paid to housekeepers at his missions. He suggested that "every *expositus* [priest] have a brother as housekeeper because, not to mention feminine whims and quirks, women demand higher wages."[17]

What Schlumpf and other monks failed to take fully into account was the implicit clericalism against which the lay brothers had to contend. A case in point was the practice of many Benedictine monasteries in the United States of offering a place of rehabilitation for diocesan priests who created disciplinary problems.[18] The fact that the burden of caring for these "priest-penitents" fell to the lay brothers did not bother the clerics in the monastery as much as it did the brothers, who bristled at one more symbol of their status of servitude. Nor did spiritual exhortations on the need to cultivate the virtue of humility lead to a greater acceptance on the part of the lay brothers.

The Lay Sister

This class system was brought over from Europe by Benedictine sisters also. The choir sister (*Frau*) was roughly equivalent to the male cleric, usually well educated and of a higher social class. She would usually teach and attend the full Divine Office in choir.[19] The lay sister (*Schwester*) lacked extensive education and was assigned to do manual labor; instead of participating in the Office, she would perform private devotions such as the rosary.[20] The positions of prioress, novice mistress, and other supervisory roles were held by choir sisters, while those of farmworker, cook, and laundry worker were assigned to the lay sisters.

In 1879 fourteen of the sixteen existing convents of American Benedictine sisters still distinguished between these two classes.[21] In 1881 the general chapter of Benedictine sisters meeting in Chicago drafted in their proposed constitution a clause which directed that the dress of all community members should be the same. More importantly, they urged that both choir sisters and lay sisters should be given a voice in chapter decisions.[22] When the new constitutions were adopted in 1882, these provisions were included.

By 1903 only four of the twenty-two Benedictine communities of women in the United States continued to observe the distinction between choir sisters and lay sisters.[23] The reason for this transition was a demographic change more than any juridical dictate: the supply of European vocations was coming to an end. In the words of Abbot Innocent Wolf of Atchison: "The institution of lay sisters dies out in America when they cannot get foreign girls any more."[24]

A comparative study shows that the tensions created by the differences between choir sisters and lay sisters in American Benedictine houses were less divisive than those among the monks. Among the women, a transition to an integrated and egalitarian daily order was already underway in the early years of the twentieth century.

A System Dismantled

By the turn of the century, the vocation of lay brother had become restricted almost entirely to those who spoke German. American-born candidates who applied to the brotherhood faced barriers on several fronts. They found it difficult to accept discrimination of persons, something that flew in the face of their accustomed democratic and egalitarian principles. They also faced a virtual closed shop of German-speaking and German-trained craftsmen, who were wary of admitting any "foreign" apprentices into their own closed community. An example of this took place at Belmont Abbey, where German lay brothers from St. Vincent clashed with English-speaking hired hands of the abbey farm and American-born monks entering the community. American candidates for the brotherhood at Belmont, especially a local black, claimed to have been hounded out of the community by the German faction.[25]

Other statistics underscore the discrimination. Abbot Innocent Wolf kept a record of the brother candidates at St. Benedict's Abbey in a twenty-year period at the end of the nineteenth century and documented that out of ninety-six who entered, only sixteen stayed, implying that the older German monks had a great deal to do with the attrition rate.[26]

If anything, the differences between the lay brothers and choir monks had become more pronounced as the century began. In a sort of territorial ordering of space, physical separation ran along strict lines of demarcation. The kitchens, agricultural areas, and trade shops became the "turf" of the brothers. The chapter room, choir area,

Brothers' quarters at St. Joseph Abbey, St. Benedict, Louisiana

and classrooms were the territory of the priests and clerics. They had separate recreation rooms and oratories, even separate cemeteries. What was obvious to many outsiders was that priests and lay brothers were separate but not equal. This was evident to those who made further investigation into the daily life of the monastery. At table the brothers were often given less and simpler fare and fewer utensils than the priests. Even in the departments and shops that were the brothers' bailiwick, priests held positions of administrative or financial responsibility. The living quarters of the lay brothers were usually substandard, often in attics with little ventilation or light, or in basements with inadequate plumbing or heating.

Much of this system of separation was even codified in the statutes of the congregations. As late as 1938, in the Declarations on the Holy Rule of the Swiss-American Congregation, a clear distinction was made between the functions of lay brothers, who were to perform manual work, and those of priests and clerics, who were to devote themselves to studies and spiritual work.[27] Weekly conferences on moral, theological, and liturgical topics were reserved only to the clerical members of the community. Even some of the interpre-

155

tations of the Rule were stretched to fit the situation, as reflected in excerpts taken from the Swiss Declarations: "Since our most Holy Father exempts from service in the kitchen those who are engaged in employments of greater importance, it is not departing from his spirit if all priests and clerics are exempted from this duty, and if only lay brothers are appointed to the work of the kitchen."[28] The document added an interesting gloss with regard to living accommodations: "Since the priests of the monastery have separate cells, in these they live and sleep. Both the clerics and lay brothers have their own common dormitories in which, as also in every corridor, a light shall burn throughout the night."[29]

During the period between the two World Wars, the crisis concerning the role of lay brothers in American Benedictine communities came to a head. By the late 1920s German brothers were no longer immigrating to the United States.[30] This trend coincided with a surge of candidates for the priesthood and religious life in the American Catholic Church. This became more observable during the Depression years, when the security of life within a religious community became more appealing to many. Some monastic communities coped with this change by initiating new vocational programs. Abbot Ignatius Esser of St. Meinrad started an oblate high school in 1933 for "American students" interested in the brotherhood.[31] The aim of the school was to provide candidates for the brotherhood; it offered a high school course of studies different from that of the minor seminary program. It was also a clear attempt to tap the immense reservoir of American-born vocations by presenting the students with an environment and formation suitable to their own cultural experience. St. Meinrad and Conception Abbeys also promoted workshops for the "brother masters" of the Swiss-American Congregation during the 1940s in an effort to incorporate some of the sociological changes already mentioned into their programs of formation.

But even as the number of German brothers dwindled, there was still operative a mentality that gave theological justification to the separation of lay brothers and priests.[32] For some observers, the sight of a community of lay brothers evoked an idealistic image of monastic life that became the subject matter for promotional and even his-

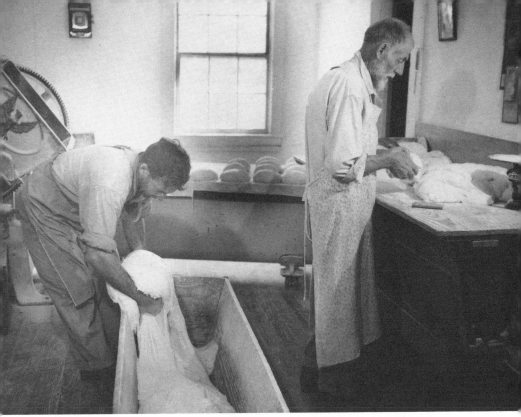

Above: Brothers Paul Ott and Benedict Sailer at work in the bakery at St. Joseph Abbey, St. Benedict, Louisiana. Below: Brother Valerian Horky of St. Procopius Abbey operates a linotype machine.

torical literature. Wrote one community historian of a Benedictine community with numerous lay brothers: "A carpenter shop, a blacksmith shop, a butcher shop, and other we-can-do-it-ourselves facilities, manned by skilled and totally dedicated lay brothers, whose goal was service, not self-centered ambition—all this created a wholesome and unique atmosphere for Christian education and monastic living."[33]

Unique it was, but by mid-century there would be many "totally dedicated brothers" disputing the wholesomeness of the atmosphere as they experienced it. It was at this juncture that a confluence of several movements signaled the end of the social system. After World War II the monasteries saw the last of German-speaking candidates for the brotherhood and the farm-and-shop economy that had kept them occupied. With the termination of many monastic farms and specialized trade shops, as well as printing presses, sawmills, and other operations, the practical basis for the existence of the lay brothers was rapidly disappearing. This was combined with an increasing awareness of social inequalities in the American society of the 1950s and 1960s and the need to eliminate discrimination and segregation. The same social sensibility that gave impetus to the civil rights movement permeated monastic walls as well.

Finally, the sweeping renewal of religious life brought about by the Second Vatican Council heralded a new theology of community relationships that eroded all the previous barriers of inequality. While the distinction between clerical and non-clerical members of monastic communities was affirmed, brothers could now receive full rights as solemnly professed members of their communities and were given equal standing at chapter meetings. In the wake of the conciliar reform in the late 1960s, the last traces of distinction in dress and living arrangements were allowed to pass out of existence, as did a social and spiritual system of separation that had marked American Benedictine life for over a century.

CHAPTER 10

Brick-and-Mortar Benedictinism

Among the descriptive phrases used by historians to describe the American Catholic Church in the last hundred years, "brick and mortar" has acquired a noted cachet. The phrase creates an image that depicts the intense effort of the Church, initiated in the last century and continued into the present one, to construct a network of institutions and edifices whose sheer number and size would reflect the solid and permanent presence of Catholics in the United States.

As with so many other aspects of American Catholic life, Benedictines found themselves becoming part of this flurry of new building, from the flimsy clapboard cabins of the founding years to the architectural showpieces of stone and marble of recent vintage. The story of all this construction is strewn with countless examples of egoism, overinvestment, and indebtedness, but these examples were countered by lasting architectural symbols of solidity, aesthetic excellence, and apostolic service, all indicative of the unique Benedictine virtue of stability of place.

An Investment in Land

One way in which the first Benedictines who came to North America distinguished themselves was in their capacity, not as builders, but as realtors. The pioneer generation was engaged to a considerable extent in purchasing tracts of land. In the case of Boniface Wim-

159

mer, it seems that the greater part of his time during the early years at St. Vincent was taken up in the purchase and transfer of land: buying up isolated plots for his four priories in Pennsylvania, using funds intended for the construction of convents for Benedictine sisters to buy land for his first foundation in Minnesota, and constantly making reference in his personal correspondence to potential real estate deals. Wimmer was no different in this respect than many of his fellow Benedictine pioneers. The first monks of St. Vincent who traveled to Minnesota made personal land claims that quickly ran into hundreds of acres and led to protracted legal battles when their claims were contested.[1]

The early problems over indebtedness that the Swiss-American communities of St. Meinrad and Mount Angel had with their European founding houses of Einsiedeln and Engelberg were illustrative of how land speculation could lead a struggling community into a cycle of buying, borrowing, and building.[2] Yet land was essential for a monastery that wanted a farm and the option of future physical expansion, and that land would not have been as available or cheap if the founders would have had to wait until financial security was their lot.

This insecurity, if not insolvency, was even more characteristic of communities of Benedictine women. They were much more limited in raising funds than the monks were; moreover, they could not count on a corps of community craftsmen to construct new buildings for them. In truth, the living conditions of some of the sisters were a source of scandal. Sod huts could hardly serve to protect them from the bone-chilling winds of Dakota winters, and a parish rectory adequate for a pastor became little more than a communal crawl space for a convent of sisters. The dependency experienced by Benedictine sisters in their founding years was physical as well as canonical. Most communities had to wait several generations before they could acquire their own land and sufficient financial resources to construct buildings that suited their needs.

In a more positive vein, one can point to the fact that most American Benedictine communities improved their land as the years went by. Even if a bit overblown in its description, the account that appeared in a local Catholic paper about how the monks of Mount Angel had enhanced the property they occupied exemplifies what often happened to the geography of a Benedictine monastery: "What was, a few years ago, prior to the occupation of the Benedictines, comparatively a howling wilderness covered with timber, is now converted into waving grain fields, orchards, vineyards and vegetable gardens, dotted here and there at convenient points with flour mills, shops and all the engineering of modern civilization."[3] The European monastic heritage of land stewardship was obviously given free play in a country where the power of positive thinking was linked with ownership of property. For the American Benedictines, accepting the responsibility for such stewardship was well worth the risk of over-speculation and mismanagement that went with it.

Construction Success and Failure

The buildings that Benedictines erected on their tracts of land were for the most part simple and spartan, reflecting the lives of their inhabitants. They were built by the monks themselves, with lay brothers serving as carpenters, masons, and skilled workers.

While the size and appearance of early monastic buildings generally conformed to Benedictine norms of poverty, it often appeared as if no sacrifice or expense was too large for the construction of a church. The abbey churches of St. Meinrad, Conception, St. Vincent, and St. John's at the end of the nineteenth century were impressive edifices by any standard, with their twin towers dominating the landscape. They were adorned with some of the best of European art, whether it was the Bavarian stained glass of St. Vincent or the Beuronese frescoes in Frowin Conrad's basilica at Conception Abbey.[4]

Because of their size and significance, those monasteries might have been expected to construct such imposing churches. What is surprising is how smaller, financially strapped communities were equally intent upon building churches of similar magnificence. Prior Augustine Wirth's project of building a large and impressive abbey church at Atchison, in anticipation of his becoming abbot of St.

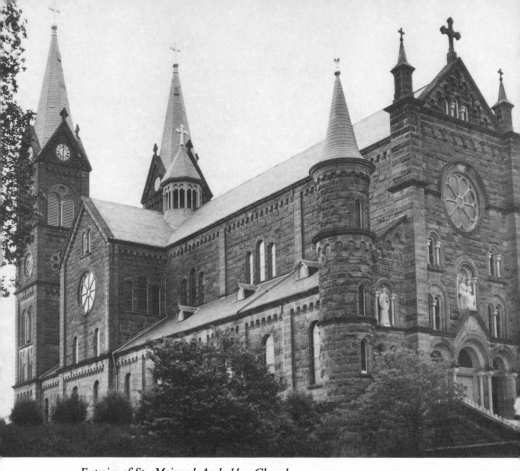

Exterior of St. Meinrad Archabbey Church

The basilica of Conception Abbey, Conception, Missouri

St. Vincent Archabbey Church
St. John's Abbey, Collegeville, Minnesota (1884)

Above: Beuronese frescoes in the basilica of Conception Abbey. Below: The cathedral church of Belmont Abbey, Belmont, North Carolina (1972)

Benedict's, bankrupted that community and moved his successor to describe the edifice as "a perpetual monument to the stubbornness and bad taste of a former prior."[5] It also committed the American Cassinese Congregation to avoid such scandals in the future. But such concern did not dampen Leo Haid's ambition to erect at Belmont Abbey in the 1890s "the largest and most resplendent Catholic Church in the state."[6] Thanks to the generous benefactions of Katharine Drexel and the labor of a sizable contingent of Belmont's monks, Haid was able to fulfill his ambition. The abbey cathedral became a showpiece in the midst of America's Bible Belt.

The building efforts of the Benedictines were not without trials. The financial panics that struck the nation in 1857, 1873, and 1893 hampered numerous construction projects. The monastic complexes were also curiously susceptible to fires and natural disasters. The monasteries of the Swiss-American Congregation in particular experienced a cycle of disastrous fires, beginning with St. Meinrad in 1887, Mount Angel in 1887, 1907, and 1926, New Subiaco in 1901 and 1927, and St. Joseph in 1907. A tornado struck Conception's new basilica in 1893, doing extensive damage. The next year St. John's Abbey bore the full brunt of a tornado that did over $60,000 damage.[7]

The one constant in all these calamities was an instinctive and indomitable will to build again. The money to do this came from a variety of sources: European monasteries and mission-aid societies; other American monastic communities; and, above all, the lay people who worshiped in the monastic churches and were dependent upon Benedictine schools for the Catholic education of their children.

The school, whether a seminary, college, or high school, was a natural adjunct to most Benedictine monasteries. Unlike the abbey church, the school was constructed along practical rather than aesthetic lines. By modern standards, the first school structures had about them a makeshift quality, often temporary and simple in style, not unlike many of the monastic buildings. This functional character was of a piece with the utilitarian nature of things American that characterized monastic building programs well into the twentieth century. Part of the reason for this was the immediate need for larger facilities for the increasing number of monks and students. Part of it was also

Vincent Wehrle, O.S.B.,
first abbot
of St. Mary's Abbey,
Richardton, North Dakota,
and bishop of Bismarck

due to the inheritance of a pioneer generation of Benedictines whose relentless drive to expand demanded physical growth to satisfy its sweeping missionary vision.

The proliferation of school buildings and residence halls coincided with the emergence of a generation of monastic superiors whose penchant for enlarging physical plants was apparently a charism needed for their office. In the first two decades of the twentieth century, the growing diversity of community apostolates led to a rash of new buildings in Benedictine communities. Hospitals for sisters, printshops for monks, powerhouses and storage buildings—all contributed to a more ambitious investment in land and buildings.

This combination of land acquisition and construction projects created difficulties and disasters for some houses. At St. Mary's Abbey in Richardton, North Dakota, a decade of financial mismanagement by Abbot Vincent Wehrle was compounded by impulsive land investments on the part of his successor, Abbot Placid Hoenerbach. The situation became so critical that the community was forced to

166

declare bankruptcy in 1924.[8] Because of similar problems, exacerbated by a fire in 1901, Sacred Heart Abbey in Oklahoma was forced to move to Shawnee in 1924 and, like Richardton, be received into the American Cassinese Congregation.

Community resources were further strained during the Great Depression. Despite bank failures and declining school enrollments, some houses not only kept their physical plant operational but continued to enlarge and plan for future needs. It was also during this period that many Benedictine houses served as models of agricultural science and ingenuity for American farmers despondent over the hard times of the Dust Bowl. From fruit orchards and reforestation programs to fish hatcheries and innovative cattle breeding, Benedictine communities made a distinctive contribution to rebuilding the confidence of a suffering agricultural sector during the thirties. Benedictine investment in the land also led monks such as Father Martin Schirber of St. John's Abbey to take an active leadership role in the National Catholic Rural Life Movement.[9]

St. Vincent Archabbey, Latrobe, Pennsylvania, before the fire of 1963

St. John's Abbey and University, Collegeville, Minnesota (1987)

St. Benedict's Abbey, Atchison, Kansas (ca. 1950)

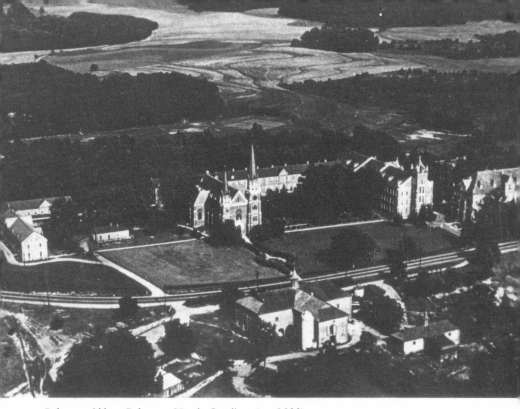

Belmont Abbey, Belmont, North Carolina (ca. 1939)

St. Procopius Abbey, Lisle, Illinois (1975)

St. Gregory's Abbey, Shawnee, Oklahoma
Assumption Abbey, Richardton, North Dakota

St. Bede Abbey, Peru, Illinois

St. Anselm's Abbey, Manchester, New Hampshire

Mount Angel Seminary and Library, Mount Angel, Oregon (1982)

St. Meinrad Archabbey, St. Meinrad, Indiana (1982)

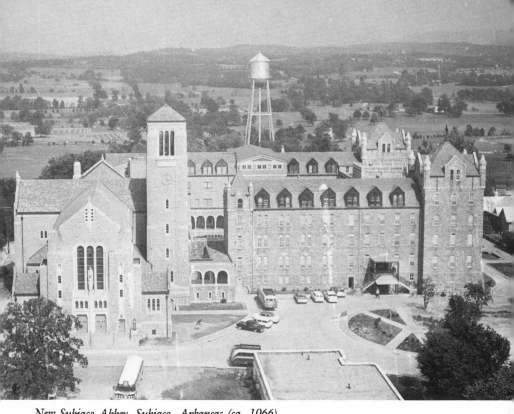

New Subiaco Abbey, Subiaco, Arkansas (ca. 1966)

St. Joseph Abbey, St. Benedict, Louisiana

Marmion Abbey, Aurora, Illinois

An Era of Architectural Sophistication and Innovation

Eventually American Benedictines entered into an era of prosperity after World War II, when, for the first time, they were able to afford the time and material resources necessary to systematically study and plan building programs, as well as to engage qualified architects for the task. Like the Catholic bishops of this era, the superiors of American Benedictine communities during this time were builders and administrators. Nonetheless, they incorporated motifs of Benedictine theology and spirituality into their programs as much as possible. Perhaps the best example of this took place at St. John's Abbey in Collegeville, Minnesota. In 1951 Abbot Baldwin Dworschak appointed a building committee to make recommendations. After a year and a half of study and meetings, the committee and the senior council decided to sound out a select group of internationally pres-

174

tigious architects on drawing up a hundred-year plan of construction for the present and future needs of the community. The famed Bauhaus architect Marcel Breuer was the eventual choice, offering a plan that Maurice Lavanoux called "a milestone in the evolution of the architecture of the Catholic Church in this country."[10]

What resulted from the St. John's "master plan" and its elaboration by Breuer was the largest construction project ever undertaken by an American Benedictine community, a series of buildings—an abbey church with an imposing bell banner, a monastic wing, a library—whose monumental scale was a testament to the last era in the American Catholic Church when such a scale could safely be associated with the word "monastic." The abbey churches built during the late 1950s at St. Benedict's in Atchison, Kansas, St. Bernard in Cullman, Alabama, and New Subiaco, in Subiaco, Arkansas, embodied much of the same monumentalism.[11]

Communities of Benedictine sisters did not remain apart from these developments. They built impressive edifices of brick, stone, and glass that rose from the Midwest tabletop surrounding Yankton, South Dakota; St. Joseph, Minnesota; and Beech Grove, Indiana; from the river bluffs of Bismarck, North Dakota; Atchison, Kansas; and Nauvoo, Illinois; and from the Great Lake ports of Erie, Pennsylvania, and Duluth, Minnesota. For the sisters, too, the period after the Second World War through the early 1960s was one in which a steady stream of young vocations prompted expanded building programs. Houses of several hundred sisters were not uncommon.

A paradigm for this new growth was Wimmer's founding monastery of St. Vincent in Latrobe, Pennsylvania. That community constructed a masssive new monastery in the early 1960s, heralding the heady optimism of the American Catholic Church in the midst of the Second Vatican Council and the modern lifestyle to which monasteries were beginning to adapt.

But this also marked the moment when the postwar building boom was coming to an end. American Benedictines in the 1960s had to deal with some of the same problems that the entire Catholic Church in the United States faced: the conversion of cavernous church spaces; adapting sanctuaries to conform to the revised liturgical standards of the conciliar renewal; finding practical and innovative means of using parochial schools emptied of students as enrollments declined; adjusting to the changed reality that monks were no longer the primary architects and builders of their communities, and at the same time attempting to translate Benedictine spiritual ideals for architects and contractors who had little awareness of Benedictine life; accepting the fact that an agricultural component of monastic institutions did not necessarily make good sense, either financially or spiritually; and searching for a philosophy of building that would project a simplicity in conformity with Benedictine tradition while preserving an aesthetic sensibility.

Most of these problems were part of the larger framework of the renewal of religious life and the decline in vocations that followed the Second Vatican Council. This renewal process indicated to many that Benedictines would have to integrate their own spiritual version of "less is more" with community complexes scaled down to a more simplified model, and also with a newly emerging ecological awareness and a need for energy conservation. New building projects did continue, but their scale and implementation were far different from those of the triumphant and monumentalist mentality that had previously held sway. This had been foreshadowed in the 1950s by the simpler monastic churches of Mount Saviour and Weston Priories and the arresting architecture of the monastery of Christ in the Desert in New Mexico.[12] The renewal process was also accompanied by the Benedictine equivalent of the experiments in communal and rustic "return to nature" that were so much a part of the American counterculture of the time, and the results of this were the closure of many community buildings and a monastic diaspora of some who wanted to live in smaller communities in cabins or rustic retreats.[13]

The results of this period of renewal are yet to be fully assessed. From the purely architectural point of view, American Benedictines have produced prize-winning buildings, from the St. Procopius abbey church and monastery to the Mount Angel library.[14] A succession of new abbey churches, from Morristown, New Jersey, and Manchester, New Hampshire, to Benet Lake, Wisconsin; Westminster, British Columbia; Lacey, Washington; Oceanside, California;

and St. Louis, Missouri, have offered a new dimension of design and elegance. Restoration projects of monastic churches of both monks and sisters have attempted to blend the old and the new with differing degrees of acceptance.[15]

In both a material and a spiritual sense, it seems clear that Benedictine men and women in the United States since the 1960s have been about the work of conversion in a most literal manner. They have adapted and changed their institutional space to fit the needs of a changing Church and community. They have reevaluated their commitment to the land and the use they make of it. They have, above all, rediscovered that behind the façade of brick and mortar, there is both a physical and a religious task of transforming the space they inhabit. It is a task that the first American Benedictines willingly accepted in the nineteenth century and one that confronts their successors even more clearly at the close of the twentieth century. In meeting that task, contemporary Benedictines would do well to draw upon both their deep historical tradition and their characteristic sensitivity to the needs of the Catholic culture in which they live.

St. Vincent Archabbey, Latrobe, Pennsylvania (1967)

Exterior and interior of St. John's Abbey Church, Collegeville, Minnesota (1961)

Interior of St. Procopius Abbey Church (1971)
Interior of Mount Angel Abbey Library (1973)

St. Anselm's Abbey Church, Manchester, New Hampshire

St. Benedict's Abbey Church, Benet Lake, Wisconsin

St. Martin's Abbey Church, Lacey, Washington

St. Bede's Worship-Assembly Building, Peru, Illinois (1974)

CHAPTER 11

Liturgy and Ecumenism

Many people who are acquainted with Benedictine life in the United States today associate that life with the Church's liturgy. They look upon individual Benedictines as liturgical experts and upon Benedictine communities as models of liturgical practice.

The task of tracing the historical growth of liturgical customs and their implementation is not an easy one. But even if the historical record does not yield any uniform evolution of liturgical practice, it does afford a fascinating glimpse at some of the factors that forged the unique identity of American Benedictine houses as centers of public prayer.

Early Models of Liturgy

The liturgical norms and usages that were established in the first Benedictine foundations in the United States were essentially derived from the standards of European monasteries. This is most immediately seen by noting the similarity between the typical daily horarium observed in European houses and that of American houses. The monks rose around 4:00 A.M. to pray Matins and Lauds. There was then an interval before the time of private Masses and the Hour of Prime. The other Little Hours (Terce and Sext) were usually said along with the conventual Mass later in the morning. The remaining Little Hour of None, as well as Vespers and Compline, showed a greater divergence in the time of celebration from house to house. In general, the basic liturgical schedule was the same in all houses; whatever was different bore the mark of the motherhouse: St. Meinrad followed the usage of Einsiedeln; St. Vincent, that of Metten; the women's houses, that of Eichstätt or Maria Rickenbach.

The correspondence of early American Benedictines indicates that they never really gave serious consideration to adapting their customs of common prayer to American conditions. However, it soon became evident that the differing demands of America's Catholic Church would require alteration of liturgical activity. For Benedictine women, this meant not only increased external activity but also a mitigated version of the Divine Office that their canonical status implied. For Benedictine monks, the ever present reality of pastoral work and commitments outside the monastery made it difficult to observe a fixed schedule.

Boniface Wimmer made it a regular practice to allow his foundations a grace period of accommodation before instituting a regular observance. Even then, exceptions to liturgical observance were made for large numbers of the monks who had commitments of missionary work or manual labor. Given these exceptions, one can say that choir attendance was satisfactory, if not always exemplary. In those cases where laxity appeared, appropriate measures were taken. For an example of frontier motivation that was effective, one can look to a recommendation given to St. Benedict's Abbey in Atchison by Abbot Alexius Edelbrock during a visitation, recommending that a priest who did not attend choir in the morning would receive no beer that day, and one who did not celebrate a private Mass would get no breakfast.[1]

Although creativity in disciplinary correctives was condoned, creative adaptation in liturgical customs invited reproach. Such was the case with Martin Marty's decision to replace the monastic Breviary at St. Meinrad and Frowin Conrad's efforts to follow Beuronese liturgical usage at Conception. Nevertheless, a wider mix of liturgical currents from the nineteenth-century monastic reform did find their way into American houses. Boniface Wimmer sent Father Ignatius Treug

of St. Vincent to study the new methods of Gregorian chant at Beuron in the 1870s.[2] A decade later, monks from St. John's and Conception introduced European methods of chant from Solesmes,
Metten, and Beuron. The Swiss-American Congregation, when it
was formed in 1881, freely adopted Beuronese statutes and incorporated the Beuronese monastic habit and liturgical *ceremoniale* as part
of its tradition.[3]

The incorporation of some of these new liturgical ideas and customs, however, ran up against the same pragmatic tendencies that
had kept the activist strain of monastic life flourishing among American Benedictines. In the choral recitation of the Divine Office, more
emphasis was placed on speed than on silent intervals, on performance
of canonical duty rather than prayerful atmosphere. Speaking of his
own community's apparent reluctance to attach a greater importance
to the Divine Office, Father Bede Maler of St. Meinrad noted: "As
long as the Little Flower and St. Rita devotions and other private
practices, customs, devotions, observances and litanies play the main
role in our abbeys, the *Opus Dei* will necessarily remain unimportant."[4]
There was a tendency in American monasteries to stress rubrical punc-
tiliousness in the performance of liturgical roles rather than historical study or pastoral sensitivity. Even so liturgically sophisticated a
superior as Abbot Bernard Locnikar of St. John's Abbey was better
known for his inauguration of Lenten reading of the Missal rubrics
than for his application of liturgical theory.[5]

American Benedictines did promote a number of highly popular
devotional practices in the late nineteenth century. Perhaps the most
prominent was Eucharistic devotion. In 1887 Father Bede Maler of
St. Meinrad discovered a set of the statutes of the Priests' Eucharistic
League, a European movement that aimed to sanctify the priesthood
through deeper devotion to the Eucharist and to encourage lay people
to do the same. The St. Meinrad monk had the full support of his
abbot, Fintan Mundwiler, in introducing the league in the United
States. In 1894 the league's first convention was held at the University of Notre Dame, with Mundwiler as one of the featured speak-
ers. In 1895 Maler began to publish the German monthly
Paradiesesfrüchte. This St. Meinrad publication, along with its Eng-

lish equivalent, *Emmanuel*, attracted large numbers of readers and new league members in the years that followed.[6]

At this same time, the Benedictine Sisters of Perpetual Adoration started their magazine, *Tabernacle and Purgatory*, attempting to "increase esteem for Holy Mass, encourage a frequent and worthy reception of holy communion and awaken and strengthen a lively faith in the real presence of our Lord in the Holy Eucharist."[7] The sisters also initiated the Association of Perpetual Adoration for people outside the community and began their work of making altar breads.

Benedictine communities made their deepest and longest lasting impact in liturgical matters on the parish level. Amid an assortment of pious private devotions often devoid of a sense of communal participation, the monastic heritage of corporate worship and common prayer was a notable advance. For all the frontier hardships endured by Benedictines in their missions and parishes, they introduced a liturgical tradition that most American Catholics had never been exposed to.

Virgil Michel and the Liturgical Movement

If the modern identification of Benedictines with the liturgy has any observable basis in recent history, it stems from their involvement in what is now commonly referred to as "the liturgical movement." Emanating from such European monastic centers as Solesmes, St. André, Maredsous, and Mont-César, this movement was already generating much interest in the late nineteenth century. At that time a number of American Benedictine monks were studying in Europe and were exposed to the ideas of the movement. Father Alcuin Deutsch of St. John's Abbey was one of them. When he was elected abbot of his community in 1922, he introduced a number of significant changes in the liturgical life of the monastery. He brought back the custom of praying the Divine Office in the abbey church rather than in a separate choir chapel. He had the altar and apse areas of the church reconstructed. He made a special point of promoting a renewed appreciation of music in the liturgy, and to this end he sent monks to the Pius X School of Liturgical Music in Manhattanville,

Virgil Michel, O.S.B.,
monk of St. John's Abbey
and leader
of the liturgical movement
in the United States

New York, to study under Dom André Mocquereau of Solesmes. He also brought over from Maredsous Abbey in Belgium the famed chant expert Dom Ermin Vitry to give instruction on the liturgy to the monks of Collegeville.[8]

The most important contribution of Deutsch in fostering the liturgical movement turned out to be his decision to send a young priest-protégé, Father Virgil Michel, to study in Rome in 1922. While a student there at the Benedictine College of Sant' Anselmo, Michel struck up a friendship with a monk of Mont-César Abbey in Belgium, the noted liturgist Dom Lambert Beauduin. Stimulated by Beauduin's ideas, Michel traveled to other Benedictine liturgical centers throughout Europe, imbibing such new concepts as the Mystical Body of Christ and the social ramifications inherent in them.[9]

By the time Virgil Michel returned from Europe in 1925, the moment and the climate were favorable for implementing the liturgical movement on the North American continent. Enlisting the assistance of such American liturgical pioneers as Fathers Martin Hellriegel, Gerald Ellard, S.J., and William Busch, Michel launched a publishing project at St. John's unprecedented in scope, one that left its mark on liturgical life in the United States as nothing before it. He started a monthly liturgical review called *Orate Fratres*, which kept English-speaking readers abreast of the latest liturgical developments. The project gave birth to The Liturgical Press, which was soon issuing a series of translations of the works of European liturgists, a "Popular Liturgical Library" of paperbacks and pamphlets, and a new series of catechetical textbooks.[10]

The peculiar genius of Michel's method of promoting the liturgical movement was that it focused on the education and participation of laypersons and employed the best of both scholarly research and modern communication.[11] The influence that the Collegeville monk had on the American Catholic Church during the 1930s is difficult to overestimate. Certainly he was instrumental in creating a new awareness of the Church's liturgical tradition among both laity and clergy. The extent of that influence can be partially measured in the words of the editor of *Commonweal*, writing in 1936 at the peak of Michel's activity:

> In a day when the great mass of American Catholics are in appalling ignorance of their religion and its fullness . . . you are holding up to our gaze the riches, the depths, the inspiration to be found by the laity in the Mass and the Divine Office. . . . For these reasons and because the priests that are coming out of the seminaries now are liturgically minded due to your influence and because of your attitude on the social question and the general impression of your excellent work of various kinds, from my vantage point I believe you are the greatest hope in the United States today for the Church.[12]

Before his untimely death in 1938, Michel brought to his monastery in Minnesota such Catholic notables as Peter Maurin, Dorothy Day, Catherine de Hueck, and Maurice Lavanoux. He also attracted European Benedictines to the United States. During the 1930s the ideas of Abbot Idelfons Herwegen and Dom Odo Casel of the German abbey of Maria Laach were transmitted by that community's prior, Dom Albert Hammenstede, as he spent time at various Benedictine abbeys in the United States. What was most surprising to Hammenstede and other foreign visitors was the way in which American monasteries had so quickly absorbed the main lines of the liturgical movement. Toward the end of his stay he wrote: "I have learned a great deal about the true monastic spirit since I came to America, and my respect for the American Benedictines has been increased enormously."[13]

Michel's mission of popularizing the liturgical movement not only propagated the previous work of European liturgical scholars, but it also gave support to the work of other American Benedictine liturgical pioneers. Father Bede Maler of St. Meinrad Archabbey, who for a quarter century had been promoting some of Michel's ideas in his monthly magazine devoted to the Eucharist, could only have been pleased with the wide distribution of liturgical publications coming out of Collegeville. Father Michael Ducey of St. Anselm's Priory, Washington, D.C., and St. Mary's Abbey, Newark, New Jersey, received indispensable support from Michel's labors in organizing the first Benedictine Liturgical Conferences and later the National Liturgical Conference. Michel's liturgical leadership has been carried forward by a number of monks of St. John's Abbey, among them Fathers Godfrey Diekmann, Paschal Botz, Michael Marx, Kilian McDonnell, and Aelred Tegels. These men helped to nurture Michel's legacy by making Collegeville a center of liturgical research and practice that first presaged and then promoted the liturgical reforms of the Second Vatican Council. Fathers Paschal Botz, Godfrey Diekmann, and William Heidt widened the publishing activity of The Liturgical Press, and *Worship* magazine (formerly *Orate Fratres*) became the standard-bearer of the liturgical movement in the United States.

In the expanding wave of liturgical reform that followed Michel's death, the monasteries of St. Meinrad and Conception became designated centers for liturgical experimentation during the years immediately preceding the Council. The work of these communities and other smaller monastic houses paved the way for the reforms in the vernacular and revisions in the Divine Office that followed in the wake of the Council. In 1968 St. John's Abbey responded to the request of the bishops of the United States to become one of three research centers for pastoral liturgical development in the American Catholic Church.[14]

Liturgical scholarship, previously a luxury offered only by European liturgical centers, now acquired a greater accessibility and demand in American Benedictine communities of men and women. The names of Fathers Aidan Kavanagh, Nathan Mitchell, Kevin Seasoltz, Gabriel Coless, and Sister Mary Collins were evidence that the Benedictine contribution and commitment to liturgical research and renewal had penetrated beyond the period of the Council.

The Ecumenical Apostolate

An offshoot of the liturgical movement that in turn generated a new and fertile field of activity for many Benedictine houses in the United States was the ecumenical movement. As appropriate as Benedictine involvement in ecumenism might seem to contemporary observers, it should not be forgotten that for most of the first century of their history in North America, Benedictines found themselves in an adversarial position with the non-Catholic majority that surrounded them. Not only the Nativists and the Know-Nothings but several generations of steadfast Lutherans, Southern Baptists, and Czech freethinkers did their best to discourage any possible ecumenical advances. Situated in such a climate, most American Benedictines were willing to respond in kind, particularly by means of the press and the pulpit. Typical of a more extreme individual response was Father Boniface Spanke of New Subiaco Abbey. As a circuit rider in his "Gospel Wagon" throughout western Arkansas just before the First World War, Spanke gained a reputation for confronting Protestant preachers in polemical exchanges.[15]

But in the inhospitable ecumenical atmosphere of the 1920s, when American Benedictines were wincing at Protestant accusations against "monkery," resistance to Prohibition, and papal connivance with the politics of Al Smith, European Benedictines were exploring and encouraging the possibility of Christian unity. In the abbeys of Chevetogne, Niederalteich, Maria Laach, and St. André, Dom Lambert Beauduin and other monks were laying the groundwork for the Catholic Church's participation in the modern ecumenical movement.

That movement first touched monastic circles in the United States in the form of an appeal made by Pope Pius XI in 1924 to the Benedictine Order. The Pontiff asked Benedictine congregations throughout the world to make special efforts on behalf of Christian unity and appealed for one monastic house in each country to take particular interest in advancing the cause of ecumenism. The Benedictine abbot primate, Fidelis von Stotzingen, while visiting St. Procopius Abbey in 1926, proposed to the community that they accept this work. The following year the monastic chapter agreed to do so.[16] The ecumenical apostolate of the St. Procopius community, particularly the work of Abbots Valentine Kohlbeck and Procopius Neuzil in furthering dialogue and promoting reconciliation with Eastern Rite Churches, was a groundbreaking endeavor.[17] It led to the foundation of Holy Trinity Monastery in Butler, Pennsylvania, in 1948 (for the Greek Ruthenian Church) and an ongoing commitment to theological and liturgical sharing with the Eastern Churches in the United States.

Monasticism's ecumenical work was not limited to the Eastern Churches. In 1946 the Anglican Benedictine monastery of Nashdom in England made a monastic foundation in Three Rivers, Michigan. The monastic community of St. Gregory's that evolved from this foundation eventually became an independent abbey, and under its superior, Abbot Benedict Reid, took an active role in ecumenical exchange with other monastic houses in the United States.

An allied apostolate that became both a source and support for the ecumenical movement during these years was the work at Newman Clubs on college campuses. Monks from St. Vincent accepted a request to staff the Newman Club at Penn State University in College Park, Pennsylvania. This coincided with a decision of the monks of St. John's Abbey to operate the Newman Club at the University of Illinois in Champaign-Urbana. As a result of this monastic presence in continuing education programs, campus liturgies, and a community-centered prayer life, many non-Catholic students were exposed to a part of the Catholic tradition that was far less abrasive than what they had been led to believe. The staying power of that monastic witness on campuses and its evolution as part of the ecu-

St. Gregory's Abbey, Three Rivers, Michigan

Institute for Ecumenical and Cultural Research, Collegeville, Minnesota

191

menical movement over the years can be seen in the decision of the abbey of St. Pius X to relocate its monastery to the campus of the University of Missouri in Columbia during the 1980s, in order to concentrate on the ministry to Newman Clubs.

Both individual and institutional involvement in the ecumenical movement became more extensive in the communities of St. Vincent and St. John's during the years leading up to the Council. Monks from St. Vincent became an important component of the "ecumenical" community of Dormition Abbey in Jerusalem. St. John's Abbey enlarged its ecumenical scope significantly in the early 1960s, sponsoring four ecumenical symposia that signified a new and more intense commitment to ecumenical dialogue.[18] Under the direction of Abbot Baldwin Dworschak and Father Kilian McDonnell, the community established the Institute for Ecumenical and Cultural Research in 1967, affording facilities where scholars could undertake prolonged study on questions of concern to contemporary ecumenists. St. John's also sent professors to teach in exchange programs with Protestant colleges, founded a chair of Jewish Studies at its university, and hosted programs involving members of other religious denominations at the monastery.

What was taking place at Collegeville was occurring on a smaller scale in other Benedictine communities across the country, fueled by the call of Pope John XXIII for an ecumenical council and a growing convergence of denominational practice in the Churches of the United States during the 1960s. Benedictine communities became favorite sites for interfaith worship and discussion, and remained so long after the initial enthusiasm engendered by Vatican II and the Decree on Ecumenism had passed. New possibilities of connecting the tradition of monastic life with Protestant denominations were explored. Even when some of these experiments fell short of their goal, as was the case with the monastic community founded by Conception Abbey in Denmark, the resultant widening of horizons on the part of all those engaged in the task was evident.

The period immediately after the Council was also a time when the highly publicized activity of Trappist Fathers Thomas Merton and Basil Pennington, as well as other monastic figures who wanted to make contact with forms of Eastern monastic tradition and non-Christian prayer forms, sparked the interest of many American Benedictines. This culminated in the establishment of the North American Board for East-West Dialogue, a joint Benedictine organization that sponsored a widening number of exchanges between American monastic communities and representatives of non-Christian Eastern monastic bodies. Mutual visits of Benedictine and Buddhist monks to monasteries in India and the United States complemented a more systematic study of the spiritual similarities and differences of both traditions.

Many longtime observers of American Benedictine monasticism recognized how widespread the repercussions of involvement in the liturgical and ecumenical movements of the twentieth century were. Benedictine communities had been transformed from embattled Catholic minorities, deriving their liturgical life from staid European traditions of the nineteenth century, to an assimilated and confident presence in the religious pluralism of twentieth-century America. But this was really nothing more than a paraphrase of the same development that took place in American Catholicism during the same period, and it pointed to one more example of how American Benedictines had become part of the living reality of the larger American Church.

CHAPTER 12

Spiritual Life and Formation

Even if the external work of missionary activity, education, liturgical expression, and ecumenical witness may have appeared as the most prominent elements of Benedictine influence in the United States, it is essential to remember that all this was made possible by the nourishment of a long tradition of spiritual formation and religious observance. The task of transmitting this revered monastic deposit of spirituality and asceticism and adapting it to an American environment that was radically different from monasticism's European origins is a crucial factor in the survival and sustenance of that tradition for subsequent generations of American Benedictines.

Unlike other religious orders, the Benedictines have always maintained a determined adherence to their autonomy, whether as a congregation or an individual monastic house. Thus one cannot easily paint with broad strokes on the canvas of Benedictine spiritual life as it developed in the United States. Yet there were distinguishing features in the spirituality and monastic formation of American Benedictines. In the nineteenth century the landscape where those features could be found consisted largely in the life of the two major congregations of monks, the American Cassinese and Swiss-American, and it is to this representative sector of monastic life that focus will first be directed.

194

The Interplay of Europe and North America

If the first generation of American Benedictines could be said to have had a distinctive spirituality, ascetical model, or devotional practice, it was derived in form and spirit from their European founders. Moreover, the Bavarian and Swiss Benedictine customs and practices, from which the Cassinese and Swiss descended, differed considerably from more structured reformed congregations of Beuron, Solesmes, and the Primitive Observance. A large number of priest-monks of Metten or Einsiedeln worked in educational and pastoral apostolates outside the community in the nineteenth century. But the scale and intensity of missionary work performed by the priest-monks of Wimmer's American Cassinese Congregation exceeded any modern European precedent and pointed to an inherent conflict between the monastic community's interior life of prayer and detachment and its exterior program of missionary evangelization, a conflict that was to be inherited by succeeding generations.

It is to Wimmer's credit that he was aware of the nature and potential consequences of this conflict, even if his methods of trying to resolve it did not always meet with approval. In his first years, Wimmer seemed firmly convinced that he could continue to conduct widespread missionary activity and still maintain a strict observance of monastic practices and common prayer. His own overriding concern for the spiritual life was expressed in a letter sent to the abbot of Metten in 1858: "If our Order would dedicate itself more to the interior life, to meditation and contemplation in the monasteries, and to the conversion of people in the outside world, there would be less danger of relaxation of discipline."[1] But what Wimmer in his first years as abbot saw as an easily compatible coordination of "contemplation and conversion" became the core of a ceaseless conflict of interest in his Cassinese houses. The predictable results of such conflict were articulated by Wimmer himself in a letter he wrote in the twilight of his life: "I fear we hold to our Rule too little; therefore God will withdraw his blessing bit by bit. There is too little spirit of the Order, etc., in most of the men. . . . The small parishes are the graves of good discipline; we should take them only out of necessity."[2]

Another dimension of this conflict that caused Wimmer to be on the receiving end of much criticism lay in the lack of adequate monastic formation given to young monks before they were sent out to do parish or missionary work. Wimmer could point to his practice of sending several St. Vincent monks to Rome and Munich for further study, at no small sacrifice to the Latrobe community.[3] Still, even Wimmer had to admit that the amount of spiritual formation and theological education received by the majority of monks at St. Vincent was far less than that of monks in European abbeys. The same critique of a too hasty and superficial monastic formation was directed toward the newly ordained priests of Wimmer's early foundations in Atchison and Collegeville. Some students for the priesthood at St. Benedict's Abbey in Atchison received only one or two years of theological studies before ordination, and often much of their time during those years was taken up with duties of prefecting or teaching in the school.[4] When criticized for not giving clerics of St. John's Abbey sufficient training in spiritual and theological formation, Abbot Alexius Edelbrock responded: "A larger and more thorough course would be desirable, yet as long as the priest is for the people, and as long as people are going to destruction for want of priests, so long it would be cruel not to have priests ordained when they possess sufficient knowledge. We must first look to what is necessary, then to what is merely desirable."[5]

The pragmatism and emphasis upon priestly ministry reflected in Edelbrock's words were only a continuation of the predominant attitude that Wimmer had imparted to the American Cassinese monks from the beginning. One of Wimmer's proposals for the monastic houses of his congregation was a highly centralized and uniform mode of life. This penchant for efficient centralization was evident in the decisions made by the first general chapters of the American Cassinese Congregation, over which Wimmer presided. In 1858 provisions were approved for a unified structure of the Divine Office and adherence to the prevailing statutes of the Bavarian Congregation. More significant was the approval of Wimmer's proposal to set up a common novitiate and house of studies at St. Vincent for all the houses in the congregation.[6] In 1862 the general chapter passed detailed directives on required reading, with a common list of books for monks in formation as well as those who had already made vows.[7] In 1867 the chapter reiterated its determination to secure a uniform monastic observance in all the houses of the congregation. Some members of that chapter may have been led to question the limits of centralization, however, when the body voted that all monks in the congregation, including novices, should wear beards.[8]

Wimmer's centralizing tendency extended beyond the boundaries of the Cassinese Congregation. Mention has already been made of his intention to incorporate all the Benedictine sisters from Eichstätt into his congregation of monks. The rebuff he received from Rome on that proposal did not dissuade him from making overtures to other Benedictines. In 1868 he proposed to Martin Marty that St. Meinrad become a member of the Cassinese Congregation, claiming: ''I gain nothing if you join us, except the duty of making the visitation and from time to time some official communication. But the Benedictine Order and your abbey gain in meaning and power.''[9] Knowing of Wimmer's tendency to acquire and consolidate personal power as superior, Marty declined the offer.

In the final accounting, Wimmer's ideal of a highly coordinated and centralized monastic congregation remained only a dream. His own Cassinese houses showed increasing resentment over his insistence on a common novitiate and clericate at St. Vincent. Upon Wimmer's death in 1887, the superiors of the congregation, led by Abbots Innocent Wolf and Leo Haid, led a move to discontinue the common novitiate. As new president of the congregation, Belmont Abbey's Leo Haid was less compelled to conform to the Bavarian constitutions and more willing to allow for autonomy and adaptation on the part of each community in structuring its monastic observance.[10]

Wimmer's successors at St. Vincent, as well as abbots such as Leo Haid and Bernard Locnikar of St. John's, did their best to preserve a disciplined monastic observance in their respective communities and cut back on pastoral commitments, but the pressure of many missionary obligations continued to make such efforts difficult long after Wimmer had departed from the scene.

The tension experienced between a cloistered spiritual life and urgent pastoral demands was not, however, peculiar to the American Cassinese Congregation. Houses of the Swiss-American Congregation felt the same conflict, with none of the Swiss superiors feeling it more keenly than Frowin Conrad of Conception Abbey.

The spiritual ideal of the monastic life that Frowin Conrad brought over to the United States in the 1870s was of a self-enclosed community, intent upon the pursuit of personal holiness and liturgical prayer. It was an ideal that frowned upon the prospect of outside parish commitments and believed that flight from the world was the proper expression of monastic spirituality. A selection of entries from Conrad's personal journal, ranging over thirty years, points out how constant his ideal remained and how difficult it was to achieve:

> I commend my *expositi* every day to the grace of God and I fear for them because of the danger to which they are exposed. May I live long enough to see all my confreres living within the monastery and see no external or internal reason drawing them out.[11]

> A great misfortune for our Order in this country is the abundance of outside activity that has nearly robbed us of the sense of genuine monastic life. We seem to be more professors and missionaries than monks, the result being that all of our activity is more pretense than truth.[12]

> I see daily more and more how necessary it is for our infant monasteries in this country to cling firmly to the established traditions of the best monasteries in Europe. It is perfectly true as some say that conditions in the New World are quite different from those of Europe, but that is every reason that true monastic spirit must not be allowed to degenerate under pressure.[13]

The rich spiritual life of Beuron remained Conrad's theoretical norm and monastic model, but he was forced to adapt that ideal to the quite different conditions that confronted him on America's frontier. Even as he supported the missionary enterprise of Martin Marty and sent monks from Conception to assist in parish and missionary work, Conrad was convinced that true Benedictine spirituality was lived inside, not outside, the cloister.

Conrad could count on some kindred spirits in the Swiss-American houses to lend support to his cause. Foremost among them was Fintan Mundwiler of St. Meinrad, who singled out some of the same spiritual tensions facing his community. Shortly after becoming abbot at St. Meinrad, he wrote:

> In general, try to keep people of the world away from the house as much as possible, since this is good for all; for I discovered years ago and continue to note how harmful it is for religious to have much to do with people of the world. The lack of monastic enclosure and separation has been for us at St. Meinrad a great obstacle already for some time and most of our problems seem to stem from it. Unfortunately, I have not yet succeeded in keeping a stricter *clausura*, but am still trying to do so. Here in the missions as well I find that the greatest evils stem from too free association with people of the world, and that as a result the monastic order is destroyed and disorder and worldliness take root.[14]

The recipient of Mundwiler's comments, Father Wolfgang Schlumpf, was at one with the opinion expressed by the St. Meinrad superior. Basing his opinion on his own experience while prior of New Subiaco Abbey, Schlumpf echoed Mundwiler's sentiments:

> If the *expositi* follow the directions of the Statutes of our Congregation their spiritual welfare will be assured and the good name and welfare of the monastery will be enhanced. . . . A Benedictine pastor should not live simply according to the ways of a secular priest, but should remain a monk under all circumstances. We must be watchful that a desire for mission life does not impede monastic life. According to my observations this desire has already seized some of the young men, so we must apply the brakes in time.[15]

Before applying these brakes, the burden of spiritual formation and direction devolved upon the person of the abbot or superior of the house. Even though the constraints of time and material resources often lessened the effectiveness and thoroughness of such formation, many young monks managed to acquire a solid grasp of the essentials of monastic life. A good example of how this took place can be seen at St. Meinrad during the abbatial tenure of Martin Marty. A scholar in his own right, Marty purchased copies of the Rule of Benedict in English and other works on Benedictine spirituality (for example, the works of Abbot Cisneros) that he used to instruct the younger monks. After the evening meal the abbot himself would lecture and examine his young monks in Latin, Greek, rhetoric, and dogmatic theology. Time was also set aside for conferences on the Rule, the Swiss constitutions, the life of Benedict, and monastic history.[16]

Marty's personal example was followed even more conscientiously by Swiss superiors such as Conrad and Mundwiler. But even their best intentions were often compromised by frequent absences from the monastery and the administrative demands of their office. Without the experiment of the American Cassinese common novitiate, the Swiss-Americans relied much more on the individual monk who was appointed as novice master or cleric master in each community. Even in the case of the priest-monk entrusted with this role, parish work and other commitments often limited the time he could give to the task of spiritual formation.

In time the Swiss-American houses developed programs of monastic formation and spiritual instruction that reflected a mixture of the customs of the European motherhouse, the individual emphasis of the master of novices and clerics, and the unique spiritual orientation of the community itself. But there was also a common core of practices found in all houses. A glance at the formalized content of monastic formation at a house like St. Meinrad at the turn of the century exemplifies this. A dominant feature was a handbook of what amounted to monastic etiquette, a detailed list of six pages regulating everything from the wearing of the habit to the manner of walking (eyes cast down and hands always under the scapular). Also prescribed was a precise program of religious exercises that included the procedure of public and private *culpa* (nonsacramental confession of faults), a general and particular examination of conscience, assigned times of spiritual and scriptural reading, and encouragement of both frequent confession and private devotions such as the Rosary and the Way of the Cross.[17] Much the same form of spiritual instruction existed at other Swiss houses, with the only exception being that particular customs or devotional practices from Engelberg prevailed at Mount Angel and Conception Abbeys, while those of Einsiedeln held sway at New Subiaco and St. Joseph Abbeys.

There was, however, a problem shared by both congregations. Whatever systematized spiritual formation was given, it extended only to the point when the monk made final profession or was ordained. There was no formal provision for monastic or theological instruction to be given after that time. This not only blocked any likelihood of continuing formation, but it also accentuated the double standard existing between the ordained and non-ordained monks, the solemnly professed and lay brothers, a situation that continued to exist in most houses up to the time of the Second Vatican Council.

The Transmission of a Spiritual Tradition

Despite these shortcomings, a form of Benedictine spirituality was imparted to the monks who passed through the formation programs, and that same spirituality was communicated to the parishes and churches where the monks ministered. The sizable number of devotional societies that existed in German parishes was often attributable to the presence of Benedictine priests.[18] Similarly, many of the popular practices of piety that were part of American Catholic parish life in the nineteenth century were fostered by Benedictine pastors. They included the singing of German and Latin hymns at Mass by both the choir and the congregation, Sunday Vespers (sung by the lay congregation) and Benediction, Marian pilgrimages, devotion to the Sacred Heart, adoration of the Blessed Sacrament, and processions for such feasts as Corpus Christi and Rogation Days.

American Benedictines also cultivated a number of devotions within their own communities, including the renewed devotion to Mary that had been part of the wider Catholic experience of the nineteenth century. The establishment of the Swiss-American Congregation in 1881 under the patronage of the Immaculate Conception and the promotion of Marian piety by many individual Benedictine houses, few of which lacked a distinctive Marian shrine, gave witness to a strong attachment to the Blessed Virgin. Renewed devotion to the Holy Spirit was seen with the establishment of the

Confraternity of the Holy Ghost at St. Vincent Archabbey in the
last decade of the nineteenth century.[19] The mix of specifically monastic observances and popular spiritual devotions is seen in a list of
recommended practices for the Swiss-American Congregation in 1924:
a half hour of meditation each morning; up to one hour of private
and public spiritual reading each day; examination of conscience in
common; adoration of the Blessed Sacrament after the common meal;
daily recitation of the Rosary; weekly reception of the sacrament of
penance; private devotions to the Sacred Heart and the Blessed Virgin; the Way of the Cross.[20] This model of spiritual practices was
followed in large part by other Benedictine congregations and communities of the time.

Another observable characteristic of formation programs was that
the uniquely Benedictine character of spiritual norms did not always
carry over into the religious instruction given to the monastic community. Such spiritual staples as *The Imitation of Christ* and the
Tyrocinium Religiosum received a degree of emphasis that often ob-
scured more monastic material. This was due to the unavailability
of adequate translations of monastic sources of spirituality and to the
lack of adequate numbers of monks or sisters to teach it. Beyond
that, a powerful preaching voice and a rugged physical constitution
were usually given higher regard in the formation of monks than any
claim to monastic scholarship.

The theological education received by most Benedictine candidates for the priesthood, with the exception of the few monks sent
to Europe, suffered from some of the same deficiencies. In the post-
Modernist era of American Catholicism, it was an education rooted
in the unquestioning acceptance of material from the theological
manuals, leaving little room for a broader sampling of spirituality or
advanced scholarship.

What held true for Benedictine monks was even more true for
Benedictine sisters in the United States. Formation in convents consisted of ascetical rigorism and rote learning of detailed duties. The
insistence was on conformity, docility, and submission to the common rule.[21] The fact that this system produced saintly women and
edifying examples of obedience is not disputed, but it seems that what-

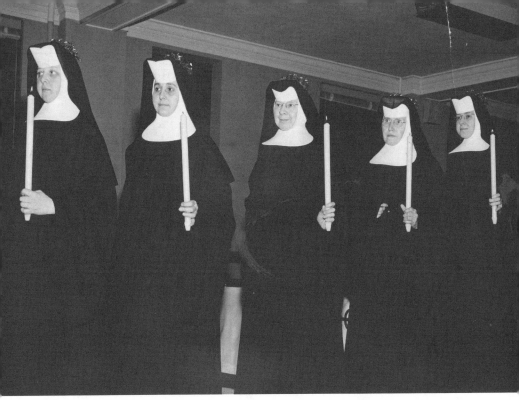

Ceremony of consecration of virgins, St. Walburga Priory, Covington, Kentucky

Benedictine prioresses and Father Paschal Botz, O.S.B., at the grave of Mother Benedicta Riepp, O.S.B., St. Joseph, Minnesota (1952)

Profession ceremony in Sacred Heart Chapel, St. Benedict's Convent, St. Joseph, Minnesota

Choral recitation of the Divine Office, St. Scholastica Priory, Chicago, Illinois

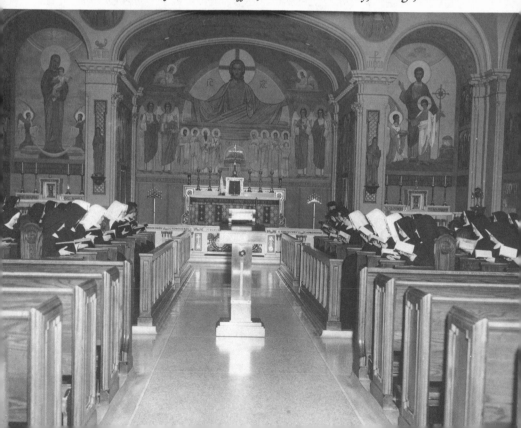

Sister Stanislaus of St. Walburga Priory teaching first grade at St. Henry School, Erlanger, Kentucky

ever deeper understanding of monastic tradition this system imparted was more often by accident than by design.

A break with this system of spiritual formation occurred in October 1957 in the form of a resolution signed by thirty-seven Benedictine prioresses, representing the four congregations of Benedictine sisters. It established the Benedictine Institute of Sacred Theology at St. Benedict Convent, St. Joseph, Minnesota. Previous to that time, even those American Benedictine sisters who had the opportunity to obtain advanced academic degrees or pursue personal studies had to do so during their summer vacation, when they were free of teaching duties. Even then the need for graduate degrees in education and specialized fields of teaching left little time for theological studies or enrichment. The problem of time constraints was compounded by a rigid "flight from the world" spirituality that looked upon everything outside the convent as a threat to the spiritual life and well-being of the community.

The Benedictine Institute of Sacred Theology attempted to remedy those weaknesses. It was intended for sisters and was connected with the faculty of St. John's University in Collegeville. Under the leadership of Father Paschal Botz and Sister Mary Anthony Wagner, the institute attracted many Benedictine women and evolved into an accredited program that offered both spiritual formation and theological scholarship.[22]

Another Benedictine project that contributed to the formation of sisters was the periodical *Sponsa Regis* (now called *Sisters Today*). This magazine began to be published by St. John's Abbey in 1929, under the editorship of Father Joseph Kreuter, who saw a need for ascetical and liturgical emphasis in the spirituality of sisters.

Opening to a Wider Public

The Benedictine Institute in Collegeville also attracted lay people, which was appropriate because almost a century earlier the St. John's community had proposed the possibility of creating closer ties between lay people and the spiritual life of the monastic community. The first publication of St. John's Abbey Press was a pamphlet written in German and English by Abbot Alexius Edelbrock to promote the Oblates of St. Benedict among the students, parishioners, and benefactors of the abbey.[23] This ancient institute of secular or lay oblates was one that dispersed the riches of Benedictine spirituality to a much wider segment of the Church. Its purpose was to have laypersons interested in the Benedictine life to affiliate themselves to a Benedictine community and develop their spiritual lives according to the monastic principles of the Rule of St. Benedict.

In 1894 Archabbot Leander Schnerr of St. Vincent revived the association of Benedictine oblates in the United States. In 1923 St. Vincent Archabbey issued *A Manual for Secular Oblates*. The movement was given further impetus by Abbot Alcuin Deutsch of St. John's Abbey in the 1920s, when he expanded the institute of secular oblates to include a greater number of laypersons and made available to them annual retreats, a monthly publication, and a lending library.[24] The oblate movement soon spread to other houses of American men and women and remains a vigorous witness to the applicability of Benedictine spirituality to the wider Church.

Abbot Columban Thuis, O.S.B., presides at monastic profession at St. Joseph Abbey, St. Benedict, Louisiana (ca. 1949)

Profession ceremony at St. Benedict's Convent, St. Joseph, Minnesota

The oblate programs developed in tandem with another lay program that took root in American Benedictine monasteries in the twentieth century—the spiritual retreat movement. St. John's Abbey took a leading role in this movement, and many smaller monastic houses were also attracted to it. Four of the new monasteries established by the Swiss-American Congregation after World War II were devoted almost exclusively to the retreat apostolate.[25] A substantial number of other Benedictine communities constructed retreat facilities to meet the needs of lay people.

The period after World War II was also one in which Benedictine houses continued to attract deeply committed monastic vocations. One is led to wonder whether this took place in spite of or because of the climate of community life and spiritual formation, but there is little doubt that an underlying monastic instinct was conveyed to many. This was due in no small part to the greater availability of monastic writings that made their way into American Benedictine houses. Guardini, Herwegen, and Casel were replacing the timeworn teaching of Tanquerey and the *Tyrocinium*. For the English-speaking world, there was also the appearance of the works of British abbots Cuthbert Butler and John Chapman, with their spiritual doctrine that was marked with a distinctively Benedictine imprint. The collected works of Abbot Columba Marmion, once they appeared in English, became the standard resource in programs of religious formation, even outside the Benedictine Order. By this time, too, many of the riches of the liturgical movement had taken root in the United States, and the increasing number of American monks who had received training in Rome at the Benedictine College of Sant' Anselmo brought back to their communities a broadened understanding of Benedictine spirituality and the monastic tradition.

The appearance of the previously mentioned American Benedictine Academy and its official journal, *The American Benedictine Review*, undergirded other changes in spiritual life and monastic formation in the postwar era. There was now a more open collaboration between Benedictine communities and more diversified opportunities for individual members of those communities to have access to resources of monastic formation and Benedictine studies.

Parochial as the original academy's meetings and some of the review's articles were,[26] they did constitute a step forward from the hidebound nature of formation that had characterized the previous century.

But the real watershed in the history of the spiritual life and formation of American Benedictines came in the decade of the 1960s, a history that will be detailed in a concluding chapter.

CHAPTER 13

The Contemplative Impulse: Failure and Success

At the center of Benedictine spiritual life in every age has been the desire to seek God. It is an aim that has traditionally been coupled with a life of separation from the world and an environment of contemplation.

The Ascendancy of the Active

If someone were charged with creating a cultural setting or climate most alien to a life of contemplation and detachment, the American society into which the first Benedictines entered would have come close to fitting that prescription. Intellectual historians have noted that the very traits of the American character that have allowed it to grow—individualism, pragmatism, productivity, and self-initiative—have also served to distance it as a nation and a people from the more patterned and established social fabric of Europe. So it was in the religious world as well. The emerging immigrant Catholic Church in the United States in the second half of the nineteenth century could be described as muscular, action-oriented, and purposeful, leaving little opening for the possibility of a contemplative monastic community, whose non-productive presence would not easily lend itself to the needs of such a Church.

This predominantly practical character of the American Catholic Church is all the more pronounced when one considers the earliest instance of monastic settlement in the United States: a group of refugee French Trappist monks, led by Father Urban Guillet, who were invited to come to Kentucky by Father Charles Nerinckx and Father Stephen Badin, two early French missionaries, in the early years of the nineteenth century. Frontier circumstances forced them to undertake missionary work and the administration of a Catholic school. The venture soon collapsed.[1] What is so arresting about this experiment is less the frontier failure of the French monks than the expectations that the Trappists would "devote their energies to active service."[2]

The incongruity of the apostolic labors of Trappist monks is a leitmotif that reappears in later foundations at Gethsemani, Kentucky, and New Melleray, Iowa. In the former, Trappistine sisters teamed with monks to assist in the operation of a boy's boarding school.[3] In the latter, two of the community members were named as bishops of the American hierarchy.[4] Protests against such pressure to adopt an active role were forwarded to the Propaganda Fide in Rome, but they produced no immediate change.[5] It is also interesting to note that the number of American-born candidates entering these two Trappist houses in the first decades of their existence was negligible.

Unlike the Trappists, who disclaimed any desire to accept parish or missionary tasks, the first American Benedictines were primarily intent upon planting an activist missionary model of monasticism rather than a cloistered and contemplative one. Such Benedictine founders as Boniface Wimmer, Benedicta Riepp, and Martin Marty all valued the community life and monastic observance that had nurtured their respective vocations, but they were also convinced that the needs of the Church in the "New World" required an activist Benedictine presence as a matter of priority.

This is not to say that there was unanimity about such a priority. A continuing movement of dissent against this activist mentality was a constant part of the history of most of the first Benedictine houses. The periodic protests at St. Vincent under Wimmer's regime cited earlier—the revolt of Peter Lechner in 1849; the dispute headed by Paul Keck, Othmar Wirtz, and Wendelin Mayer in 1862; the demand to conform to Beuron led by James Zilliox and Andrew Hintenach in 1879—all carried with them a determination to withdraw from missionary work and lead a more cloistered monastic life.

It is too facile an explanation to say that the majority of these protests were put down principally because of the force of Wimmer's personality. Evidence abounds that the American bishops, members of Roman congregations, and indeed the majority of the American monks themselves, were willing to support the missionary model of monasticism, given the exigencies of the Church's mission in the nineteenth century.

The most vocal and critical chorus of voices that disagreed with the activist bent of American monks came from the monasteries of Europe. There the Wolter brothers of Beuron, particularly Placid Wolter, carried on an extensive campaign of protest, inveighing against what they saw as the unmonastic impulsiveness and "Americanism" of Wimmer and Marty.[6]

As noted earlier, these European critics had their advocates in American houses. Frowin Conrad of Conception probably stands out as the most singular example of a superior who wanted "a real monastery," one that did not commit large numbers of its members to missionary work away from the abbey. Yet there is perhaps no better indicator of how strong the undertow of the activist strain of monasticism in the United States was than the fact that not even as dedicated a contemplative spirit as Conrad could stay its momentum during his years as abbot.

Conrad was not alone in this struggle. Other superiors reacted against what they saw as the founding abbot's overactive commitments by cutting back on pastoral involvement and missionary activity, but with scant success. Such was the case with Archabbot Andrew Hintenach, successor to Wimmer at St. Vincent. After four years of attempting to pull back from many of Wimmer's expansionist activities, Hintenach resigned. A contemporary of Hintenach's, Abbot Bernard Locnikar of St. John's Abbey, underwent a similar experience. Following the advice of his friend and mentor Frowin Conrad, Locnikar attempted to implement a stricter claustral life at Collegeville and to place a greater emphasis on the celebration of the Divine Office and the community liturgy. In an ironic twist of events, most of his energy was devoted to settling a dispute with his diocesan bishop over the administration of parishes and missions. That dispute and the tornado of 1894 that ravaged the Minnesota monastery brought Locnikar to an early grave only four years after his election.[7]

One instance in which the contemplative critics could point to at least partial success in checking the momentum of missionary monasticism was in the resignation of Abbot Alexius Edelbrock of St. John's Abbey in 1889. As in the case of complaints against Wimmer, Edelbrock's former prior, Father Bernard Locnikar, and his former novice master, Father Alfred Mayer, were in the forefront of those who accused him of being absent from the monastery too much and of giving too much attention to money matters and missionary activity, to the detriment of the Collegeville community's interior monastic life and spiritual formation. Another of the burrs in Wimmer's own side, Abbot James Zilliox of St. Mary's Abbey, contributed to the chain of criticism that led to Edelbrock's resignation. The St. Mary's abbot, who had headed a special visitation of the St. John's community, summarized the grievances in a letter to Edelbrock:

> It is my own observation, that the guiding spirit in St. John's Abbey is one of intense external activity, expanding materially and embracing as much as possible of things external. I believe your own person is the best representative of both the monks and the nuns in this regard. . . . Whatever may be said of all this external activity, as actually existing, or also as to the correctness of principle in it, I will only say that too much of it harms, and that it seems that there is too much of it to be consistent with monks and nuns of the Rule of St. Benedict, and that the spiritual advancement of all parties concerned seems at present to be more than questionable. This point is fundamental.[8]

Edelbrock's resignation was due to a set of factors more complex than a cabal of contemplative monks. It was also triggered by renegade priest-monks and Americanizing bishops.[9] Nonetheless, the Edelbrock affair marked a time when some circles in the American hierarchy and Roman ranks of Benedictine leadership were expressing reservations about the unchecked character of missionary activity.

Contemplative Challenges to Missionary Monasticism

In 1888 the Redemptorist bishop of Portland, Oregon, William Gross, wrote a letter to Abbot Anselm Villiger of Engelberg Abbey in Switzerland. Speaking of the work of the Mount Angel monastic community in his diocese, the prelate joined in the lament over the possible dangers of not fostering the contemplative dimension of community life:

> I consider it to be a very great mistake to allow the Benedictine Fathers to look after parishes. . . . They are always among the people of the world, and what this leads to God only knows. The great inclination toward freedom and independence in America alone is enough to penetrate a man's thinking even though he is not in the midst of it, but when he is, he will lose, without noticing it, all love for religious life and all interest in the choir and school. He does not even wish to think about returning to monastic life with its choir obligation and other usages.[10]

The same admonition to avoid taking over too many parishes and the exhortation to preserve a deeper claustral prayer life was conveyed in a letter sent by the first abbot primate of the Benedictine Order, Hildebrand de Hemptinne of Maredsous Abbey, to the Swiss-American Congregation in 1904.[11] Thirty years later another abbot primate had the same message for American Benedictines: "It is of greatest importance that our abbeys in America should develop the inner cloistral life more and more and place the greatest importance on that. There is great danger that the 'pioneer stage' will last too long, at least in its effects."[12]

The pioneer stage was, in fact, passing. It should not seem surprising that in the midst of so much concern over the lack of a more contemplative monastic life in the United States, some experiments to put it into effect would be initiated. Possibly the most famous of these was the community of New Cluny in Wetaug, Illinois, headed by Oswald Moosmueller. Moosmueller, despite his position as one of the key figures in Boniface Wimmer's network of missionary monasteries, had long indicated his fascination for the medieval ideals of the Benedictine Abbey of Cluny, particularly as those ideals had been revived in the monastic reform of Prosper Guéranger and Maurus

Wolter. It was this contemplative and scholarly spirit that the St. Vincent monk wanted to animate the community he established in 1892 near the small southern Illinois town of Wetaug.

Just before his resignation as abbot of the St. Vincent community, Andrew Hintenach had given Moosmueller permission to found his community. Its principal work was to be the celebration each day of the full liturgical round. It also was to be engaged in the literary activity of translating the *Acta Sanctorum* of the Bollandists from Latin into German, a task carried out by means of a monthly journal called *Die Legende*.[13] Moosmueller assembled a number of lay brothers to help with what he imagined would be a self-sufficient farm. He also attracted a substantial number of clerical candidates from different Cassinese houses who were interested in investigating the promise of a more contemplative community life. Exemplary as Moosmueller's personal goal and subsequent efforts as superior were, the combination of poor location, inadequate funds, and bad management spelled the community's early demise.

A measure of how foreign such a life of cloistered contemplation was to the American spirit at the end of the nineteenth century was manifested in a letter sent by a diocesan priest of the Belleville Diocese (where New Cluny was located) to his bishop:

> All the students have left Cluny, the undeserving one who received minor orders at your hands has obtained a three month's furlough to canvass Chicago and other places for that pious fraud known as the *Legende*. He will impose on charitable and good-natured priests and their flocks, telling them the proceeds are to be employed in the education of poor boys for the priesthood, while as a matter of fact it must be used to pay off Engelbert's huge barn and stable. With all the money obtained heretofore through their pious imposition, they have not treated one young man justly who came to them with a vocation and sincere heart. Cluny has proven in this trial of the last five years under the combined mismanagement of Revs. Oswald and Engelbert a complete failure. . . . Ten industrious families would not only live comfortably but would save money on the land that these Benedictines are holding and cannot make it yield enough of potatoes and wheat for 15 or 20 persons. Then they canvass the country to have the people for sweet charity's sake buy that stale *Legende*.[14]

The Father Engelbert (Leist) mentioned in the letter had been assigned to the parish in Wetaug even before Moosmueller's arrival and obviously had not ingratiated himself with the local clergy. Neither the academic nor the agricultural achievements of New Cluny impressed the inhabitants of the local community of Catholics, and the Protestants saw nothing but a symbol of all that had been caricatured in the papist monkery of the Middle Ages. With Moosmueller's death in 1901, members of New Cluny decided to leave Wetaug. With the help of monks of St. John's Abbey, they trekked to Canada's prairie province of Saskatchewan, where they supported themselves by printing, agriculture, and pastoral work. They founded the German-Catholic colony of St. Peter's and the Benedictine abbey nullius of St. Peter as a monastery of the American Cassinese Congregation.[15]

Not so much an experiment as an evolving community commitment was the decision of the Benedictine sisters in Clyde, Missouri, to relinquish their external apostolates in the first part of the twentieth century and establish themselves as the Congregation of Perpetual Adoration. Their principal work would be a life of community prayer and Eucharistic adoration, with only internal ministries such as the making of altar breads and church vestments and the printing of devotional literature allowed under the umbrella of community apostolate. But the other three major congregations of Benedictine sisters in the United States showed that contemplative interests were still the exception as they continued their active apostolic commitments.[16]

The American Catholic Church and its monastic component in the first part of the twentieth century offered little promise for contemplative community life to take root. It was a climate in which the accent was on sacramental service to a rapidly growing body of faithful who clamored for confessors and catechists rather than contemplative and cloistered monastic communities. But by the middle of the century the climate underwent a change as the Church displayed a greater receptivity to the contemplative impulse. This change was reflected intellectually in the renewed aesthetic attraction of the

*Thomas Merton
(Father Louis, O.C.S.O.),
Abbey of
Our Lady of Gethsemani,
Trappist, Kentucky*

Middle Ages and concretely in the appearance of several new monastic foundations.

The Postwar Flowering of Contemplative Communities

After several failed attempts at starting a contemplative house in the United States, a German monk from the abbey of Maria Laach, Father Damasus Winzen, founded the community of Mount Saviour in Elmira, New York, in 1950. Apart from the rich heritage of monastic tradition that Winzen transmitted from his European experience as a Benedictine, he introduced at Mount Saviour an emphasis upon manual work and community prayer, and deemphasized priestly and missionary activity. Another European Benedictine, Father Leo Rudloff, had similar intentions in founding the community of Weston Priory in Vermont in 1952.[17]

Part of this new appeal of contemplative monastic life stemmed from the publication of Thomas Merton's *Seven Storey Mountain* in 1948. Merton's bestselling autobiography moved numerous veterans of World War II to join Trappist monasteries in the late forties and

217

early fifties, triggering an interest in monastic life and the contemplative vocation among a new generation of American Catholics.

Benedictine women were also beneficiaries of new foundations that advertised themselves as cloistered and contemplative. Almost a century after their arrival in the United States, Benedictine sisters from Eichstätt founded houses in Boulder, Colorado (1935), and Greensburg, Pennsylvania (1943), communities that explicitly adopted a more enclosed form of monastic observance. Sisters from the abbey of Jouarre in France founded the convent of Regina Laudis at Bethlehem, Connecticut (1947), to live a contemplative life.

The contemplative quest became even more diversified during the 1960s with the appearance of various experiments with the eremitical life. In the wake of the publicity attracted by Thomas Merton's retreat to his Gethsemani hermitage, monasteries of men and women constructed their own hermitages to allow for greater individual expression of the contemplative spirit in their communities.

The popularity of monastic houses as retreat centers helped to spur the growth of new branches of Benedictinism in the United States during this era. A Carthusian community in Sky Farm, Vermont; Camaldolese monks in Big Sur, California; the community of Christ in the Desert in Abiquiu, New Mexico, and their daughter foundation of La Soledad in Mexico—all offered remote sites for retreatants who wanted the setting of a contemplative community where they could encounter silence and separation from the outside world. Even among the older Benedictine congregations, newer communities tended to concentrate more on serving as retreat centers than on the more traditional apostolates of education and parish ministry. The Swiss-American abbeys in Benet Lake, Wisconsin; Columbia (formerly Pevely), Missouri; Hingham, Massachusetts; and Oceanside, California, were all founded after World War II and followed in this path.

Many houses of Benedictine women that had formerly conducted schools converted their buildings into retreat houses. This coincided with the appearance of a still wider range of contemplative communities among the sisters. After the Second Vatican Council, Trappistine houses across the country—from Wrentham, Massachusetts,

Renovated choir and sanctuary of Gethsemani Abbey Church, Trappist, Kentucky

Renovated abbey church, New Melleray Abbey, Dubuque, Iowa (1980)

Trappist Abbey of Gethsemani, Trappist, Kentucky (1933)

Glastonbury Abbey, Hingham, Massachusetts

St. Benedict's Abbey, Benet Lake, Wisconsin

Prince of Peace Abbey Church, Oceanside, California (1988)

to Dubuque, Iowa, to Redwoods, California—saw new vocations streaming to their communities even as other women religious were leaving their convents in large numbers. Small communities of sisters in Sand Springs, Oklahoma; Windsor, New York; and Big Horn, Wyoming, harked back to a simpler monastic regimen while welcoming others to share their contemplative life.

The traditional dress and monastic observance of Benedictine sisters in Petersham, Massachusetts, and Boulder, Colorado, found a receptive response from young women who preferred the perennial character of a contemplative monasticism to what many saw as the confused identity of other communities of religious women. Newer offshoots of the Benedictine tradition, such as the Benedictine Sisters of Jesus Christ Crucified, saw that their enclosed existence was in no way at odds with the spiritual environment of the United States, and they established their first community of Regina Mundi Priory in Devon, Pennsylvania, in 1955.

By the second half of the twentieth century it seemed that the American character, which had initially been so reluctant to concede

222

any place to the contemplative charism of monastic life, now embraced it wholeheartedly. Whether this was a sign of a new maturity of American Benedictine life or merely the temporary testing of a new religious experience only the passing of years could determine, but confirmation could be given that the alternative forms of monastic expression had expanded considerably from the activist missionary model of the nineteenth century.

CHAPTER 14

Expansion and Diversification in a New Century

The initial phase of Benedictine growth in the United States was closely aligned with a pastoral ministry to particular immigrant groups and a practical response to the urgent needs of the American Catholic Church of the nineteenth century. As the horizons and pregnant power of that Church and the American Republic were amplified at the turn of the century, so were the presence and the potential of Benedictines on the North American continent. What the spirit of Manifest Destiny of the mid-nineteenth century had done to lend support to the westward movement of American Benedictines, the surge of imperialist sentiment and overseas expansion among American citizens at the end of the century did to effect the flowering of new monastic foundations and an ever greater variety of ministerial work.

The Beginnings of Foreign Missionary Work

This enlarged horizon of commitment and expansion had its remote origin in the twilight of Boniface Wimmer's life. During his last years he sent monks from his home abbey and Benedictine sisters from Elizabeth, New Jersey, to staff a missionary foundation in Ecuador. Even though Wimmer's successor abandoned the project in 1889, the patriarch's plans for foreign foundations were taken up by others. In that same year Abbot Hilary Pfraengle of St. Mary's Abbey in Newark had visited the Bahama Islands at the invitation

224

of Archbishop Michael Corrigan of New York. Abbot Hilary, a true son of Wimmer, announced plans for a monastic missionary house in Nassau. But it fell to another of Wimmer's spiritual sons to pursue the plans. Abbot Alexius Edelbrock, who had recently resigned as abbot of St. John's and was residing in New York City, sent Father Chrysostom Schreiner to Nassau in 1891 and encouraged the new abbot of St. John's to provide the parishes and school there with what personnel he could afford.[1]

Wimmer's dynamic vision of missionary monasticism stirred others outside his own communities as well. Michael Kruse, who had been a student at St. Vincent, later became abbot of São Bento monastery in São Paulo, Brazil. One of the most influential Benedictine missionaries on the Latin American continent in the early twentieth century, Kruse credited Wimmer with inspiring him to work in the missions.[2]

That spirit of Wimmer carried over into the new century and was a suitable concomitant for an American Catholic Church which in 1908 lost its formal status as a "missionary" nation and was now willing to embark on its own missionary stage. In that same year, when the first American Catholic Missionary Congress was convoked in Chicago, six American Benedictine abbots were in attendance.[3] Their presence at that congress registered a further step in the missionary momentum that was now so much a part of the heritage of American Benedictine men and women. There was now a maturing sense of carrying the Benedictine charism beyond the territorial frontiers of the United States and a joining of forces with fellow American Christians and Catholic missionaries in spreading the gospel. This more mature missionary commitment was found in the houses of both men and women, and one can select some graphic examples of the unfolding of that commitment, charting its progress through the new century.

Collegeville: A Model of Missionary Growth

The community of St. John's Abbey was well into the second half-century of its existence when its capitulars met in 1921 to elect

Alcuin Deutsch, O.S.B.,
fifth abbot
of St. John's Abbey,
Collegeville, Minnesota

Prior Alcuin Deutsch as their fifth abbot. A product of Benedictine education from his earliest years, the new abbot was representative of the evolving personality of the Collegeville community. Proud of his immigrant heritage and his identity as an American citizen, and having integrated a European Benedictine tradition with American values of hard work and administrative competence, he was ready to accept responsibility for a host of new monastic opportunities requiring commitments whose scope would have given pause even to Boniface Wimmer. It was one thing to speak of brick-and-mortar growth, quite another to extend the geographic and spiritual boundaries of a community to include almost the entire globe and to undertake the founding of new daughter houses and the rescue of other monasteries that were on the verge of collapse.

The role of intervention and rehabilitation of other Benedictine communities was not one actively sought by the monks or the abbot of St. John's, but it constituted an inestimable service at a time when overexpansion and mismanagement had put a number of American monasteries on the brink of extinction. It was also a natu-

226

ral byproduct of the motto of Alcuin Deutsch, taken from the monastic model of St. Martin of Tours: "Non recuso laborem."[4]

In 1928 Abbot Alcuin was named apostolic administrator of Sacred Heart Abbey in Oklahoma. Earlier in that decade Deutsch had sent monks from St. John's to Sacred Heart to serve as superiors of the abbey and teachers at the school. At Deutsch's instigation, a decision was made to relocate the abbey to the site of its college in Shawnee, Oklahoma, in 1929. With St. John's monks in leadership positions during the difficult Depression decade that followed, the community and college acquired a spiritual and fiscal stability, and became affiliated with the American Cassinese Congregation.

Mention has already been made of the financial failure of St. Mary's Abbey in Richardton, North Dakota. When the communities of the Swiss-American Congregation refused to accept responsibility for St. Mary's bankruptcy, the future of the Dakota abbey was placed in jeopardy. In 1926 Abbot Alcuin Deutsch was named administrator of the abbey by Rome. Under the leadership of Deutsch's personal secretary, Father Cuthbert Goeb, the community regained its financial footing and was restored to the status of an independent abbey in 1931. Goeb was made abbot, and the monastery chapter voted to become part of the American Cassinese Congregation in 1932.[5]

As president of the American Cassinese Congregation beginning in 1932, Deutsch faced another crisis with a monastery in his own jurisdiction. At the general chapter of the Cassinese Congregation in 1930, Abbot Cyprian Bradley of Holy Cross Abbey in Canon City, Colorado, asked the assembled abbots to assist him in extricating his community from a huge debt and imminent insolvency.[6] The abbots agreed, but with the condition that he resign and that Father Leonard Schwinn, a monk of St. Benedict's Abbey in Atchison, be appointed administrator. More important for the immediate survival of Holy Cross, St. John's Abbey pledged the sum of $100,000 to help the Colorado community.[7]

The role of Abbot Alcuin and the St. John's community as monastic troubleshooters was not limited to American Benedictine houses. In the decade of the 1920s, Archabbot Aurelius Stehle of St. Vincent, assisted by the monks of his monastery and Benedictine sisters from St. Joseph, Minnesota, had established a Catholic university in Peking, China, with the prospect of a future monastic foundation there. After having given support to the Peking enterprise at the general chapter of 1930, Deutsch sent his prior, Father Basil Stegmann, to China, with the intention of laying the groundwork for an independent Benedictine community, consisting of monks of the American Cassinese Congregation then serving on the faculty of the university. After much discussion and struggle, Deutsch decided in 1933 to petition Rome to transfer control of the university to the Divine Word Missionaries, thus ending official sponsorship of the venture on the part of the American Cassinese Congregation.[8]

This did not mean that St. John's vision of monastic expansion was no longer fixed across the Pacific Ocean. In 1940 Abbot Alcuin received a request from the abbot president of the Congregation of the Primitive Observance and the archbishop of Manila to incorporate the Abbey of Santa Maria di Montserrat in the Philippines into the American Cassinese Congregation and to take over the administration of the community's school, San Beda College. The geographical distance and the debt of the Manila monastery, to say nothing of the uncertain political climate in the Philippines on the eve of World War II, caused Deutsch to turn down the offer. But in October of that year he acceded to a request from Rome to become apostolic administrator of the Manila house. During the ensuing years, despite the difficulties imposed by Japanese occupation, Deutsch put San Beda College on firm financial ground and, with the help of monks from St. John's and St. Benedict's Abbey in Atchison, was able to make necessary modifications in the life of the community of Santa Maria, so that it voted in 1947 to maintain its affiliation with the Congregation of the Primitive Observance.[9]

In the same year that Deutsch relinquished his role as apostolic administrator of the Manila abbey, the St. John's Abbey chapter voted to support a Japanese foundation to be located in the still battle-scarred city of Tokyo. The parish of St. Anselm was placed in the hands of Benedictines, and its first community was made up of a St. John's monk who had been a chaplain in the Pacific theater during the war, two Beuronese monks who had belonged to an earlier Japa-

Interior and exterior of St. Anselm's Priory Church, Tokyo, Japan

Benedictine Priory of St. Procopius Abbey in Chiayi, Taiwan
Abadía del Tepeyac, Tlalnepantla, Mexico

St. Augustine's Priory, Nassau, Bahamas

Abadía de San Antonio Abad, Humacao, Puerto Rico

nese priory near Tokyo before the war, and a Benedictine missionary from Belgium who had worked in China. The two Beuronese
monks transferred their stability to St. John's Abbey and became the
core of the dependent priory of St. Anselm.[10]

The St. John's community was not alone in its Far Eastern out-
reach. Another Minnesota Benedictine house, St. Benedict's Convent in St. Joseph, made foundations after World War II in Sapporo,
Japan, and Tanshui, Taiwan. China was also the setting for an earlier effort to erect a Benedictine mission and monastery. In 1936 two
sisters from St. Benedict's Convent and three monks from St.
Procopius Abbey left the United States to join the sisters from St.
Benedict's who were conducting a dispensary and the monks from
St. Vincent who were teaching at the Church-sponsored Kwang Fu
school in the Kaifeng vicariate. Within a year the Benedictines were
subjected to a student riot, an earthquake, the Japanese occupation
of the district, and the serious illness of several community members.

In 1941 the Benedictines opted to move their operation to the
American vicariate of Chowtsun. Before that could be accomplished,
they were interned by the Japanese in Kaifeng on the day of the attack on Pearl Harbor, and they remained in Japanese custody until
1943.[11] The Communist takeover of mainland China after the war
effectively blocked any further attempt at Benedictine settlement
there. But three Benedictine foundations in Taiwan followed from
that experience: St. Benedict Monastery, founded by St. Benedict's
Convent in Tanshui; Benedictine Priory, established by St. Procopius
Abbey in Chiayi; and Wimmer Priory, founded by St. Vincent
Archabbey in Taipei.

The foreign expansion orchestrated by St. John's under Alcuin
Deutsch turned southward in 1946. Even before that date a number of American Benedictine monks had made soundings regarding
the possibility of a foundation in Mexico. Father Alcuin Heibel of
Mount Angel Abbey had served as trailblazer in the 1930s and 1940s,
searching for a suitable monastic site in Mexico. In this project he
had the support of Abbot Alcuin and Abbot Martin Veth of St.
Benedict's Abbey in starting a missionary community. He was aided
in his efforts by Father Lambert Dehner of St. Benedict's Abbey and

Father Clarus Graves of St. John's. In 1944 they also won the backing of Sister Lucy Dooley, prioress of the community of Mount St. Scholastica in Atchison. Through their combined efforts, Benedictines undertook direction of the Catholic school of Tepeyac, and by 1946 they had five hundred students in their charge. When the St. Benedict's Abbey chapter declined to continue staffing the Tepeyac school in 1946, the monks of St. John's accepted the responsibility and further committed themselves to establish a Benedictine monastery in Mexico. With a new influx of monastic personnel and a new site for the monastery, the growth of the community of Tepeyac continued, culminating in its independence as an abbey in 1971.[12]

In 1946 the monks of St. John's received another appeal from south of the border. Bishop James Davis of San Juan, Puerto Rico, turned to the Collegeville community to make a monastic foundation and direct a school and parish in Humacao, Puerto Rico. Like the community in Tepeyac, the Benedictines of San Antonio Abad experienced continued growth in their school and monastery, eventually achieving the status of an independent abbey in 1984.

St. John's monastic expansion culminated with the establishment of St. Augustine's Priory in the diocese of Nassau in the Bahamas in 1948, a half century after monks from Minnesota had first started their mission work there. Running on a line from Mexico and the Caribbean to the stretches of the Atlantic, there was now a stable Benedictine presence carrying on the commitment of Wimmer's missionary vision.

This spirit of boundless possibility and eagerness to expand the frontiers of American Benedictinism was not unique to St. John's Abbey, even if its size and the magnitude of its undertakings gave it a privileged rank among communities in the United States during the first half of the twentieth century.

The Growth of the Swiss-American Congregation

During this same period Swiss-American monasteries were spawning a second generation of new houses. Under Abbot Ignatius Esser, St. Meinrad continued to grow in numbers in the decades after the

First World War, allowing it to provide personnel for an orderly succession of daughter foundations. After benefiting from an initial influx of monks from the St. Meinrad motherhouse, the following communities acquired the status of independent abbeys: Marmion Abbey, Aurora, Illinois, in 1947; Blue Cloud Abbey, Marvin, South Dakota, in 1954; and Prince of Peace Abbey, Oceanside, California, in 1983.

Conception Abbey, under Abbot Stephen Schappler, was also able to establish new foundations that were successful in developing into autonomous monasteries. St. Pius X Abbey in Missouri, founded in 1951, and Mount Michael Abbey in Nebraska, founded in 1956, were examples of a more restricted geographical expansion. Conception Abbey's own sister monastery of Mount Angel also laid the basis for an independent branch when it started Westminster Abbey in Mission City, British Columbia, in 1939.

The other two Swiss-American monasteries of the nineteenth century, New Subiaco Abbey, Subiaco, Arkansas, and St. Joseph Abbey, St. Benedict, Louisiana, completed the cycle of generational growth by founding Corpus Christi Abbey, Corpus Christi, Texas, and the Abbey of Jesus Christ Crucified, Esquipulas, Guatemala, which became abbeys in 1961 and 1982, respectively.

The figure in the Swiss-American Congregation who perhaps best personified the spirit of expansion and opportunity that marked the new century was a monk of Conception Abbey, Father Richard Felix. His was in many respects a twentieth-century version of Boniface Wimmer, filled with projects and plans, radiating an intense zeal for the work of evangelization, and creating new communities to spread the Benedictine way of life. As the founder of St. Benedict's Priory in Benet Lake, Wisconsin in 1945, Felix outlined his plan for a new Benedictine congregation that would rely upon the most advanced means of communication for the work of catechesis, preaching, and fund-raising. Use of mass mailings, modern media, and missions to the unchurched were only a few of the techniques he outlined.

The vision of a new missionary congregation of monks grew from an earlier organization of Felix's, the St. Benedict's Home Mission Society. The society's purpose was to found "little centers of monastic

*Richard Felix, O.S.B.,
abbot of
St. Benedict's Abbey,
Benet Lake, Wisconsin*

life'' in areas of the United States where there was a shortage of priests. It also attempted to provide for the education of priesthood candidates in Latin America and to establish agricultural and industrial schools for minority groups.[13] Felix put his ideal into practice after his election as abbot of Benet Lake in 1952. He founded priories in Reading, Pennsylvania; Pecos, New Mexico; and Hingham, Massachusetts. He also began a Benedictine House of Studies in a Chicago ghetto. This new congregation was to include Mexico and Central America as well. Community experiments and schools in Costa Rica, Nicaragua, and El Salvador fell victim to problems of politics and personnel. But the Mexican priory founded in 1958 survived as the Priory of St. Benedict in Morelia.

Felix's activist model of leadership, eager to "found first, think later," was a variant of the missionary model of monasticism whose positive side was boldness in experimentation and whose negative side was a compulsion to expand without always calculating the community's readiness or willingness to follow. Just how consistent the vision of Richard Felix and other "founding" types of the twentieth century were with the actual resources of their monastic communities will only be fully established by the course of subsequent history.

St. Benedict Monastery, Tanshui, Taiwan

Foundations of Benedictine Women and New Congregations

Contemporaneous with the broadening base of Benedictine monks, the numerical growth of American Benedictine sisters and the evolution of independent congregations in the twentieth century placed them also in a position for further expansion. This was especially evident in the decade after World War II. St. Benedict's Convent in St. Joseph, Minnesota, was perhaps the most notable example of this expansion, establishing independent foundations in Bismarck, North Dakota; Eau Claire, Wisconsin; St. Paul, Minnesota; and Olympia, Washington. Later in 1975 dependent priory status was granted to the convent's missions in Japan, Taiwan, the Bahamas, Puerto Rico, and in Manchester, New Hampshire. A dependent priory was also established in Ogden, Utah, in 1980. The dependent priory in Sapporo, Japan, became independent in 1985 and the one in Tanshui, Taiwan, achieved independence in 1988.

That same willingness to integrate a wider vision of Benedictine ministry and mobility is reflected in the growth of the communities

Immaculate Conception Convent, Ferdinand, Indiana

of other congregations of sisters. In the Congregation of St. Gertrude, Immaculate Conception Convent in Ferdinand, Indiana, planted new roots as near as Indianapolis (Beech Grove) and as distant as Guatemala (Cobán) and Peru (Moropón). In the Congregation of St. Scholastica, the sisters of Mount St. Scholastica in Atchison, Kansas, complemented new foundations in the American West with houses in Mexico City and Mineiros, Brazil.

While American Benedictines were spreading throughout the Americas and the Far East, they were being enriched in turn with a fresh infusion of traditions from outside the United States. The English Benedictine Congregation of monks founded new American communities in Washington, D.C. (St. Anselm's Abbey), Portsmouth, Rhode Island (Portsmouth Abbey), and St. Louis, Missouri (St. Louis Abbey). These houses soon gained a distinguished reputation for their college preparatory schools. They also contributed to a high level of monastic scholarship with such names as Fathers Mark Sheridan, Joseph Jensen, Patrick Granfield, Julian Stead, and Timothy Horner. The congregation's Benedictine sisters from Stan-

237

Above: First monastic building at St. Anselm's Abbey, Washington, D.C. Below: Abbey church and cloister, St. Anselm's Abbey, Washington, D.C.

brook, England, were also instrumental in providing personnel and formation for the American priory of St. Scholastica, founded in Petersham, Massachusetts, in 1980.

German monks from the Missionary Congregation of St. Ottilien settled in Newton, New Jersey, in 1924 and became St. Paul's Abbey in 1947, providing yet another missionary monastic model for American Benedictines. The female counterpart of the St. Ottilien Congregation, the Missionary Sisters of Tutzing, founded a house in Norfolk, Nebraska, in 1923.

Another twentieth-century foreign influence came from Italy in the form of foundations made in Michigan and New Jersey by the Sylvestrine Congregation. Also, the Monte Oliveto Congregation founded a priory in Lake Charles, Louisiana, and later accepted Our Lady of Guadalupe Abbey, Pecos, New Mexico, into the congregation.

An American Home for Political Refugees

The attraction of the United States as a haven for victims of war and revolution brought a stream of Benedictine refugees in the course of the twentieth century, adding even more variety to the monastic melting pot of North America. In 1906 the Mexican revolution forced Benedictine monks of Silos, Spain, to flee their missionary community in Mexico and seek sanctuary at St. Joseph Abbey in Louisiana. In the 1930s St. Benedict's Abbey in Atchison welcomed a large group of Augustinian refugees from the Spanish Civil War.

The number of monks from German abbeys and the influence of their presence in the United States during the Nazi takeover has already been noted.[14]

The impact of the Second World War on American Benedictines carried over into the Communist takeover of China and the countries of Eastern Europe. From China came monks of the Congregation of the Annunciation; in 1947 they found a new home in the community of Valyermo in the southern California desert.

Another refugee monastic community that found a home in California came from Hungary in 1957. Near Palo Alto monks of the Hungarian Congregation established Woodside Priory. The priory was later accepted as a member of the American Cassinese Congregation under St. Anselm's Abbey in Manchester, New Hampshire.

When monks from St. Procopius Abbey were forced to leave the Czech monastery of Broumov in 1950 as a result of the Communist government's confiscation of their property, the Illinois monastery concentrated its efforts on sponsoring the emigration of Czechs who suffered from religious persecution.[15]

The cross-fertilization between different monastic traditions that took place in American Benedictine communities during these years served to leaven them and to expand the provincial outlook that had previously characterized so many monastic houses.

The Missionary Thrust to Latin America

Another sign of this maturity and widened vision of Benedictine communities can be seen in the chief monastic missionary movement of the second half of the twentieth century: the migration of Benedictines from communities in the United States to Latin America. Inspired by the exhortation of Pope John XXIII to have the religious communities of North America send ten percent of their membership to supply the needs of the Church in Latin America, Benedictines displayed their immense energy as they reacted to the request from Rome in the 1960s.

By the end of the 1960s, Benedictine communities from the United States had established foundations across Latin America. St. Vincent Archabbey fulfilled their founder's ambitions for a Benedictine house in South America by taking over responsibility for the Brazilian Congregation's St. Benedict Priory in Vinhedo, Brazil, in 1964. St. Benedict's Abbey, one of the original promoters of a missionary monastery in Mexico, founded St. Joseph's Priory in Mineiros, Brazil, in 1962. Monks of that priory were joined by sisters from the community of Mount St. Scholastica in Atchison. In that same year another community of the American Cassinese Congregation, Assumption Abbey, founded Tibati Priory in Bogotá, Colombia. Thirteen sisters from convents of the Congregation of St. Gertrude formed the solid core of the teaching staff of the Colegio San Carlos, which was operated by the Bogotá Benedictines.[16]

Coordinated missionary activity also marked the progress of the Latin American foundations of the Swiss-American Congregation. Apart from an attempt by St. Meinrad Archabbey to create a permanent priory in Peru, the focus of Swiss-American communities was in Mexico and Central America. An early foothold had been made by the houses in Morelia, Mexico (1958), and Esquipulas, Guatemala (1959), as foundations of the abbeys of Benet Lake and St. Joseph respectively. The Morelia priory was given a Mexican companion in the form of the Priory of Our Lady of the Angels, founded by Mount Angel Abbey in Cuernavaca in 1966. The Guatemalan Benedictine presence was widened to include Blue Cloud Abbey's Resurrection Priory (Cobán) in 1964 and Marmion Abbey's St. Joseph's Priory (Sololá) in 1965. Benedictine sisters from Ferdinand, Indiana, also came to work in Cobán, and sisters from Watertown, South Dakota, settled in Izabal. The Central American constellation of houses of the Swiss-American Congregation was completed with New Subiaco Abbey's founding of Holy Family Priory in Cayo, Belize, in 1971.

Abbey of Jesus Christ Crucified, Esquipulas, Guatemala

Priory of St. Benedict, Abbot, Morelia, Mexico

Priory of St. Joseph, Sololá, Guatemala

The challenge posed by the Latin American Church resembled that faced by American Benedictines a century earlier: adapting to a new culture, learning a new language, and encountering Catholic communities in need of pastoral and catechetical assistance. The challenge was compounded by the stark poverty of the Third World, an uncertain political climate, and the problem of finding the means of establishing an indigenous monastic life.[17] Twentieth-century American Benedictines brought to this challenge much of the same spiritual armory that their forebears possessed: a revered religious tradition, a widely recognized reputation for pastoral and educational work, and a renewed commitment to serve the oppressed. In return, they were exposed to currents of theology and ecclesiology in Latin America that were changing the contours of the Roman Catholic Church. In the process of transmitting their monastic tradition to this environment, American Benedictines found that tradition animated and transformed. The missionary movement in Latin America also added one more rich deposit to that tradition, whose rate of acceleration seemed to advance in tandem with the rapid changes taking place in the Catholic Church and throughout the world during the same time frame.

Thus, amid the expansion and diversification of American Benedictine life in the twentieth century, one can perceive more complex and challenging components of its history and identity. The confluence of historical events and the evolving spiritual and theological renewal that were part of this phenomenon came to a head in the turbulent decade of the 1960s, a period that was a watershed for the whole twentieth-century experience of American Benedictines, spiritually and historically, and one that will receive attention in the final chapter.

CHAPTER 15

Entry into a New Era

The posture of any historian before the immediate past is properly one of caution. Not only is the perspective a partial and segmented one, but the orbit of historical causality initiated by any movement or individual within one's own lifetime is of its very nature incomplete. Nonetheless, the critical place occupied by the events of the 1960s and the flashpoint they became for subsequent monastic life require more than a passing comment for anyone wishing to obtain a fuller understanding of American Benedictine history. A reflection on this period of reform and renewal will not remove or reduce the ambiguity of its impact, but it will at least show how crucial a role that period played in the unfolding of that history.

The Challenging Events of the 1960s

The decade of the 1960s saw the intersection of several forces affecting the orientation of Benedictine life in the United States. The social upheaval that took place during this decade, difficult to document in objective fashion, left a lasting imprint on all institutions in American society, monasticism included. The character of the decade's opening years, marked by the heady euphoria of having a young Catholic president, the stirring idealism of the civil rights movement, the promise of the elimination of poverty, and the role of the United States as the watchdog of peace and world police officer, was changed by the decade's end into the somber reality of political assassination as the price of public life, race riots, a growing socio-economic disparity, the decline of the United States as a world power, and the disillusionment brought about by the Vietnam War. Campus protests, the feminist movement, and a developing distrust of both civil and religious authority only served to deepen the social rift.

Monasticism has been influenced by the social history of every age, but that influence was quickened in an age when communications media and the very apostolates of Benedictine communities provided instant access to American culture within the cloisters of Benedictine houses. In this light, it is not surprising that the social changes of the 1960s deeply affected the fixed monastic tradition that had long dictated the mode of life in most American monastic communities.

American Benedictines were not alone in experiencing the seismic shock of the events of the 1960s. European monks also were exposed to student protest, the sexual revolution, and political disillusionment that was comparable in its influence to the social shift that took place in the United States in the same period.

The unprecedented upheaval witnessed in the American Catholic Church during the decade of the 1960s rivaled the radical changes that took place in secular culture. One should not be too quick to assign the sole cause of this upheaval to Vatican II. Currents of theological reform and renewal of religious life were at work in channels distinct in time and place from what was taking place in Rome from 1962 to 1965. But the Council did become a lightning rod and symbol of all that change, and whatever verdict one attaches to the methods of monastic renewal that followed in its wake, that verdict can be fairly rendered only by an understanding of how Pope John's Ecumenical Council served to initiate and promote the entire renewal process.

It should be noted that a number of American Benedictines participated in the planning and work of the Council. In 1960 Abbot Ambrose Ondrak of St. Procopius Abbey was appointed consultor of the Pontifical Theological Commission, charged with preparing the conciliar agenda.[1] Two monks of St. John's Abbey, Fathers Ul-

Baldwin Dworschak, O.S.B.   *David Melancon, O.S.B.*

ric Beste and Godfrey Diekmann, served as *periti* in the areas of canon law and liturgy respectively, and were joined at the Council's last session by their abbot, Baldwin Dworschak, who had just been elected president of the American Cassinese Congregation.[2] In their capacity as abbots nullius, Walter Coggin of Belmont Abbey and Jerome Weber of St. Peter's Abbey were present throughout the course of the Council as voting members. Abbot David Melancon, president of the Swiss-American Congregation, attended the final Council session in 1965. Many more American Benedictines who were students in Rome at this time were exposed to the theological debate and ecumenical atmosphere of the Council and carried the spirit of *aggiornamento* back to their communities in a very concrete way.

Along with that spirit and new theological vocabulary came a mandate to renew religious life, more particularly to hold extraordinary general chapters for each congregation of Benedictines to implement the renewal through a revision of constitutions and a reform of community structures.[3]

246

First International Symposium of Benedictine Women in Rome (October 1987). Left to right: Anselm Hammerling, O.S.B.; Johnette Putnam, O.S.B.; Joan Chittister, O.S.B.; Karen Joseph, O.S.B.; Margaret Michaud, O.S.B.

The two major congregations of American Benedictines met in their general chapters from 1966 to 1969, producing two documents that capsulized most of the major problems and controversies swirling around the volatile issue of monastic renewal.[4] If these statements on Benedictine life after the Council did not give any definitive answers to the new structures and reformed spirituality demanded by the renewal, they did articulate the variety of responses made to the conciliar mandate, as well as a willingness to initiate practical reforms to comply with it.

Benedictine women were also tackling the renewal process head-on. Many of the sweeping changes instituted by the general chapters of the Federation of St. Scholastica in the period from 1966 to 1974 were documented in the controversial *Climb Along the Cutting Edge*.[5] Somewhat more representative of the wider response given by American Benedictine sisters was the joint statement on monastic values, *Upon This Tradition*.[6] The changes in lifestyle and ministry reflected in these documents were sources of prolonged debate

247

on the nature of monastic life for women in a changed contemporary culture and postconciliar Church, a debate that carried over into the process of writing new constitutions for congregations of Benedictine sisters.

American Benedictine participation in the larger renewal process was reflected in the debate and decrees of the Congress of Abbots of the worldwide Benedictine Confederation held in Rome in 1967. The election of an American monk, Abbot Rembert Weakland of St. Vincent Archabbey, as abbot primate was testimony to the new direction and leadership in monastic renewal that many Benedictines sensed were coming from the United States.

For all the earnest efforts made by American Benedictines to implement the process of renewal in the years immediately after the Council, the most noticeable outward change in Benedictine life during this period was a decline in the membership of monastic communities. The two major American Benedictine congregations once again served as reliable indicators of this decline. In 1965 the American Cassinese Congregation numbered 2045 members; in 1985 the number was 1462. In 1965 the total of Swiss-American monks was 972; in 1985 it had dropped to 812. Communities of Benedictine women experienced an even sharper drop in numbers.[7] This erosion of what had up to the time of the Council been an uninterrupted growth in American Benedictine houses was due to the departure of many professed members and the abrupt termination of large novitiate classes. The Benedictines were affected by the same phenomenon that was taking place in other religious communities in the United States and throughout the world. Although this decline soon bottomed out and some communities experienced a resurgence of vocations in the seventies and eighties, the effect on the morale and renewal of monastic houses was hard to overestimate.

Responses to Renewal

The change in numbers was in many ways linked to the changes taking place in monastic life itself. Part of that change was identified with a renewal process that antedated the Council. As only one example of this, the restructuring of the Divine Office and the evident concern for adapting community prayer life to contemporary circumstances had received impetus long before the Council as a result of the liturgical movement. The Constitution on the Sacred Liturgy and the work of committees in each American Benedictine congregation after the Council only affirmed and implemented the changes that had been proposed years earlier. Basic liturgical changes such as the use of vernacular in the Divine Office and Eucharistic concelebration in turn created an environment open to further experimentation, ranging from entire communities practicing centering prayer and espousing the charismatic renewal to the multiplication of different forms of private prayer and meditation.

Reassessment of community apostolates was often a more wrenching experience of change. The decision to close many parishes, schools, and missions was not easy for a monastic community nor for the people who had been served by these apostolates. One of the reasons for these closings was the sheer lack of personnel. There was also a change in the orientation of community apostolates and ministries to meet what some saw as the new demands of a postconciliar Church. This new orientation was in opposition to the earlier expression of American Benedictine life, which had a centrifugal character, with active apostolates branching out from the monastic community. The monastery was now viewed more as a centripetal force, serving as a spiritual center that attracted an entire spectrum of people by virtue of its liturgy, its facilities for spiritual retreat, its environment of solitude and space. Vast acreage that had once been prized for providing agricultural self-sufficiency or space for more buildings was now valued as a buffer between the breakneck pace of urban and suburban society and the slower rhythms of silence and prayer it offered the American Catholic layperson.

This new orientation indicated one more way in which American Benedictines both affected the life of Catholics in the United States and saw themselves as serving the changing needs of the Catholic faithful, a body of believers who had now achieved educational levels comparable to those of members of mainline Protestant denominations and had been integrated into the wider social framework of American culture.

A New Era of Monastic Scholarship

The educational level of American Catholics was matched by positive advances in study and scholarship by American Benedictines in the period after the Council. The exhortation of the Council fathers for religious communities to return to the spirit and aim of their founders had already been anticipated in many circles by a renewed interest in research on the Benedictine Rule and its sources.[8] For many years this work had been the preserve of European monks, with the writing of someone such as Thomas Merton before the Council constituting the exception rather than the rule in American monasteries. But by the 1960s Merton's writings found their way into the libraries and formation programs of European monasteries, combining as they did a firm understanding of monastic tradition with a candid willingness to confront the problems of the present day. At the same time, Merton was joined by American Benedictine scholars such as Fathers Claude Peifer, Ambrose Wathen, and Terrence Kardong, all of whom showed themselves to be competent and creative commentators on the Benedictine Rule and spirituality.[9] The culmination of much of this new intellectual flowering was the joint effort of American Benedictine men and women in publishing an authoritative translation and historical commentary on the Rule of Benedict to commemorate the fifteen hundredth celebration of St. Benedict's birth in 1980.[10]

This manifestation of monastic scholarship on the part of American Benedictines was seen on a wider scale in the postconciliar period. Cistercian Publications, Kalamazoo, Michigan, began issuing a long and impressive series of volumes on monastic spirituality and history under the sponsorship of the Cistercian Order in the United States. Cistercians also sponsored specialized journals such as *Liturgy* and *Hallel*. A younger corps of monks in the American Cassinese Congregation gave expression to their interest in Benedictine topics through reviews such as *Confluence* and *The Scriptorium*. Another distinctively American and independent voice of scholarship that appeared during the period of monastic renewal was *Monastic Studies*. This journal carried on the tradition of Father Damasus Winzen of

Mount Saviour and Father John Main of the English Benedictine Congregation by devoting itself to the study of Benedictine spirituality.

The pages of the *American Benedictine Review*, both during and after the Council, displayed some of the diversity of Benedictine positions in the debate on the merits and methods of renewal. During the period of the Council the emphasis of the *Review*, under the vigorous editorship of Father Colman Barry of St. John's Abbey, reflected both his own expertise in the area of monastic history and a more concentrated interest in the themes of the Council itself. The articles of Father Ignatius Hunt of Conception Abbey on Scripture, of Father Polycarp Sherwood of St. Meinrad Archabbey on patristics, and those of a growing number of Benedictine commentators were indicative of this.[11] Beginning in 1964, under the editorial direction of Sister Teresa Ann Doyle of Atchison, the *Review* stimulated a "Call for Monastic Scholars" and provided a forum for what was an extended public debate on the nature of monasticism and the Benedictine charism. Subsequent scholarly studies remained a testament to the candid and concrete manner in which much of the renewal discussion was conducted.[12]

Monks were not the only ones engaged in monastic studies and scholarship. Sisters Imogene Baker and Augusta Raabe were part of the principal editorial staff for the *RB 1980* project. The community of sisters at Mount St. Scholastica in Atchison published *Benedictines*, a semiannual journal on monastic themes, and also sponsored their own Institute of Monastic Life, both of which represented a distinctive voice of women interested in Benedictine studies. The founding of the contemplative community of St. Scholastica's Priory in Massachusetts in the 1970s formed the fertile ground for a yearly monastic review, *Word and Spirit*, published by the Benedictine nuns of that house. Benedictine women were also coming out of postgraduate programs in spirituality and patristics with credible professional credentials during the period after the Council.

Another practical realization of the renewal's effect on monastic institutions was the many new organizations that seemed to multiply in the postconciliar years. Annual workshops for superiors and novice masters brought together members of all the major congregations and communities of Benedictine monks. The Conference of American Benedictine Prioresses was an unprecedented demonstration of a collaborative leadership effort on the part of Benedictine women. The Swiss-American Congregation sponsored a yearly Monastic Institute from 1973 to 1983 for the purpose of studying specific monastic topics in conjunction with a qualified faculty, while sharing in the common life of a host monastic community. The American Cassinese Congregation initiated a summer formation program for junior monks along the same lines during this period. In the 1970s a revamped and revitalized American Benedictine Academy provided a unique forum in which both men and women of American Benedictine communities could discuss common concerns.

Forging a Postconciliar Identity

At the heart of much of this scholarly activity and process of renewal, along with the changes that accompanied them, was the effort to clarify Benedictine identity. In fact, the search for monastic identity was something of a leitmotif of postconciliar monastic renewal. It was a search that generated its own cottage industry of commentators, whose insights provided helpful clues in trying to discover what some of the common currents in the renewal process of each community were.[13]

What was being accomplished in American Benedictine houses during this postconciliar period was nothing short of a self-questioning of the entire monastic world view and a reformulation of each community's reason for existence. That such questioning led to excesses and overreactions in certain instances is clearly borne out by historical hindsight. But given the redefinition of Church and world brought about by Vatican Council II in its dogmatic and pastoral constitutions, *Lumen Gentium* and *Gaudium et Spes*, and given the revolutionary upheavals that had taken place in American society, it was to be expected that the duration and demands of the ensuing change would be of such magnitude.

As the pace of renewal subsided, it was evident that the features of American Benedictine life had changed as a result of that renewal. The original idea of "flight from the world" had been turned inside out by what many interpreted as the Council's embrace of the world. For a substantial number of Benedictines, that vision implied a new monastic stance on the margins of American society, serving as a spiritual oasis and prophetic critic for a culture that demanded neither flight nor fight. For others, the roller coaster of monastic renewal pointed only to the need for a restoration of previously held Benedictine values.

Regardless of the particular interpretation given to the spiritual role of Benedictine communities, the physical features of those communities underwent a face-lift. The ethnic and European stamp of monastic life that had marked the first generation of American Benedictines had disappeared. Culturally closed communities of Bavarian and Swiss Benedictines gave way to a more cosmopolitan network of monastic communities, comfortably assimilated into the heterogeneous fabric of American society.

This face-lift was no less apparent in the features of the American Catholic Church, which after the Council contained a dizzying variety of elements that could hardly have been anticipated a century earlier. Demographic, social, and theological shifts transformed it into an entity at once more supple, outspoken, diversified, and mature. Much the same could be said of monasticism.

The Benedictines of the postconciliar era had certainly become more diverse, not only in membership but in their monastic orientation. Their membership reflected the higher educational and socioeconomic levels of the American Catholic laity in general, as well as a variety of backgrounds, ages, and professional experience.

The renewal process also matured the Benedictine Order in the United States in observable and subtle ways. A number of outstanding leaders of monastic communities were raised to prominence as a result of their work in renewal. A check of the episcopal appointments and lists of presiders over organizations of religious women in the decades after the Council affirms the recognition given to the charism of leadership exercised by the Benedictine Order in the wider Church.

Perhaps less observable was the way in which Benedictines, by virtue of their acceptance of the challenge of renewal, came to a deeper understanding of the Church and the order in which they lived out their vocation. In the process they reminded the Church of how essential its monastic arm was in the role of reading and discerning the signs of the times.

Within that same renewal process, American Benedictines rediscovered and reaffirmed many of their lasting monastic values. They also found themselves once again facing some of the same questions that their predecessors had grappled with: maintaining an equilibrium between a life of separation from the world and active ministry in that same world; accepting the tension of living an enclosed life in a stable monastic community while being responsive to the Church's need to draw resources from the same community; striking a balance between serving as a spiritual influence on American society and not being transformed in turn by the secular values of that society. The context in which these questions were addressed, however, was significantly different from that which had existed a century earlier. The unfailing optimism of an earlier era had given way to the hard reality of communities top-heavy with retired members, a condition that forced some Benedictine communities to question the possibility of their continued existence as they approached the millennium.

Even in the bleakest of periods of their history, American Benedictines displayed a remarkable resilience and a sure sense of spiritual vigor and physical survival. Part of that was due to their firm links with the taproot of their monastic tradition, a tradition that over the centuries had proven adept at surmounting a recurring series of problems and pitfalls. Part of it was also due to an ability to sense and adapt to the needs of a constantly evolving American Catholic Church. Insofar as American Benedictines can retain their ability to remain firmly rooted in that monastic tradition and deeply aware of their own history as part of the Catholic Church in the United States, their capacity to continue as an effective presence in that Church seems assured.

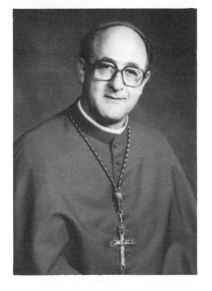

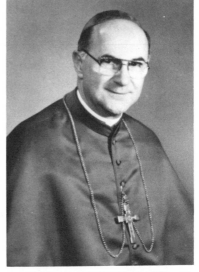

Clockwise: Archbishop Rembert Weakland, O.S.B., Milwaukee, Wisconsin; Archbishop Daniel Kucera, O.S.B., Dubuque, Iowa; Bishop Joseph Gerry, O.S.B., Portland, Maine; Bishop Daniel Buechlein, O.S.B., Memphis, Tennessee; Bishop Jerome Hanus, O.S.B., St. Cloud, Minnesota.

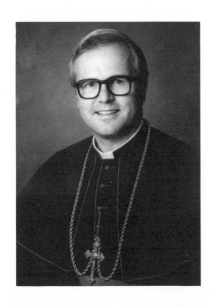

Notes

ABBREVIATIONS

AAA	Assumption Abbey Archives
AEA	Archives of Einsiedeln Abbey
APF	Archives of the Propaganda Fide
CAA	Conception Abbey Archives
EAA	Engelberg Abbey Archives
HCAA	Holy Cross Abbey Archives
LMA	Ludwig-Missionsverein Archives
MAAA	Mount Angel Abbey Archives
MMAA	Mount Michael Abbey Archives
NSAA	New Subiaco Abbey Archives
SHCA	Sacred Heart Convent Archives
SJAA	St. John's Abbey Archives
SMAA	St. Meinrad Archabbey Archives
SPAA	St. Procopius Abbey Archives
SVAA	St. Vincent Archabbey Archives
UNDA	University of Notre Dame Archives

NOTES TO THE INTRODUCTION

1. Two such works that were of invaluable help in writing this volume were Colman Barry's community history, *Worship and Work: Saint John's Abbey and University 1856–1980* (Collegeville, Minn.: The Liturgical Press, 1980) and Jerome Oetgen's *An American Abbot: Boniface Wimmer, O.S.B.* (Latrobe, Pa.: The Archabbey Press, 1976).

2. Two works of accomplished monastic historians of the twentieth century that serve as models are David Knowles, *Christian Monasticism* (New York: McGraw-Hill, 1969), and Louis Lekai, *Cistercians: Ideal and Reality* (Kent, Ohio: Kent State University Press, 1977).

257

NOTES TO CHAPTER 1

1. Daniel Misonne, "La restauration monastique du XIX siècle," *Revue Bénédictine* 83 (1973) 37–38, and Louis Soltner, *Solesmes et Dom Guéranger (1805–1875)* (Solesmes: Editions de Solesmes, 1974).

2. Benedict Rietz, "Les principes fondamentaux de la vie monastique et bénédictine d'après D. Maurus Wolter (1825–1890)," *Théologie de la vie monastique* (Ligugé, 1961), and Louis Soltner, "Beuron und Dom Guéranger," *Erbe und Auftrag* 51 (1975) 5–10.

3. Giovanni Lunardi, *Pietro Casaretto e gli inizi della Congregazione Sublacense (1810–1880)* (Montserrat, Spain: Publicaciones de l'abadía de Montserrat, 1972); idem, "The Missionary Spirit of Abbot Casaretto," *Tjurunga* 8 (1974) 35–36.

4. Denis Huerre, *Jean-Baptiste Muard: Fondateur de la Pierre-qui-Vire* (St. Léger-Vauban: Les Presses Monastiques, 1978).

5. David Lunn, "The English Benedictines in the Nineteenth Century," *Tjurunga* 8 (1974) 25–32.

6. Maurice Freemyer, "Ullathorne and Guéranger and the Revival of Benedictine Monasticism: 1815–1850" (M.A. thesis, University of Notre Dame, 1953) 20–21; Frances O'Donoghue, *The Bishop of Botany Bay* (Sydney: University Press, 1982); Alexander Austin, "Archbishop Ullathorne," *Benedict's Disciples* (London: The Trinity Press, 1980) 308–326.

7. *Acta Capitulorum Generalium, 1790–1900*, Downside Abbey Archives, copy in Belmont Abbey Library, England.

8. *Der Fünfarmige Leuchter: Beitrage zum Werden und Wirken der Benediktinerkongregation von St. Ottilien*, ed. Frederick Renner (St. Ottilien, 1971).

9. Letter of Monsignor Gamboni to Abbot Casaretto, 28 August 1872, Archives of Sant' Ambrogio Monastery, Rome.

10. Kenneth Scott Latourette, *A History of the Expansion of Christianity* (New York: Harper & Brothers, 1943); Daniel Rees, "The Benedictine Revival in the Nineteenth Century," ed. D. H. Farmer (Leominster: F. Wright Books, 1980) 282–307.

11. Philip Gleason, "Mass and Maypole Revisited," *Catholic Historical Review* 57 (1971) 265.

12. This was especially the case during the pontificate of Camaldolese Pope Gregory XVI. See "Las misiones desde 1840 hasta 1870," *Manual de historia de la Iglesia* 7, ed. Hubert Jedin (Barcelona: Herder, 1978), 797–827; Roger Aubert, "XIX Century Monastic Restoration in Western Europe," *Tjurunga* 8 (1974) 5–24.

13. Letter of Abbot Martin Marty to Father Benno of Einsiedeln, 10 September 1874, SMAA.

14. While the history of the English Benedictine monk-bishops of Australia has been well documented, the story of the Spanish monk Rosando Salvado's work in Western Australia has only recently been given deserved attention in E. J. Stormon, ed. and trans., *The Salvado Memoirs* (Nedlands, W. A.: University of Western Australia Press, 1977); George Russo, *Lord Abbot of the Wilderness: The Life and Times of Bishop Salvado* (Melbourne: The Polding Press, 1980).

15. Letter of Badin to Bishop Edward Fenwick of Cincinnati, 2 August 1826, UNDA.

16. Lemke was a Prussian-born priest from the diocese of Regensburg who had worked as a missionary in the United States with German-speaking settlers in Pennsylvania in the 1830s and 1840s. See Lawrence Flick, "Biographical Sketch of Rev. Peter Lemke, O.S.B., 1796–1882," *American Catholic Society Records* 9 (1897) 129–192; Willibald Mathäser, *Haudegen Gottes* (Würzburg: Kommissionsverlag Echter, 1971).

17. Letter of Martin Marty, dated 7 August 1876, appearing in the *Wahrheitsfreund* of Cincinnati, 4 April 1877.

18. Microfilm copies of all the requests made to the three major immigrant aid societies by American missionaries can be found in the archives of the University of Notre Dame. See also Theodore Roemer, *The Ludwig-Missionsverein and the Church in the United States, 1838–1918* (Washington: Catholic University of America, 1933); *Ten Decades of Alms* (St. Louis: B. Herder Book Co., 1942).

19. Edmund Hogan, "The Congregation of the Holy Ghost and the Evolution of the Modern Irish Missionary Movement," *Catholic Historical Review* 70 (1984) 1–13.

20. Joseph Murphy, *Tenacious Monks* (Shawnee, Okla.: Benedictine Color Press, 1974) 33–38.

21. The Ludwig-Missionsverein Archives in Munich provide ample documentation of these letters. See also Joseph Schabert, "The Ludwig-Missionsverein," *Catholic Historical Review* 11 (1922) 25–30.

22. Letter of Müller to Henni, 1 March 1847, as cited in Roemer, "The Ludwig-Missionsverein and the Church," 34.

NOTES TO CHAPTER 2

1. Jerome Oetgen's *An American Abbot: Boniface Wimmer, O.S.B.* (Latrobe, Pa.: The Archabbey Press, 1976) remains the best work on Wimmer.

2. Oetgen, *An American Abbot*, 44–45.

3. Letter of Wimmer to Abbot Gregory Scherr, 26 January 1846, as cited in Jerome Oetgen, "Boniface Wimmer and the Founding of St. Vincent Abbey," *American Benedictine Review* 21 (1971) 151.

4. As cited in Colman Barry, *Worship and Work: Saint John's Abbey and University 1856–1980* (Collegeville, Minn.: The Liturgical Press, 1980) 420.

5. Letter of Wimmer to Abbot Gregory Scherr, 13 January 1848, as cited in Basilius Doppelfeld, *Mönchtum und kirchlicher Heilsdienst* (Münsterschwarzach, Germany: Vier-Turme-Verlag, 1974) 241.

6. *The John Carroll Papers,* ed. Thomas O'Brien Hanley (Notre Dame: University of Notre Dame Press, 1976) 2:129.

7. Henry Szarnicki, "The Episcopate of Michael O'Connor, First Bishop of Pittsburgh, 1843–1860," (Ph.D. diss., Washington: Catholic University, 1971) 161–244,

8. Letter of Bishop O'Connor to Wimmer, 14 April 1847, SVAA.

9. Letter of Bishop O'Connor to Tobias Kirby, 13 August 1851, Pittsburgh Diocesan Archives, microfilm copy in UNDA.

10. Letter of Bishop O'Connor to Bernard Smith, 20 November 1851, microfilm copy of Smith letters in UNDA.
11. See letters of 14 July 1851, 19 August 1851, and May 1857 in APF.
12. Szarnicki, "The Episcopate of Michael O'Connor," 174.
13. Letter of Wimmer to King Ludwig I, 4 June 1855, translated copy in SVAA.
14. Brief of 24 August, 1855, APF.
15. Oetgen, "Boniface Wimmer and the Founding of St. Vincent Archabbey," 163.
16. Letter of Wimmer to Leiss, 12 March 1849, Archives of Scheyern Abbey, as cited in Oetgen, *An American Abbot*, 79.
17. *Ibid.*, 79.
18. Transcript of the general chapter proceedings, SVAA.
19. As first prior of St. Vincent's foundation in Minnesota, Wirtz had collected a coterie of like-minded monks who wanted to declare the Minnesota community an independent abbey whose life would be contemplative and based upon the monastic statutes of the medieval Abbey of Cluny. It was not to be the last American Cassinese community wanting to imitate this medieval model.
20. Edward Malone, "Letters from Placidus Wolter to Frowin Conrad," *American Benedictine Review* 16 (1965) 316.
21. Wrote Wimmer: "F. James has brought all this trouble into our house with his praising of Beuron and his criticism of life at St. Vincent's." Letter of Wimmer to Alexius Edelbrock, 9 September 1882, SVAA.
22. Oetgen, *An American Abbot*, 274–276.
23. Letter of Wimmer to Frowin Conrad, 25 December 1881, translated copy in CAA.

NOTES TO CHAPTER 3

1. Letter of Wimmer to the directors of the Ludwig-Missionsverein, 1848 (no specific date given), translated copy in SVAA.
2. Letter of Wimmer to King Ludwig I, 9 April 1859, translated copy in SVAA.
3. Letter of Wimmer to Edelbrock, 17 March 1876, SVAA.
4. Letter of Wimmer to the directors of the Ludwig-Missionsverein, 26 February 1857, translated copy in SVAA.
5. Letter of Wimmer to Abbot Lang, February 1877, as cited in Jerome Oetgen, "Boniface Wimmer and the American Benedictines, 1877– 1887," *American Benedictine Review* 25 (1974) 2.
6. Jerome Oetgen, *An American Abbot: Boniface Wimmer, O.S.B.* (Latrobe, Pa.: The Archabbey Press, 1976) 62–68.
7. Report of Wimmer to the directors of the Ludwig-Missionsverein, 1856, LMA.
8. Colman Barry, *Worship and Work: Saint John's Abbey and University 1856–1980* (Collegeville, Minn.: The Liturgical Press, 1980) 97.
9. The difficulties of these early years are fully documented in Peter Beckman, *Kansas Monks* (Atchison, Kans.: Abbey Student Press, 1957).
10. Letter of Wimmer to Abbot Utto Lang, 8 November 1858, as cited in Jerome Oetgen, *An American Abbot: Boniface Wimmer, O.S.B.* (Latrobe, Pa.: The Archabbey Press, 1976) 145. Original in Metten Abbey Archives.

11. Letter of Wimmer to King Ludwig I, 4 July 1853, translated copy in SVAA.
12. Letter of Augustine d'Asti to Archbishop John Odin of New Orleans, 1 July 1861, UNDA.
13. Oetgen, *An American Abbot*, 186.
14. Paschal Baumstein, *My Lord of Belmont: A Biography of Leo Haid* (Belmont, N.C.: Herald House, 1985) 32–33.
15. *Ibid.*, 20–26.
16. Records of abbatial election of 11 February 1885, SVAA.
17. Jerome Oetgen, "The Origins of the Benedictine Order in Georgia," *Georgia Historical Quarterly* 53 (1969) 165–183.
18. Baumstein, *My Lord of Belmont*, 59–62.
19. *Ibid.*, 89.
20. Oetgen, *An American Abbot*, 253.
21. *Ibid.*, 254.
22. *Ibid.*, 285.

NOTES TO CHAPTER 4

1. See the letter of Athanasius Tschopp to a "confrere," 24 December 1852, in AEA, translated copy in SMAA.
2. Brief #10005, APF. Abbot Schmid had actually proposed that the foundation at St. Meinrad be given the status of an abbey nullius, but Bishop St. Palais argued against it, feeling that the parishes served by St. Meinrad might acquire too much autonomy. See the letter of Bishop St. Palais to Abbot Schmid, 4 October 1854, AEA.
3. Letter of Father Ulrich Christen to the dean of Einsiedeln, 1853 (no specific date), in AEA, translated copy in SMAA.
4. Letter of Schwerzmann to Abbot Schmid, 26 May 1854, AEA, copy in SMAA.
5. Letter of Bachmann to Father Augustine of Einsiedeln, 16 January 1854, AEA, copy in SMAA.
6. Basilius Doppelfeld, *Mönchtum und kirchlicher Heilsdienst* (Münsterschwarzach, Germany: Vier-Turme-Verlag, 1974) 102–105.
7. See letter of Father Bede O'Connor to Abbot Schmid, 19 August 1854, SMAA.
8. Albert Kleber, *History of St. Meinrad Archabbey, 1854–1954* (St. Meinrad, Ind.: Archabbey Press, 1954) 94.
9. Letter of Abbot Schmid to Father Athanasius, 14 February 1856, SMAA.
10. Letter of Father Isidore Hobi to Einsiedeln, 1858, AEA, copy in SMAA; Doppelfeld, *Mönchtum und kirchlicher Heilsdienst*, 116.
11. Statement addressed to Abbot Schmid, Ferdinand, Indiana, April 1858, AEA, translated copy in SMAA.
12. Letter of Athanasius Tschopp to Ulrich Christen, 15 October 1858, AEA, copy in SMAA.
13. Letter of Bishop St. Palais to Abbot Schmid, 19 October 1860, SMAA.
14. Joel Rippinger, "Martin Marty: Monk, Abbot, Missionary and Bishop," *American Benedictine Review* 33 (1982) 227.

15. Ildephonse Betschart, *Der Apostel der Sioux-Indianer, Bischof Martinus Marty, O.S.B., 1834–1896* (Einsiedeln, 1934), translated for personal use by Sister Stanislaus Van Well (Yankton, S. Dak., 1979) 15.

16. Marty's main sources of financial aid in Europe were the Ludwig-Missionsverein in Munich and the Leopoldine Society in Vienna. See letters found in AEA, copies in SMAA.

17. Letter of Marty to Abbot Schmid, 13 November 1861, AEA, translated copy in SMAA. Emphasis in original.

18. Letter of Marty to Abbot Schmid, 16 July 1861, AEA, translated copy in SMAA.

19. Kleber, *History of St. Meinrad*, 214–217.

20. They include *The Catholic Church in the United States* (St. Meinrad, 1865); *Der heilige Benedikt und seine Order, von einem Benediktiner in St. Meinrad* (St. Meinrad, 1874); *Dr. Johann Martin Henni: Erster Bischof von Milwaukee* (Chicago, 1888).

21. Claudia Duratschek, *The Beginnings of Catholicism in South Dakota* (Washington: Catholic University of America Press, 1943) 223.

22. See Kleber, *History of St. Meinrad*, 250–254, and Joel Rippinger, "From Old World to New: The Origins and Development of St. Meinrad and Conception Abbeys in the Nineteenth Century," (Rome, 1976) 18–22, for two accounts of the controversy. Correspondence between Marty and Father Frowin Conrad of Conception reveals that Marty had given some hint of his decision to his former classmate before it went into effect.

23. Letter of Caspar Seiler to Abbot Basil Oberholzer of Einsiedeln, 6 August 1877, as cited in Kleber, *History of St. Meinrad*, 237.

24. Letter of Placid Wolter to Frowin Conrad, 11 September 1874, CAA, as cited and translated in Edward Malone, "Documents: Placidus Wolter and the American Benedictines," *American Benedictine Review* 16 (1965) 319–325.

25. Kleber, *History of St. Meinrad*, 255–257. Much to the consternation of Einsiedeln, they were obliged to purchase and send to St. Meinrad at no little expense an entire set of monastic breviaries, since Marty had donated all the old ones to Conception Abbey.

26. Letter of Marty to Frowin Conrad, 28 December 1872, CAA.

27. The letter is undated, SMAA.

28. Letter of Schlumpf to Dean Ildephonse, 31 August 1877, AEA, translated copy in SMAA.

29. Letter of Mundwiler to Frowin Conrad, 7 November 1881, CAA.

30. Letter of Bishop Hogan to Marty, 8 November 1872, Archives of Mount Michael Abbey.

31. Edward Malone, *A History of Conception Colony, Abbey and Schools* (Omaha, Nebr.: Interstate Printing, 1971) 48–49.

32. Observed Conrad after his visit to the German monastery: "We have observed the Beuron *Ceremoniale* as far as we can and we have also studied their statutes. No monastery had made such a good impression on me as that of Beuron, because in no other place was I able to find a way of life based so solidly on the

traditions of our Holy Order." Entry in Conrad's Journal for 1 February 1875, CAA. It is worth noting that Conrad, in spite of his numerous requests, could not obtain the *Ceremoniale* and *Graduale* of Engelberg during this same time.

33. Letter of Conrad to Abbot Villiger, 3 September 1871, EAA, copy in CAA.
34. Letter of Villiger to Frowin Conrad, June 1873, CAA.
35. Letter of Conrad to Abbot Villiger, 15 June 1873, EAA.
36. Malone, *A History of Conception*, 65–80.
37. *Ibid.*, 106–107, where Malone offers a translated version of the letter in full.
38. Journal entry of 27 November 1876, CAA.
39. Letter of Conrad to Abbot Villiger, 14 June 1877, EAA.
40. Journal entry of 5 April 1878, CAA.
41. Journal entry of 13 July 1881, CAA.
42. Journal entry of 30 November 1876, CAA.
43. Letter of Odermatt to Abbot Villiger, 19 October 1881, MAAA.
44. Unpublished manuscript of Father Ambrose Zenner, "Pages from Mt. Angel's early history," MAAA.
45. Letter of Frei to Abbot Villiger, 2 December 1881, EAA, copy in MAAA.
46. Gerard Steckler, "The Founding of Mt. Angel Abbey," *Oregon Historical Quarterly* (December 1969) 312. The monks from St. John's, after a period of investigating the possibilities of a foundation, refused the offer of Seghers, but eventually a Cassinese community did take root in the Northwest, with monks from Collegeville coming to Lacey, Washington, in 1895.
47. Tagebuch of Abbot Anselm Villiger, 5 September 1882, EAA, translated copy in MAAA.
48. Journal entry of 26 September 1882, CAA.
49. Odermatt was not alone in his letter-writing campaign. Father Barnabas Held of Engelberg Abbey also corresponded with the Leopoldine Society in Vienna, asking for assistance for the new Oregon foundation and insisting that the Catholics in "free" Switzerland believed it was necessary to prepare to move to a new homeland if conditions grew worse. Letter of Held to Coelestin Gaenglbauer, archbishop of Vienna, 7 July 1882, microfilm copy of Leopoldine Society Papers, UNDA.
50. Lawrence McCrank, *Mt. Angel Abbey: A Centennial History of the Benedictine Community and Its Library, 1882–1982* (Wilmington, Del.: Scholarly Resources, 1983) 26–27. Ironically, the building program of Mount Angel proceeded without interruption during this same period.
51. Tagebuch of Abbot Anselm Villiger, entry of 3 August 1887, MAA.
52. Martin Pollard, "Abbey Chronicle, 1901" in MAA.
53. Conrad relates this throughout his journal for the first part of July 1901.
54. Only eight years earlier the community of Mount Angel had seriously entertained the possibility of joining the American Cassinese Congregation, a proposal that caused much alarm and no little distress in circles at Engelberg and Conception. See Villiger's Tagebuch and Pollard, "Abbey Chronicle," MAA.
55. In his *History of St. Meinrad*, 345, Kleber attributes the plan to Anton Hellmich, the chief editor of the German daily *Amerika*.

56. Hugh Assenmacher, *A Place Called Subiaco* (Little Rock, Ark.: Rose Publishing Co., 1977) 8.
57. *Ibid.*, 9.
58. *Ibid.*, 12.
59. When Hennemann died of tuberculosis soon after this, his superiors refused to accept responsibility for his debts, and the monastic community of St. Meinrad was forced to take possession of the property. See the microfilm account of Luke Gruswe to the Leopoldine Society in 1895, UNDA.
60. Agnes Voth, *Green Olive Branch* (Chicago: Franciscan Herald Press, 1973) 50–80. Weibel had hoped to found a permanent community of monks as a political refuge for his Swiss monastery, which, unlike Einsiedeln and Engelberg, had been suppressed by the Swiss government.
61. Letter of Mundwiler to Abbot Oberholzer of Einsiedeln, 13 August 1882, AEA, translated copy in AAA.
62. Letter of Father Matthew Sättele to the dean of Einsiedeln, 24 July 1885, translated copy in NSAA.
63. Assenmacher devotes a substantial part of his book (*A Place Called Subiaco*, 104–115) to Father Gall and his charges, seeing their arrival at New Subiaco as a crucial turn in the road for the community.
64. At the time it was given abbatial status, New Subiaco had more capitulars from Einsiedeln than from St. Meinrad, and this was reflected in the abbey's first generation of leadership.
65. Letter of Ignatius Conrad to Abbot Oberholzer, 13 September 1894, AEA, copy in NSAA.
66. What was originally a high school in Corpus Christi in 1927 became the basis for a monastic community that today is Corpus Christi Abbey.
67. Jonathan DeFrange, *Century of Grace: A Pictorial History of St. Joseph Abbey and Seminary* (St. Benedict, La., 1989) 2.

NOTES TO CHAPTER 5

1. Two examples worthy of note are Incarnata Girgen, *Behind the Beginnings* (St. Joseph, Minn.: St. Benedict's Convent, 1981), and Judith Sutera, *True Daughters: Monastic Identity and American Benedictine Women's History* (Atchison, Kans.: Benedictine College Press, 1987). See also Ephrem Hollermann's unpublished doctoral dissertation, "The Reshaping of a Tradition: American Benedictine Women, 1852-1881," for a description of the evolution of the first generation of American Benedictine women.
2. Jerome Oetgen, *An American Abbot: Boniface Wimmer, O.S.B.* (Latrobe, Pa.: The Archabbey Press, 1976) 98.
3. Letter of Wimmer to Archbishop Reisach, 1 January 1852, SVAA. Reisach had also formerly been the bishop of Eichstätt and thus knew the Benedictine community there quite well.
4. Girgen, *Behind the Beginnings*, 16.
5. *Ibid.*, 27, and Regina Baska, *The Benedictine Congregation of St. Scholastica: Its Foundation and Development, 1852-1903* (Washington: Catholic University Press, 1935) 25–26.

6. Grace McDonald, *With Lamps Burning* (St. Joseph, Minn.: St. Benedict's Priory Press, 1957) 14.
7. Letter of Wimmer to Scherr, 6 July 1853, as cited in Willibald Mathäser, *Haudegen Gottes* (Würzburg: Kommissionsverlag Echter, 1971) 60.
8. Letter of Wimmer to King Ludwig I, 9 April 1859, Royal Archives of Munich, as cited in Oetgen, *An American Abbot*, 154.
9. *Ibid.*, 160.
10. Girgen, *Behind the Beginnings*, 110–113.
11. The original statement of Riepp's points of difference is found in the Baraga Collection of the archives of St. Benedict's Convent, St. Joseph, Minnesota. Among the questions raised by Riepp were Wimmer's right to decide which candidates entered the novitiate and which novices made final profession; whether Wimmer had the right to choose superiors for the sisters; and whether the St. Vincent superior had the authority to control the sisters' financial affairs.
12. Girgen, *Behind the Beginnings*, 113–121.
13. Later Wimmer relented and reinstated Scherbauer when she made her submission.
14. Girgen, *Behind the Beginnings*, 98–99. It was a reprise of the action Wimmer had taken with the money intended for the convent of St. Marys in 1853.
15. Chronicle of St. Joseph's Convent, St. Marys, Pennsylvania. No date given. Translated copy in the archives of St. Joseph's Convent.
16. In a letter of 30 December 1861, shortly before her death, Riepp wrote to Boniface Wimmer requesting pardon for all the offenses he had to bear on her account. SVAA.
17. Between 1852 and 1879, sixty-five sisters died in American Benedictine convents, a death rate of 12 percent. Even more disturbing is the fact that 87 percent of those who died were younger than thirty years of age. See Jerome Oetgen, "Benedictine Women in Nineteenth-Century America," *American Benedictine Review* 34 (1983) 412, and Jay Dolan, *The American Catholic Experience* (Garden City, N.Y.: Doubleday, 1985) 121–122.
18. For a historical perspective, see Mary Ewens, *The Role of the Nun in Nineteenth-Century America* (New York: Arno Press, 1978) and Margaret Thompson, "To Serve the People of God: Nineteenth-Century Sisters and the Creation of an American Religious Life," Paper in the Cushwa Center Series, University of Notre Dame (February 1987). For a theological background, see Regina Vidal Celna, "Evolución Histórica de la Institución de Clausura en el Monocato Feminino," *Cistercium* 170 and 171 (1986) 113–124 and 297–338.
19. Chronicle of Sister Nepomucene Ludwig, archives of St. Joseph Convent, St. Marys, Pennsylvania.
20. Brief of Wimmer to Cardinal Barnabo, 4 July 1858, APF.
21. Roman document of 6 December 1859, SVAA. In 1866 the sisters were finally given permission to say the Little Office of the Blessed Virgin. There was no definitive response with regard to permission to teach in state schools.
22. Baska, *The Congregation of St. Scholastica*, 122–126.
23. Letter of Wimmer to Cardinal Barnabo, 24 June 1867, SVAA, and Sutera, *True Daughters*, 40. After the Second Plenary Council had failed to take ac-

tion, Propaganda Fide suggested that Wimmer ask the bishops of the dioceses in which the sisters were established if they would agree to setting up a congregation. See the letter of Wimmer to Propaganda Fide, 4 April 1867, APF.

24. Fink felt that something had to be done for all the Benedictine convents in the United States "in order to protect the sisters from the undue influence of bishops and abbots." See the letter of Fink to Abbot Bernard Smith, 7 December 1880, UNDA.

25. Letter of Theresa Vogel to all superiors, 5 June 1879, archives of St. Joseph Convent. See also Sutera, *True Daughters*, 74.

26. Letter of Fink to Abbot Bernard Smith, 7 December 1880, microfilm copy in UNDA.

27. This was the first and largest of the congregations to be approved, consisting of ten communities and following for the most part the constitutions and norms of the American Cassinese Congregation of monks. Sutera, *True Daughters*, 98–103.

28. Mary Annehem, "A Study of Catholicism in Covington, Kentucky, 1830–1868" (M.A. thesis, University of Notre Dame, 1946) 72–74, and Mary Catherine Bramlage, "Origin, History, and Educational Activities of the Benedictine Sisters of Covington, Kentucky" (M.A. thesis, University of Notre Dame, 1938).

29. See the letter of Wimmer to Sister Hildegard, 5 August 1887, translated copy in SVAA.

30. Letter of Wimmer to Ludwig-Missionsverein, 19 September 1886, translated copy in SVAA.

31. Diary of Sister Luitgard, archives of St. Joseph Convent.

32. *Ibid.*

33. Joan Chittister, "American Benedictine Women in the Pre- and Post-Conciliar Church," *The Continuing Quest for God*, ed. William Skudlarek (Collegeville, Minn.: The Liturgical Press, 1982) 186.

34. McDonald, *With Lamps Burning*, 94.

35. Oetgen, "Nineteenth-Century Benedictine Women," 416, and McDonald, *With Lamps Burning*, 97–98.

36. Oetgen, "Nineteenth-Century Benedictine Women," 416. Under Ireland, Benedictine sisters were not the only ones to suffer. The School Sisters of St. Francis, consisting mostly of German immigrants, were opposed by the St. Paul prelate because he considered their cultural and linguistic traditions opposed to "Americanism." See Marvin O'Connell, *John Ireland and the American Church* (St. Paul, Minn.: Minnesota Historical Society Press, 1988) 197–198.

37. McDonald, *With Lamps Burning*, 150–152. A more detailed background for Zardetti's actions is found in Vincent Yzermans, *Frontier Bishop of St. Cloud* (Waite Park, Minn.: Park Press, 1988).

38. Joan Chittister and others, *Climb Along the Cutting Edge: An Analysis of Change in Religious Life* (New York: Paulist Press, 1977) 76.

39. Dolores Dowling, *In Your Midst: The Story of the Benedictine Sisters of Perpetual Adoration* (St. Louis: Printery, 1988) has served as an indispensable source for the Swiss beginnings. See pp. 1–6.

40. Sister Gertrude Leüpi was superior at Maria Rickenbach since 1858 and was an advocate of the expedition. For a more detailed treatment of her life, see Moritz Jaeger, *Sr. Gertrude Leüpi* (Kanisius Verlag, 1974). There is also an unpublished English translation of this work by Alexander Leutkemeyer.

41. The sisters were told by Father Adelhelm that they would be expected not only to provide a school for the Catholic children of the area but also to serve as housekeepers, stablehands, gardeners, cooks, collection counters, and choir members for Masses as well. It was obviously a far cry from the stable monastic life they had known in Switzerland. See Dowling, *In Your Midst*, 19.

42. The convent in Ferdinand, just a short distance from the community at St. Meinrad, was founded by sisters from Covington, Kentucky, in 1867 at the request of Marty. See F. Dudine, *The Castle on the Hill* (Milwaukee, Wis.: Bruce, 1967).

43. Edward Malone, *A History of Conception Colony, Abbey and Schools* (Omaha, Nebr.: Interstate Printing, 1971) 83.

44. Letter of Villiger to Frowin Conrad, 1 June 1875, CAA.

45. Malone, *A History of Conception*, 112.

46. Letter of Marty to Conrad, 18 December 1880, CAA.

47. Letter of Marty to Abbot Schmid, 11 July 1866, SMAA.

48. Letter of Marty to Conrad, 18 December 1889, CAA.

49. Claudia Duratschek, *Under the Shadow of His Wings* (Aberdeen, S. Dak.: North Plains Press, 1971) 129, and the letter of Mother Gertrude Leüpi to Conrad, 20 December 1886, CAA.

50. Letter of Conrad to Abbot Villiger, 25 June 1884, EAA.

51. Letter of Conrad to Abbot Villiger, 24 July 1884, EAA.

52. Letter of Conrad to Abbot Villiger, 30 June 1887, copy in CAA.

53. Letter of Conrad to Abbot Villiger, 19 April 1893, EAA.

54. Dowling, *In Your Midst*, 40–78.

55. Letter of Weibel to Conrad, 16 February 1892, CAA.

56. Mary Agnes Voth, "Mother Beatrice Renggli, O.S.B., Foundress of the American Olivetan Sisters, Jonesboro, Arkansas," *American Benedictine Review* 25 (1974) 403, 406. None of these obstacles interfered with Mother Beatrice's subsequent work of founding a flood of missions and schools. She remained a mainstay of her community until her death in 1942 at the age of ninety-four.

57. Sermons of Bonaventure Binzegger, NSA.

58. Craft, a half-Mohawk Indian who had been ordained in 1878 and appointed by Marty to serve the Sioux at the Fort Berthold Reservation, was stabbed in the back at the Battle of Wounded Knee in December 1890. During his convalescence in a hospital in Yankton, Craft talked several Indian women who were interested in joining the Benedictines in Yankton to accompany him back to his church at Elbowoods, where he intended to organize them into an order of American Indian sisters. See Terrence Kardong, *A History of the Diocese of Bismarck* (Richardton, N. Dak.: Assumption Abbey Press, 1985) 49–50.

59. Letter of Craft to Daniel Hudson, C.S.C., 15 April 1898, UNDA.

60. The houses of Maria Rickenbach and Einsiedeln both served as centers of recruitment for the American houses.

61. Oetgen, "Nineteenth-Century American Benedictine Women," 421.

NOTES TO CHAPTER 6

1. Letter of Cardinal Antonelli to Didier, 28 April 1790, APF, copy in UNDA. Three years later Propaganda recommended Father Wolfgang Froelich, a Bavarian Benedictine who had volunteered for the missions, to Bishop John Carroll, but there is no indication that Froelich made the journey.

2. Camillus Maes, *The Life of Rev. Charles Nerinckx* (Cincinnati: R. Clarke & Co., 1880) 48–49, 157. The story of the first Trappists who came to the United States under Father Urban Guillet will be taken up later.

3. Roger Baudier, *The Catholic Church in Louisiana* (New Orleans, 1939) 311.

4. Jon Alexander and David Williams, "Andreas Bernardus Smolnikar: American Catholic Apostate and Millennial Prophet," *American Benedictine Review* 35 (1984) 50–63.

5. A complete microfilm list of all the requests can be found in the archives of the University of Notre Dame. See also Theodore Roemer, *Ten Decades of Alms* (St. Louis: B. Herder Book Co., 1942).

6. Letter of Wimmer to Father Salzbacher, 8 November 1845, as cited in the *Illustrated History of St. Vincent Archabbey*, 122, SVAA.

7. Letter of Marty to the dean of Einsiedeln, 1 January 1861, AEA, copy in SMAA.

8. Letter of Peter to Abbot Bernard Smith, 26 November 1857, microfilm copy of Smith letters in the North American College, Rome.

9. Excerpts from Villiger's diary entry of 29 August 1883, translated copy in MAAA.

10. Colman Barry, *Worship and Work: Saint John's Abbey and University 1856–1980* (Collegeville, Minn.: The Liturgical Press, 1980) 52.

11. Basilius Doppelfeld, *Mönchtum und kirchlicher Heilsdienst* (Münsterschwarzach, Germany: Vier-Turme-Verlag, 1974) 181.

12. Barry, *Worship and Work*, 90–91.

13. James Reardon, *The Catholic Church in the Diocese of St. Paul* (St. Paul: North Central Publishing Co., 1952) 173–174. *The Wanderer* published today is a descendant of that paper, although it has long since lost its original ethnic associations.

14. Letter of Bede Maler to Abbot Bernard Smith, 8 May 1890, microfilm copy in UNDA. The *Panier* popularized devotion to the Holy Face but ceased publication when that devotion was condemned by the Holy Office in 1892.

15. The Bohemian Benedictine Press, as it was officially known, was founded in 1889 and was a vital element in preserving the faith of Chicago's Catholic Czech community. See Charles Shanabruch, *Chicago's Catholics: The Evolution of an American Identity* (Notre Dame, Ind.: University of Notre Dame Press, 1981), and Vitus Buresh, *The Procopian Chronicle: St. Procopius Abbey, 1885–1985* (Lisle, Ill.: St. Procopius Abbey, 1985).

16. Joseph Murphy, *Tenacious Monks* (Shawnee, Okla.: The Benedictine Color Press, 1974) 180–181.

17. For a more detailed treatment of the influence of this presence, see Colman Barry, *The Catholic Church and German Americans* (Milwaukee, Wis.: Bruce, 1953).
18. Joseph Cada, *Czech-American Catholics 1850–1920* (Lisle, Ill.: Benedictine Abbey Press, 1964) 53.
19. Jay Dolan, *The American Catholic Experience*, 155.
20. Buresh, *The Procopian Chronicle*, 4. The bishop had also written to the Jesuits and Franciscans with no apparent response.
21. *Ibid.*, 18–19, and Peter Mizera, *Czech Benedictines in America, 1877–1961* (Lisle, Ill.: Center for Slav Culture, 1969) 135–140.
22. Buresh, *The Procopian Chronicle*, 21.
23. *Ibid.*, 23. Later, Sister Ludmilla Neuzil, sister of Benedictine Father Procopius Neuzil, founded the Benedictine convent of the Sacred Heart in Lisle, Illinois.
24. Shanabruch's *Chicago Catholics* (p. 49) notes that while only 25 percent of New York City's Czech Catholics kept their faith during the first generation's time in America, over 50 percent of the Chicago Czech population remained Catholic.
25. Buresh, *The Procopian Chronicle*, 70.
26. In the chapter decision of 17 April 1925, the St. Procopius monks rejected an alternative resolution from the Priests' Association of Aurora, Illinois, to establish and conduct a Catholic high school in that city. Ironically, Benedictine monks from St. Meinrad would accept a similar offer eight years later and establish Marmion Abbey. Chapter minutes, SPAA.
27. Martin Burne, "Holy Cross Abbey—One Hundred Years," *American Benedictine Review* 37 (1986) 426, and vol. 1 of the Chronicle of Benedictines in Colorado, HCAA.
28. Letter of Marty to Father McCarthy, 23 September 1884, UNDA.
29. Joel Rippinger, "From Old World to New: The Origins and Development of St. Meinrad and Conception Abbeys in the Nineteenth Century" (Rome, 1976) 46–47.
30. Claudia Duratschek, *The Beginnings of Catholicism in South Dakota* (Washington: Catholic University of America Press, 1943) 245.
31. Benjamin Blied, *Three Archbishops of Milwaukee* (Milwaukee, 1955) 33.
32. Duratschek, *Beginnings*, 244–245.
33. Letter of Wimmer to Abbot Alexius Edelbrock, 13 February 1875, SJAA.
34. From an article by Edelbrock in the *Northwestern Chronicle*, 18 August 1887, as cited in Barry, *Worship and Work*, 149. Edelbrock promoted the celebration of St. Patrick's Day in the school at St. John's and persuaded the monastic chapter to discontinue the German custom of serving beer to the students on certain days. He also distinguished himself by using English almost exclusively in his correspondence.
35. Reading at table was in German, and many American-born Benedictines were required to learn German in order to communicate with their "founding" generation. Like so many of the vestiges of German culture inside American monasteries, the German language largely disappeared with World War I.
36. Charles O'Fahey, "Gibbons, Ireland, Keane: The Evolution of a Liberal Catholic Rhetoric in America," (Ph.D. diss., University of Minnesota, 1980) 119–120.

37. James Moynihan, *The Life of Archbishop Ireland* (New York: Arno Press Reprint, 1976) 16–17. For a view that explains how Ireland used his Roman agent, Monsignor Denis O'Connell, against the Benedictines, see Gerald Fogarty, "Denis J. O'Connell, Americanist Agent to the Vatican, 1885–1903" (Ph.D. diss., Yale University, 1969).

38. Relations between Edelbrock and Ireland deteriorated when Denis O'Connell harbored and encouraged Abbot Alexius' principal adversary in the community, Father Othmar Erren. See Marvin O'Connell, *John Ireland and the American Church* (St. Paul, Minn.: Minnesota Historical Society Press, 1988) 256.

39. Letter of Edelbrock to Abbot Bernard Smith, 9 February 1885, microfilm copy in UNDA.

40. Letter of Hobi to Dean Ildephonse of Einsiedeln, 22 February 1893, AEA, copy in SMAA. For a full presentation of Ireland's Faribault Plan, see "Archbishop Ireland Explains His Stand on Public and Parochial Schools, December, 1890," in *Documents of American Catholic History*, ed. John Tracy Ellis (Wilmington, Del.: Michael Glazier, 1987) 2:473–479.

41. Letter of Mundwiler to Dean Ildephonse of Einsiedeln, 3 December 1893, AEA, translated copy in SMAA.

42. Letter of Wimmer to Father Schwerzmann, 8 August 1854, AEA, translated copy in SMAA.

43. Incarnata Girgen, *Behind the Beginnings* (St. Joseph, Minn.: St. Benedict's Convent, 1981) 45.

44. Letter of Riepp to Archbishop Karl Reisach, 20 May 1855, as cited in Girgen, *Behind the Beginnings*, 45.

45. Letter of Marty to the dean of Einsiedeln, 1 January 1861, AEA, translated copy in SVAA.

46. Letter of Wimmer to King Ludwig I, 29 November 1856, translated copy in SVAA.

47. Letter of Wimmer to King Ludwig I, 2 December 1862, translated copy in SVAA. The actual document of release, issued by the War Department and dated 28 November 1862, is found in SVAA. Worthy of mention, however, is the fact that a number of monks of St. Vincent continued to be drafted after the agreement had been struck, and the community had to pay the regular exemption fee of five hundred dollars. Moreover, in June 1863 Wimmer needed to negotiate another agreement when the draft laws were revised.

48. Letter of Marty to Abbot Schmid, 13 October 1864, AEA, translated copy in SMAA.

49. J. J. O'Connell, *Catholicity in the Carolinas and Georgia* (New York: D. J. Sadlier, 1879) 480.

50. Aloysius Plaisance, "Emmeran Bliemel, O.S.B., Heroic Confederate Chaplain," *American Benedictine Review* 17 (1966) 209–216.

51. Diary of Sister Luitgard Schraudt, St. Joseph's Convent, St. Marys, Pa.

52. Grace McDonald, *With Lamps Burning* (St. Joseph, Minn.: St. Benedict's Priory Press, 1957) 65.

53. *Ibid.*, 113.

54. Chronicle of St. Joseph Convent, St. Marys, Pa.

55. Letter of Hobi to Dean Ildephonse of Einsiedeln, 22 February 1893, AEA, copy in SMAA.

56. Zurcher's references to the Catholic Church's temperance laws alluded to the Catholic Total Abstinence Union, a society founded in 1872 that accommodated prevailing Protestant prejudices against alcohol. See James Hennesey, *American Catholics* (New York: Oxford University Press, 1981) 184; George Zurcher, *Monks and Their Decline* (Buffalo, 1898) 36.

57. Letter of Marty to Peter Rosen, C.S.C., 1 June 1884, UNDA.

58. Pastoral letter of Marty from the *Dakota Catholic* (20 April 1889) 3. Microfilm copy in SHCA.

59. Letter of Marty to Father Pius Boehm, September 1891, SMAA.

60. Colman Barry, *Upon These Rocks: Catholics in the Bahamas* (Collegeville, Minn.: St. John's Abbey Press, 1973) 198. Variants of the previous ethnic pride did linger, even if they were seasoned with patriotism. For example, the National Alliance of Czech Catholics sponsored Benedictine Father Alphonse Bishop of St. Procopius as Catholic chaplain of the Czechoslovak Legion fighting in France during World War I.

NOTES TO CHAPTER 7

1. Basilius Doppelfeld, *Mönchtum und kirchlicher Heilsdienst* (Münsterschwarzach, Germany: Vier-Turme-Verlag, 1974) 305–306, and the letter of Boniface Wimmer to the Ludwig-Missionsverein, 2 July 1846, SVAA.

2. Letter of Chrysostom Foffa to Abbot Schmid, 31 December 1857, as cited in Albert Kleber, *A History of St. Meinrad Archabbey* (St. Meinrad, Ind.: Archabbey Press, 1954) 122.

3. Letter of Odermatt to Abbot Villiger, 15 August 1881, MAAA.

4. Résumé of Marty to Einsiedeln Abbey (no date given), SMAA.

5. Jeremy Hall, "The Character of Benedictine Higher Education," in *The Continuing Quest for God*, ed. William Skudlarek (Collegeville, Minn.: The Liturgical Press, 1982) 205–206.

6. Letter of Wimmer to Ludwig-Missionsverein, 7 November 1851, LMA, as cited in Jerome Oetgen, *An American Abbot: Boniface Wimmer, O.S.B.* (Latrobe, Pa.: The Archabbey Press, 1976) 85.

7. Peter Beckman, *Kansas Monks* (Atchison, Kans.: Abbey Student Press, 1957) 147.

8. Catalogue of Mount Angel College, 188–189, MAAA.

9. Felix Fellner, "Archabbot Boniface Wimmer as an Educator," unpublished manuscript in SVAA.

10. All these publications were in German: *Europaer in Amerika vor Columbus* (Regensburg, 1879); *Bonifaz Wimmer Erzabt von St. Vincent in Pennsylvania* (New York, 1891); *Der Geschichtsfreund* (twenty-four volumes, 1882–1883); and *Die Legende* (seven volumes, 1892–1898). For more of the life of Moosmueller, see Jerome Oetgen, "Oswald Moosmueller: Monk and Missionary," *American Benedictine Review* 27 (1976) 1–35.

11. Marty's books were published in English and German and had a wide distribution, thanks to the Benziger publishing house. See Joel Rippinger, "Martin Marty: Monk, Abbot, Missionary, Bishop—II," *American Benedictine Review* 33 (1982) 385–386.

12. Letter of Marty to the dean of Einsiedeln, 1 January 1886, AEA, copy in SMAA.

13. In the 1922 constitutions of the Benedictine Congregation of St. Scholastica, this priority was underscored by a description of the apostolate of the communities as "the education of the young, both in their academies and in their parish schools." See *Declarations and Constitutions of the Congregation of St. Scholastica* (Atchison, Kans., 1922).

14. The importance that many Benedictines attached to Catholic elementary schools can be seen in Bishop Louis Fink's practice of not allowing any child to make first communion unless he or she had attended a Catholic school for at least two years, and of not ordaining anyone a priest unless he had received a Catholic elementary education. See the letter of Father Kuhls to James McMaster, 17 January 1881, UNDA.

15. Some Benedictines anticipated the Cahensly petition. In 1890 the monks of Subiaco, Arkansas, were instrumental in organizing the German Roman-Catholic Staatsverband, an organization that promoted German-Catholic parochial schools. See Hugh Assenmacher, *A Place Called Subiaco: A History of the Benedictine Monks in Arkansas* (Little Rock, Ark.: Rose Publishing Co., 1977) 160, and Colman Barry, *The Catholic Church and German Americans* (Milwaukee: Bruce, 1953) 155.

16. Letter of Haid to Abbot Bernard Smith, 19 March 1892, microfilm of Bernard Smith letters, library of the North American College, Rome.

17. Letter of Isidore Hobi to Dean Ildephonse of Einsiedeln, 21 November 1893, AEA, copy in SMAA.

18. From the catalogue of St. Benedict's College, Atchison, Kansas, 1874–1875.

19. Letter of Leo Huebscher to Henry Brownson, undated (sometime in the 1880s), UNDA.

20. Letter of Huber to Archabbot Schnerr, 26 April 1899, SVAA.

21. Incarnata Girgen, "The Schools of American Cassinese Benedictines in the United States: Their Foundation, Development and Character," (Ph.D. diss., St. Louis University, 1944) 315–316.

22. Journal entry of 19 June 1902, CAA.

23. Colman Barry, *Worship and Work: Saint John's Abbey and University 1856–1980* (Collegeville, Minn.: The Liturgical Press, 1980) 228.

24. *Ibid.,* 284.

25. Vitus Buresh, *The Procopian Chronicle: St. Procopius Abbey, 1885–1985* (Lisle, Ill.: St. Procopius Abbey, 1985) 61–62. Archabbot Aurelius Stehle of St. Vincent was quite receptive to this plan, for he considered the University of Chicago "a hot-bed of atheists and even while the price of instruction may be very low, we may pay for going there." Letter of Stehle to Abbot Helmstetter, 18 December 1920, SVAA.

26. *Ibid.,* 64. Included in this group were the famous scientists and brothers Fathers Hilary and Edmund Jurica. They both received doctoral degrees from the Uni-

versity of Chicago and established a reputation throughout the country for their innovative use of audiovisual materials in the natural sciences.

27. Peter Collins, "St. Benedict and Education," *Review for Religious* 39 (1980) 673.
28. See Debora Wilson, "Benedictine Higher Education and the Development of American Higher Education," (Ph.D. diss., University of Michigan, 1969).
29. Grace McDonald, *With Lamps Burning* (St. Joseph, Minn.: St. Benedict's Priory Press, 1957) 178.
30. St. John's, St. Benedict's, St. Mary's, St. Procopius, St. Bede, St. Andrew's, Holy Cross, and St. Mary's, Morristown, New Jersey.
31. Those remaining in operation are Marmion, Mount Michael, and New Subiaco.
32. St. Anselm's (Washington, D.C.), Portsmouth (Rhode Island), St. Louis, and Woodside (California) respectively.

NOTES TO CHAPTER 8

1. Letter from Marty, appearing in the *Wahrheitsfreund* of Cincinnati, 7 August 1876.
2. Letter of Brouillet to the administrator of the diocese of Omaha, 11 May 1876, microfilm copy from the archives of the Omaha Archdiocese in CAA.
3. Letter of Marty to the Bureau of Catholic Indian Missions, 9 October 1878, Marquette University Archives.
4. This was immediately after Custer's massacre at the Battle of Little Big Horn and General Phil Sheridan had been mustered from Missouri to enforce security in the territory in the face of Sitting Bull's action. For accounts of Marty's activity, see Robert Karolevitz, *Bishop Martin Marty* (Freeman, S. Dak.: Pine Hill Press, 1980) 65–68, and Sister Stanislaus Van Well's translation of Ildephonse Betschart, *Der Apostel der Sioux-Indianer, Bischof Martinus Marty, O.S.B., 1834–1896* (Einsiedeln, 1934), translated for personal use (Yankton, S. Dak., 1979) 54–58.
5. Letter of Marty to Abbot Oberholzer, 27 November 1878, AEA, translated copy in SMAA.
6. Letter of Stadler to Abbot Oberholzer, 5 January 1877, AEA, translated copy in SMAA.
7. Letter of Schlumpf to Dean Ildephonse of Einsiedeln, 31 August 1877, NSAA.
8. Susan Peterson, "From Paradise to Praise: The Presentation Sisters in Dakota 1880–1896," *South Dakota History* 10 (1980) 213.
9. Karolevitz, *Bishop Martin Marty*, 98–100, and Consuela Marie Duffy, *Katharine Drexel* (Cornwell Heights, Pa.: Mother Katharine Drexel Guild, 1966) 79–80.
10. Letter of Drexel to Father Peter Behrman, 22 July 1922, copy in SHCA.
11. On this subject, see the letters of Vincent Wehrle to Einsiedeln (translated copies in AAA) and the unfortunate story of Marty's harboring of a renegade priest from Collegeville, Othmar Erren (documented in correspondence from SJAA).
12. See letter of J. B. Genin to James McMaster, 6 September 1878, UNDA.
13. Letter of Marty to Drexel, 8 November 1891, copy in SHCA.
14. Appointed by President Benjamin Harrison in 1889 to serve on a special commission to negotiate for the cession of the lands of the Chippewa tribe, Marty

was piqued when he discovered that the government had reneged on the agreed settlement. For the background of the controversy, see Francis Paul Prucha, *The Churches and the Indian Schools, 1888–1912* (Lincoln, Nebr.: University of Nebraska Press, 1979), and Henry Warner Bowden, *American Indians and Christian Missions: Studies in Cultural Conflict* (Chicago: University of Chicago Press, 1981).

15. Letter of Marty to Edward Angerer of the Leopoldine Society, 24 March 1895, microfilm copy in UNDA.

16. Colman Barry, *Worship and Work: Saint John's Abbey and University 1856–1980* (Collegeville, Minn.: The Liturgical Press, 1980) 128, 136.

17. After witnessing the naming of three Benedictines as bishops during the 1870s in the largely Indian episcopal jurisdictions (Louis Fink of Kansas and the Indian Territory, Rupert Seidenbusch of the Northern Minnesota Vicariate, and Martin Marty of the Dakota Territory), Wimmer was ready to declare: "It seems that both the Black and Red men will and must become the object of particular attention and care of the Sons of St. Benedict." Wimmer to Abbot Alexius Edelbrock, 12 March 1881, SJAA.

18. Barry, *Worship and Work*, 136–138.

19. *Ibid.*, 146–147, and Father Benno Watrin's manuscript history of the Benedictine mission to the Chippewa, SJAA.

20. Joseph Murphy, *Tenacious Monks: The Oklahoma Benedictines, 1875–1975* (Shawnee, Okla.: Benedictine Color Press, 1974) 58–59.

21. *Ibid.*, 65–66.

22. Letter of Robot to Abbot Wimmer, 7 February 1879, SVAA.

23. Abbey Chronicle of Martin Pollard for 1900, MAAA.

24. Letter of Adelhelm Odermatt to Leopoldine Society, 14 November 1901, microfilm copy in UNDA.

25. Letter of Odermatt to the Ludwig-Missionsverein, 17 March 1900, LMA.

26. See the statement of the NCCB, "The Church and American Indians: Toward Dialogue and Respect," *Origins* (19 May 1977) 766.

27. Jay Dolan, *The American Catholic Experience* (Garden City, N.Y.: Doubleday, 1985) 359–360.

28. Letter of Hobi to Dean Ildephonse of Einsiedeln, 11 December 1881, AEA, translated copy in SMAA.

29. Letter of Bishop Gross to Propaganda Fide, 30 June 1879, microfilm copy of Propaganda Fide letters in UNDA.

30. Jerome Oetgen, *An American Abbot: Boniface Wimmer, O.S.B.* (Latrobe, Pa.: The Archabbey Press, 1976) 259–260.

31. Letter of Wimmer to Bishop Lynch, 23 April 1866, archives of the diocese of Charleston, copy in SVAA.

32. Letter of Fink to Edward Angerer of the Leopoldine Society, 20 October 1881, microfilm copy in UNDA.

33. Letter of Haid to Abbot Andrew Hintenach, 8 April 1889, SVAA.

34. Letter of Haid to Drexel, 24 June 1893, archives of the Sisters of the Blessed Sacrament for Indians and Colored People.

35. Agnes Voth, *Green Olive Branch* (Chicago: Franciscan Herald Press, 1973) 55.
36. Letter of Father Matthew Sättele to the Leopoldine Society, 16 October 1896, microfilm copy in UNDA.
37. Barry, *Worship and Work*, 315–316.
38. Memorandum of Father Alexander Korte, 1946, SJAA.
39. Hugh Assenmacher, *A Place Called Subiaco: A History of the Benedictine Monks in Arkansas* (Little Rock, Ark.: Rose Publishing Co., 1977) 399.
40. Father Hardin's Martin Center in Indianapolis has been a major social and cultural center for black Catholics for almost two decades. Father Davis' contribution to scholarship in the area of the history of black Catholics in the United States is well known. He was also instrumental in having the archives of the National Office of Black Catholics located in his home monastery of St. Meinrad.

NOTES TO CHAPTER 9

1. Bruce Lescher, "Laybrothers: Questions Then, Questions Now," *Cistercian Studies* 23 (1988) 63–85.
2. In an article for the *Sion* of 8 November 1845, Wimmer had already proposed his idea of letting the brothers he would bring to America receive instruction so that they could serve as catechists, especially to the children and elderly. See Felix Fellner, *Abbot Boniface and His Monks* (Latrobe, Pa., 1956) 49, SVAA.
3. Jerome Oetgen, *An American Abbot: Boniface Wimmer, O.S.B.* (Latrobe, Pa.: The Archabbey Press, 1976) 80–81.
4. Sailer to Pope Pius IX, 30 April 1861, APF.
5. Oetgen, *An American Abbot*, 174.
6. St. Vincent's chapter report of 2 October 1861, SVAA.
7. Wimmer to Cardinal Barnabo, 15 June 1855, APF.
8. Letter of Wimmer to Martin Marty, 30 March 1861, translated copy in SVAA.
9. Albert Kleber, *A History of St. Meinrad Archabbey, 1854–1954* (St. Meinrad, Ind.: Archabbey Press, 1954) 65.
10. Letter of Father Isidore Hobi to Abbot Schmid (no date), AEA, copy in SMAA.
11. Kleber, *A History of St. Meinrad Archabbey*, 242–244.
12. Letter of Marty to the dean of Einsiedeln, 31 March 1876, AEA, translated copy in SMAA.
13. Letter of Hobi to Abbot Oberholzer, 14 June 1877, AEA, copy in SMAA.
14. Letter of Mundwiler to Abbot Oberholzer, 13 January 1878, AEA, copy in SMAA.
15. Journal entry of 1 January 1875, CAA.
16. From the papers of Brother Eugene Barry, as cited in Peter Beckman, *Kansas Monks* (Atchison, Kans.: Abbey Student Press, 1957) 177.
17. Letter of Schlumpf to Abbot Oberholzer, 29 June 1886, NSAA.
18. This was another field of activity inaugurated by Boniface Wimmer at the Second Plenary Council of Baltimore in 1866 when he consented to a request made by several bishops. Monasteries of both major congregations of monks in the United States continued to perform this "penitential service" for many years afterward.

19. Judith Sutera, *True Daughters: Monastic Identity and American Benedictine Women's History* (Atchison, Kans.: Benedictine College Press, 1987) 52.

20. Jerome Oetgen, "Benedictine Women in Nineteenth-Century America," *American Benedictine Review* 34 (1983) 422.

21. Helen Herbstritt, "History of the First American Convent and the Work of God," (M.A. thesis, Rensselaer, Ind., 1985) 9.

22. Victorine Fenton, "The English Monastic Liturgy of the Hours in North America" (Ph.D. diss., University of Iowa, 1983).

23. Mary Faith Schuster, *The Meaning of the Mountain* (Baltimore: Helicon Press, 1963) 80–81.

24. Letter of Wolf to Abbot Primate Hildebrand de Hemptinne, 3 March 1910, as cited in Sutera, *True Daughters,* 53.

25. *Paschal Baumstein, My Lord of Belmont: A Biography of Leo Haid* (Belmont, N.C.: Herald House, 1985) 69.

26. Beckman, *Kansas Monks,* 176. The historian of St. Benedict's Abbey also comments on how German had become the language of the "laybrother" communities of other monasteries, creating a barrier for outsiders, 223.

27. *Declarations on the Holy Rule* (Conception, Mo.: Conception Abbey, 1938) 38–39. A similar justification of this division was made with regard to women by Abbot Anselm Villiger of Engelberg. Writing to the superior of a Benedictine convent in Uniontown, Oregon, he insisted upon separation and gave the following rationale in his journal: "The institute of lay Sisters is to be maintained also in America because it rests on very old traditions and has always existed in the motherhouse, because abandonment of its organizational features would loosen the bond of solidarity, because in a country where there is such great demand for external activity it seems necessary that some persons be burdened with fewer prayer obligations so they can devote themselves more freely to active service." Excerpts from journal entry of 13 November 1884, MAAA.

28. *Ibid.,* 29.

29. *Ibid.,* 18.

30. Mount Angel Abbey Chronicle of Martin Pollard, MAAA.

31. Ildephonse Kreidler, "The Fostering of Religious Vocations for the Brotherhood," (M.A. thesis, University of Notre Dame, 1933).

32. A good example of this from the viewpoint of canon law is Thomas Brockhaus, "Religious Who Are Known as Conversi," (Ph.D. diss., Catholic University of America, 1946).

33. Vitus Buresh, *The Procopian Chronicle: St. Procopius Abbey, 1885–1985* (Lisle, Ill.: St. Procopius Abbey, 1985) 58.

NOTES TO CHAPTER 10

1. Magnus Mayr, "History of the Benedictines in Minnesota," translated copy of manuscript in SJAA and Colman Barry, *Worship and Work: Saint John's Abbey and University 1856–1980* (Collegeville, Minn.: The Liturgical Press, 1980) 76–78.

2. The journal of Abbot Anselm Villiger during the early years of Mount Angel is in many respects a detailed account of that cycle.

3. From the *Catholic Sentinel* of 30 June 1887, copy in MAAA.

4. Edward Malone, *A History of Conception Colony, Abbey, and Schools* (Omaha, Nebr.: Interstate Printing, 1971) 131. Frowin Conrad is representative of the monastic mentality that could lament the expense of two days' travel costs of $6.00 and yet speak glowingly of an abbey church that would cost $150,000.

5. Peter Beckman, *Kansas Monks* (Atchison, Kans.: Abbey Student Press, 1957) 77–78, and the letter of Wolf to Edelbrock, 4 March 1880, in SJAA.

6. Paschal Baumstein, *My Lord of Belmont: A Biography of Leo Haid* (Belmont, N.C.: Herald House, 1985) 122.

7. Colman Barry, *Worship and Work: Saint John's Abbey and University 1856–1980* (Collegeville, Minn.: The Liturgical Press, 1980) 219.

8. Valerian Odermann, "Abbot Placid Hoenerbach and the Bankruptcy of St. Mary's Abbey, Richardton," *American Benedictine Review* 29 (1978) 100–104.

9. Barry, *Worship and Work*, 288.

10. Maurice Lavanoux, "Collegeville Revisited," *Liturgical Arts* 22 (1954) 46. At St. John's University in the early 1950s the addition of a department of sacred art, including tracks in architecture and sculpture, advanced a tradition of liturgical art and monastic architecture that acquired momentum in succeeding years.

11. Howard Niebling, "Monastic Churches Erected by American Benedictines Since World War II—Part I," *American Benedictine Review* 26 (1975) 182–202.

12. Howard Niebling, "Monastic Churches Erected by American Benedictines Since World War II—Part II," *American Benedictine Review* 26 (1975) 298–317.

13. Some of the motives and consequences that were part of this movement will be treated at greater length in a subsequent chapter on the contemplative impulse. A help in describing this movement is found in García Colombás, "A Simple and Contemporary Monastery," *American Benedictine Review* 17 (1966) 51–59; Juana Rasch, "A Survey of New Monastic Trends," *American Benedictine Review* 18 (1967) 252–269; Mark Sheridan, "Towards a Contemporary Self-definition of Monasticism," *American Benedictine Review* 19 (1968) 452–482.

14. One of the most impressive accomplishments of the American Benedictines during the 1960s was their ability to enlist the top architects of the time, a roster that included, in addition to Breuer, Alvar Aalto, Pietro Belluschi, Victor Christ-Janer, Edward Dart, George Nakashima, and Stanley Tigerman. See Michael Komechak, "St. Procopius Abbey in Lisle: Modern Expression of a Monastic Ideal," *The Benedictines of Lisle: Centennial Celebration of a Monastic Land Ideal* (Lisle, Ill.: Illinois Benedictine College, 1986) 45–62.

15. The restoration of the archabbey church at St. Meinrad from 1968 to 1970 and of the chapel of St. Benedict's Convent in St. Joseph, Minnesota, in the early 1980s serve as prominent examples.

NOTES TO CHAPTER 11

1. Peter Beckman, *Kansas Monks* (Atchison, Kans.: Abbey Student Press, 1957) 108. Abbot Alexius' community at St. John's had a rule that any monk who

missed morning Office could not attend the community *haustus* in the afternoon.

2. Jerome Oetgen, *An American Abbot: Boniface Wimmer, O.S.B.* (Latrobe, Pa.: The Archabbey Press, 1976) 266.

3. Letter of Fintan Mundwiler to Abbot Bernard Locnikar, 14 October 1890, SJAA.

4. Letter of Maler to Abbot Alcuin Deutsch, 4 February 1926, as cited in Paul Marx, *Virgil Michel and the Liturgical Movement* (Collegeville, Minn.: The Liturgical Press, 1957) 89.

5. Colman Barry, *Worship and Work: Saint John's Abbey and University 1856–1980* (Collegeville, Minn.: The Liturgical Press, 1980) 213.

6. Albert Kleber, *A History of St. Meinrad Archabbey, 1854–1954* (St. Meinrad, Ind.: Archabbey Press, 1954) 391–392.

7. Dolores Dowling, *In Your Midst: The Story of the Benedictine Sisters of Perpetual Adoration* (St. Louis: Printery, 1988) 57.

8. Beckman, *Kansas Monks*, 305. An indication of the change in the liturgical and musical education of American Benedictines was their preference for the Pius X School of Liturgical Music in Manhattanville, New York, over European abbeys.

9. See Virgil Michel, "The Apostolate," *Orate Fratres* 3 (February 24, 1929) 121–123. For a broader examination of Michel's activity and its influence, see Marx, *Virgil Michel; Worship* 62:3 (May 1988); R. W. Franklin and Robert L. Spaeth, *Virgil Michel: American Catholic* (Collegeville, Minn.: The Liturgical Press, 1988).

10. Barry, *Worship and Work*, 268.

11. See David Beauduin, "A Personalist Approach to Catechetics," *Worship* 62 (May 1988) 237–249; Archbishop John Roach, "Virgil Michel's Prophetic Vision," *Origins* 18 (September 8, 1988) 203–207. Also Joseph Chinnici, "Virgil Michel: The Priesthood of the Faithful," *Living Stones: The History and Structure of Catholic Spiritual Life in the United States* (New York: Macmillan, 1989).

12. Letter of Edward Skillin to Abbot Alcuin Deutsch, 19 December 1936, SJAA.

13. Letter of Hammenstede to Abbot Alcuin Deutsch, 3 October 1943, as cited in Barry, *Worship and Work*, 499. The Maria Laach influence worked both ways. Abbot Martin Veth of Atchison, after visiting the German abbey in 1925, adopted Abbot Herwegen's practice of regularly giving his monks a spiritual conference. See Beckman, *Kansas Monks*, 294. Personal interview with Father Burkhard Neunheuser.

14. Barry, *Worship and Work*, 353.

15. Hugh Assenmacher, *A Place Called Subiaco: A History of the Benedictine Monks in Arkansas* (Little Rock, Ark.: Rose Publishing Co., 1977) 244–250. Principally because of the passions aroused by Spanke's stump oratory, he was asked by his bishop to return to the abbey, where he contented himself with perfecting such inventions as a "congregational-singing director" mechanism, a remote-control lawnmower, and temperature-controlled window openers.

16. Chapter records of St. Procopius Abbey. The papal appeal was contained in the decree *Equidem Verba* of 21 March 1924.

17. Vitus Buresh, *The Procopian Chronicle: St. Procopius Abbey, 1885–1985* (Lisle, Ill.: St. Procopius Abbey, 1985) 88–93.
18. See the *Scriptorium* 24 (Collegeville, Minn.: St. John's Abbey, 1985) 120–127. The four were sponsored by the American Benedictine Academy (1960), the Ecumenical Institute on the Spiritual Life (1965), *Worship* magazine (1966), and the Institute for Ecumenical and Cultural Research (1970).

NOTES TO CHAPTER 12

1. Letter of Wimmer to Abbot Utto Lang, 27 July 1858, copy in SVAA.
2. Letter of Wimmer to Abbot Innocent Wolf, 18 April 1885, as cited in Peter Beckman, *Kansas Monks* (Atchison, Kans.: Abbey Student Press, 1957) 207.
3. Letter of Wimmer to Abbot Bernard Smith, 18 October 1866, microfilm copy in UNDA. Wimmer also expressed his intention to Abbot Smith of having a permanent house of studies in Rome for Benedictine students from the United States.
4. Beckman, *Kansas Monks*, 174, 225.
5. Statement of Edelbrock in response to the apostolic visitation at St. John's, May 1889, SJAA.
6. Chapter records of September 1858, SVAA.
7. All monks were encouraged to read regularly the Sacred Scriptures, the *Rule* of Benedict, the *Imitation of Christ*, and several other spiritual volumes, the most important of which was the *Tyrocinium Religiosum.* SVAA.
8. Chapter records of 17–19 August 1867, SVAA.
9. Letter of Wimmer to Martin Marty, 19 September 1868, AEA, translated copy in SMAA.
10. Some things did remain the same. Haid authorized a German and English translation of the *Tyrocinium*, encouraging his fellow superiors to use them for the instruction of laybrothers. See the letter of Haid to the Cassinese abbots, 24 April 1890, SVAA.
11. Journal entry of 5 January 1886, CAA.
12. Journal entry of 22 July 1891, CAA.
13. Letter of Conrad to Abbot Placid Wolter, 19 September 1906, MMAA, as cited in Edward Malone, *A History of Conception Colony, Abbey, and Schools* (Omaha, Nebr.: Interstate Printing, 1971) 72.
14. Letter of Mundwiler to Father Wolfgang Schlumpf, 14 May 1881, AEA, copy in AAA.
15. Letter of Schlumpf to Abbot Oberholzer, 24 August 1888, NSAA.
16. From a personal chronicle of Martin Marty, 22 June 1870 to 26 March 1873, SMAA.
17. Fraters' Chronicle and formation booklet (1907), SMAA.
18. Ann Taves, *The Household of Faith: Roman Catholic Devotions in Mid-Nineteenth-Century America* (Notre Dame Ind.: University of Notre Dame Press, 1986) 17.
19. Joseph Chinnici, *Devotion to the Holy Spirit in American Catholicism* (New York: Paulist Press, 1985) 61.
20. Part of the declarations of the Swiss-American general chapter, archives of the Swiss-American Congregation. See also *The Novice Manual: A Collection of Prayers*

and Instructions for Novices (St. Meinrad, Ind.: St. Meinrad Archabbey, 1927). To examine the influence of Marian piety in these spiritual programs, see Barbara Corrado Pope, "Immaculate and Powerful: The Marian Revival in the Nineteenth Century," *Immaculate and Powerful: The Female in Sacred Image and Social Reality* (Boston, 1985) 173–200.

21. See Joan Chittister and others, *Climb Along the Cutting Edge: An Analysis of Change in Religious Life* (New York: Paulist Press, 1977) 9–18 for a good summary of the content of this formation.

22. The program had its genesis in the form of a resolution in October 1957, signed by thirty-seven Benedictine prioresses representing the four congregations of Benedictine sisters in the United States. The resolution established the Benedictine Institute of Sacred Theology at St. Benedict's Convent, St. Joseph, Minnesota. See Audrey Morran, "A History and Chronology of the Benedictine Institute of Sacred Theology," (M.A. thesis, St. John's University, Collegeville, Minn., 1964) 32.

23. Alexius Edelbrock, *Associations of St. Benedict and Bruderschaft des Heil. Benedictus* (St. Paul, 1887).

24. Colman Barry, *Worship and Work: Saint John's Abbey and University 1856–1980* (Collegeville, Minn.: The Liturgical Press, 1980) 261.

25. St. Benedict's Abbey (Wisconsin), St. Pius X Abbey (Missouri), Our Lady of Glastonbury Abbey (Massachusetts), and Prince of Peace Abbey (California).

26. Bonaventure Schwinn, "Editorials," *American Benedictine Review* 1 (1950) 8.

NOTES TO CHAPTER 13

1. Ramona Mattingly, "The Catholic Church on the Kentucky Frontier, 1785–1812," (Ph.D. diss., Catholic University of America, 1936) 70–77, and material from the archives of Gethsemani Abbey.

2. Letter of Father William DuBourg to Father Simon Bruté, 1 September 1813, UNDA. The failure was occasioned by land debts and a fire, as well as difficulty in administering the school.

3. See the agreement of 14 March 1866 drawn up between Sister Elizabeth M. Angela and Bishop Lavialle, Bernard Smith Papers, microfilm copy in UNDA.

4. James O'Gorman was named vicar apostolic of the Nebraska Territory and Clement Smyth bishop of Dubuque, Iowa.

5. See Finbar Kenneally, *U.S. Documents in the Propaganda Fide Archives*, first series, vol. 2, #840, 131.

6. Edward Malone, "Documents: Placidus Wolter and the American Benedictines," *American Benedictine Review* 16 (1965) 310–325.

7. Colman Barry, *Worship and Work: Saint John's Abbey and University 1856–1980* (Collegeville, Minn.: The Liturgical Press, 1980) 213–217.

8. Letter of Zilliox to Abbot Alexius Edelbrock, 27 August 1887, SJAA.

9. The broader sweep of the story, particularly the influential roles played by Father Othmar Erren and Archbishop John Ireland in Edelbrock's resignation, are given extended treatment in Barry, *Worship and Work*, 163–196.

10. Letter of Gross to Abbot Villiger, 24 February 1888, copy in UNDA.

11. Archives of the Swiss-American Congregation.
12. Circular letter of Abbot Primate Fidelis von Stotzingen, 27 December 1934, archives of the Abbot Primate, Sant' Anselmo, Rome.
13. A fine portrait of the entire history of New Cluny is found in Jerome Oetgen, "Oswald Moosmueller: Monk and Missionary," *American Benedictine Review* 27 (1976) 1–35.
14. Letter of Father C. J. Eschmann to Bishop John Janssen, 29 June 1897, copy in SVAA.
15. Peter Windschiegl, *Fifty Golden Years, 1903–1953: A Brief History of the Order of St. Benedict in the Abbacy Nullius of St. Peter, Muenster, Saskatchewan* (Muenster, Sask.: St. Peter's Abbey, 1953).
16. Later contemplative movements within these communities will be considered in the concluding chapter, which deals with monasticism after Vatican Council II.
17. See Leo Rudloff, "Weston Priory," *American Benedictine Review* 4 (1953) 262–265, and also Rudloff and John Hammond, "The Weston Story: An Interview," *American Benedictine Review* 13 (1962) 390–400.

NOTES TO CHAPTER 14

1. Colman Barry, *Upon These Rocks: Catholics in the Bahamas* (Collegeville, Minn.: St. John's Abbey Press, 1973).
2. Felix Fellner, *Boniface Wimmer and His Monks* (Latrobe, Pa., 1956) 709, SVAA.
3. They were Vincent Wehrle of St. Mary's (North Dakota), Innocent Wolf of St. Benedict's, Frowin Conrad of Conception, Charles Mohr of St. Leo's, Nepomucene Jaeger of St. Procopius, and Paul Schaeuble of St. Joseph's. See *The First American Catholic Missionary Congress* (Chicago, 1909).
4. Colman Barry very fittingly adapted this motto ("No Task Refused") for the chapter of his history of St. John's that deals with this period of expansion. See *Worship and Work: Saint John's Abbey and University 1856–1980* (Collegeville, Minn.: The Liturgical Press, 1980) 255–327.
5. Chapter minutes of St. Mary's Abbey, AAA.
6. General chapter record of September 1930, SVAA.
7. Chronicle of Holy Cross Abbey, HCAA.
8. Barry, *Worship and Work*, 309.
9. *Ibid.*, 301–302.
10. *Ibid.*, 319.
11. Grace McDonald, *With Lamps Burning* (St. Joseph, Minn.: St. Benedict's Priory Press, 1957) 275–276, and Vitus Buresh, *The Procopian Chronicle: St. Procopius Abbey, 1885–1985* (Lisle, Ill.: St. Procopius Abbey, 1985) 100–106.
12. Placid Reitmeier, ed., *La Orden Benedictina en Mexico* (Tepeyac, 1983) 19–22, and Gordon Bodenwein, "The Benedictines in Mexico," *American Benedictine Review* 8 (1957) 197–214.
13. Reitmeier, *La Orden Benedictina en Mexico*, 14.
14. Perhaps the best known of these was Father Damasus Winzen, whose role as a propagator of the spiritual tradition of his abbey of Maria Laach and founder

of the community of Mount Saviour had a formative effect on American Benedictine monasticism after World War II.

15. Buresh, *The Procopian Chronicle*, 111–112.

16. Valerian Odermann, ed., *Los Benedictinos en Bogotá, 1960–1985* (Bogotá, 1985) 48–49.

17. Odo Zimmermann, "Report on Second Latin American Monastic Encounter," *American Benedictine Review* 27 (1976) 164–170, and Fernando Rivas, "El impacto del Concilio Vaticano II en la vida monastica en América Latina," *Cuadernos Monásticos* 82 (1987) 281–299.

NOTES TO CHAPTER 15

1. Vitus Buresh, *The Procopian Chronicle: St. Procopius Abbey, 1885–1985* (Lisle, Ill.: St. Procopius Abbey, 1985) 120.

2. Colman Barry, *Worship and Work: Saint John's Abbey and University 1856–1980* (Collegeville, Minn.: The Liturgical Press, 1980) 349. All the American Benedictine monks were represented at the Council through the abbot president of their respective congregation.

3. See the decree *Ecclesiae Sanctae* of 6 August 1966, "Norms for Implementing the Decree on the Up-to-Date Renewal of Religious Life," *Vatican Council II: The Conciliar and Post Conciliar Documents* (Collegeville, Minn.: The Liturgical Press, 1984) 1:624–626, and Robert Homan Winthrop, "Norm and Tradition in American Benedictine Monasticism," (Ph.D. diss., University of Minnesota, 1981).

4. The American Cassinese Congregation issued *Renew and Create: A Statement on the American Cassinese Benedictine Monastic Life* in June 1969. The Swiss-American Congregation published *A Covenant of Peace* in October 1969. The English Benedictine Congregation's renewal statement, *Consider Your Call* (London: SPCK, 1978), issued ten years later, had the help of American monks from communities belonging to the English Benedictine Congregation.

5. Some of the reasons for this controversy are enumerated in Ambrose Wathen, "The Chase—The Climb—The Cross," *American Benedictine Review* 29 (1978) 205–226.

6. The first volume of this document, issued in 1975, was concerned with monastic life in general; the second, which came out in 1978, concentrated on prayer and the Liturgy of the Hours.

7. In 1969 the Congregation of St. Scholastica had a total of 2,607 members; in 1985 it numbered 1,822. In 1969 the Congregation of St. Gertrude counted 2,187 sisters; in 1985 that figure had diminished to 1,567. The Congregation of St. Benedict had 2,129 sisters in 1969; the figure was reduced to 1,451 by 1985. Statistics for the Congregation of Perpetual Adoration were less drastic, totaling 264 in 1969 and 200 in 1985. See the *Catalogus Monasteriorum, O.S.B.* (Rome, 1985).

8. The conciliar document on the renewal of religious life, the decree *Perfectae Caritatis* (no. 2b), provided the touchstone for much of this research. See Flannery, *Vatican Council II*, 1:612.

9. Father Claude Peifer's *Monastic Spirituality* (New York: Sheed and Ward, 1966) was really the first fruit of the conciliar call for a return to the sources and remained a definitive work in formation programs of English-speaking Benedictines. The writing and teaching of Father Ambrose Wathen reached an international audience by virtue of his tenure at the College of Sant' Anselmo in Rome. Father Terrence Kardong, through his editorship of the *American Benedictine Review*, scholarly articles and books on Benedictine sources and history, and his widely popular commentary on the Rule, *Together unto Everlasting Life* (Richardton, N. Dak.: Assumption Abbey Press, 1984), made monastic scholarship accessible to many more American Benedictines.

10. *RB 1980: The Rule of St. Benedict in Latin and English with Notes* (Collegeville: The Liturgical Press, 1981), a work guided by the unflagging labor of general editor Father Timothy Fry of St. Benedict's Abbey, Atchison, Kansas.

11. Besides the *American Benedictine Review*, The Liturgical Press at Collegeville, with its periodical *The Bible Today* and other popular publications, promoted Scripture study and made the results of modern biblical research available to a widespread audience. Between 1983 and 1989 it published *The Collegeville Bible Commentary* in a series of thirty-six booklets and later in a single volume.

12. A sampling of some of these articles would include in sequence: Ronald Roloff and Wilfred Tunink, "Omnibus: Purity of Heart and the Modern Monk," 13 (1962); Claude Peifer and Ronald Roloff, "Purity of Heart and the Modern Monk," 14 (1963); Claude Peifer, "Monastic Renewal: *Ressourcement* and *Aggiornamento*," 17 (1966); Daniel Kucera, "The Challenge of Renewal," 18 (1967); Mark Sheridan, "Towards a Contemporary Self-definition of Monasticism," 19 (1968).

13. Here, too, the pages of the *American Benedictine Review* provided a forum for these commentators. Two representative examples of this discussion from the discipline of the social sciences were Richard Endress, "Monastic Community: A Social Scientific Appraisal," 28 (1977) 41–66, and Cuthbert Whitley, "An Effort at Monastic Recovery: A Sociological Interpretation," 29 (1978) 1–32.

Annotated Bibliography

Assenmacher, Hugh, O.S.B. *A Place Called Subiaco: A History of the Benedictine Monks in Arkansas.* Little Rock, Ark.: Rose Publishing Co., 1977.

Though lacking in footnotes, Father Hugh's account is a thorough, readable review of the history of New Subiaco Abbey and a careful account of the difficulties as well as the development of the community.

Barry, Colman, O.S.B. *The Catholic Church and German Americans.* Milwaukee: Bruce, 1953.

Father Colman's first monograph ably documents the background of the controversy surrounding German Catholic immigrants and the elements in the American Catholic Church that opposed the demands for separate German parishes and retention of the German language in schools and church. This work covers the period through World War I and provides a valuable appendix of source documents.

_____. *Worship and Work: Saint John's Abbey and University 1856–1980.* Collegeville, Minn.: The Liturgical Press, 1980.

Originally written to commemorate the centennial observance of the St. John's foundation, this volume remains a model of research and critical interpretation for monastic history.

_____. *Upon These Rocks: Catholics in the Bahamas.* Collegeville, Minn.: St. John's Abbey Press, 1973.

This book gives a comprehensive account of the growth of the Catholic Church in the Bahamas and the role played in its development by the Benedictines of St. John's Abbey.

Baska, Regina, O.S.B. *The Benedictine Congregation of St. Scholastica: Its Foundation and Development, 1852–1930*. Washington, D.C.: Catholic University Press, 1935.

Written as a doctoral dissertation, this still serves as a landmark work of investigation, detailing the evolution of the largest congregation of American Benedictine women.

Baumstein, Paschal, O.S.B. *My Lord of Belmont: A Biography of Leo Haid*. Belmont, N.C.: Herald House, 1985.

This biography is not only a penetrating portrait of a key figure in American Benedictine history but an extensively researched study of the community of Belmont in its first decades.

Beckman, Peter, O.S.B. *Kansas Monks*. Atchison, Kans.: Abbey Student Press, 1957.

Father Peter's history of St. Benedict's Abbey is an expanded version of his doctoral dissertation on the Catholic Church in frontier Kansas. His narrative highlights some of the legendary figures who made that history: Wimmer, Wolf, Lemke, Wirth, Moosmueller, and Fink.

Buresh, Vitus, O.S.B. *The Procopian Chronicle: St. Procopius Abbey, 1885–1985*. Lisle, Ill.: St. Procopius Abbey, 1985.

Father Vitus assembles a vast array of sources in this centennial history. His understanding of the Czech language and of his community's history is evident throughout. It is representative of the genre of commemorative history and includes many of its provincial qualities.

Doppelfeld, Basilius, O.S.B. *Mönchtum und kirchlicher Heilsdienst*. Münsterschwarzach, Germany: Vier-Turme-Verlag, 1974.

Written by a monk of the German abbey of Münsterschwarzach, this book utilizes a socio-historical method in analyzing the motivation and goals behind the founders of the first American Benedictine communities, underlining the importance of missionary and pastoral activity.

Dowling, Dolores, O.S.B. *In Your Midst: The Story of the Benedictine Sisters of Perpetual Adoration*. St. Louis: Printery, 1988.

The sole secondary source available on the history of this congregation, Sister Dolores' work presents a balanced and informative interpretation of the origins and early experience of the Sisters of Perpetual Adoration.

Duratschek, Claudia, O.S.B. *Under the Shadow of His Wings*. Aberdeen, S. Dak.: North Plains Press, 1971.

Sister Claudia, one of the first of American Benedictine sisters to be trained as a historian, wrote this history of her congregation's motherhouse in Yankton, South Dakota, emphasizing its missionary and educational apostolate to the American Indians.

Endress, Richard. *The Enduring Vision: Stability and Change in an American Benedictine Monastery*. Ann Arbor, Mich.: University Microfilms, 1974.

This unique work, written as a doctoral dissertation by an anthropologist, considers the impact of the Second Vatican Council on the community of St. Meinrad. It gives a provocative and probing analysis of some of the constitutive structures of monastic community and their adaptive capability.

Fellner, Felix, O.S.B. *Abbot Boniface and His Monks*. Latrobe, Pa., 1956. Privately published in five volumes.

This narrative of St. Vincent's early years comes close to divinizing Wimmer and is rich in colorful detail.

Girgen, Incarnata, O.S.B. *Behind the Beginnings: Benedictine Women in America*. St. Joseph, Minn.: St. Benedict's Convent, 1981.

The fruit of the author's many years of research (using primary sources in European and North American archives), this book is much more limited in scope than its title indicates. It focuses on the misunderstandings that took place between Boniface Wimmer and Benedictine sisters Benedicta Riepp and Willibalda Scherbauer, two of the first missionaries from the community of Eichstätt. The author presents the dispute from the point of view of the sisters involved and in so doing fills a previously existing vacuum of historical interpretation.

Kardong, Terrence, O.S.B. *The Benedictines*. Wilmington, Del.: Michael Glazier, 1988.

The last two chapters of this overview of Benedictine spirituality and history focus on issues that have affected the life of American Benedictines since Vatican Council II.

Kleber, Albert, O.S.B. *A History of St. Meinrad Archabbey, 1854–1954.* St. Meinrad, Ind.: Archabbey Press, 1954.

The author, community archivist at St. Meinrad for many years, provides an abundance of information and anecdotes but fails to situate the history of St. Meinrad in the wider context of American Catholic or Benedictine life, and is often highly subjective in his judgment of monks and events.

McCrank, Lawrence. *Mt. Angel Abbey: A Centennial History of the Benedictine Community and Its Library, 1882–1982.* Wilmington, Del.: Scholarly Resources, Inc., 1983.

The Mount Angel community was not well served by this volume, which manifests numerous examples of shoddy research and hasty writing. Nonetheless, it does permit the reader to appreciate the faith and vision of the founders of Mount Angel, as well as the impressive service they have rendered to the Church of the Northwest.

McDonald, Grace, O.S.B. *With Lamps Burning.* St. Joseph, Minn.: St. Benedict's Priory Press, 1957.

Sister Grace did for her community of St. Benedict what Colman Barry did for St. John's, that is, offer a sweeping and insightful portrait of a century of her convent's history, using a wide variety of primary sources.

Malone, Edward, O.S.B. *A History of Conception Colony, Abbey, and Schools.* Omaha, Nebr.: Interstate Printing, 1971.

The author presents the history of Conception Abbey in an episodic fashion, revealing a marked sensitivity to the early differences between Engelberg Abbey and its American daughterhouse, along with astute appraisals of the principal figures: Anselm Villiger, Frowin Conrad, and Adelhelm Odermatt. The book's treatment of the period of the twentieth century suffers by comparison.

Mathäser, Willibald, O.S.B., ed., *Haudegen Gottes: Das Leben des Peter H. Lemke.* Würzburg: Kommissionsverlag Echter Gesamtherstellung, 1971.

In publishing the memoirs of Lemke, Father Willibald brings to our attention one of the truly colorful figures of the founding era of American Benedictinism.

Murphy, Joseph, O.S.B. *Tenacious Monks: The Oklahoma Benedictines (1875–1975)*. Shawnee, Okla.: Benedictine Color Press, 1974.

Another in the line of centennial community histories, this one has the advantage of being written by a trained monastic historian.

Oetgen, Jerome. *An American Abbot: Boniface Wimmer, O.S.B.* Latrobe, Pa.: The Archabbey Press, 1976.

The work of this former member of the St. Vincent monastic community is more than just a biography of the founder of the American Benedictines. It enlists a diverse array of primary and secondary sources and provides a vivid picture of both the European origins of St. Vincent and the first half century of its development.

Schuster, Faith, O.S.B. *The Meaning of the Mountain*. Baltimore: Helicon Press, 1953.

Though lacking many historical-critical features, Sister Faith's history of the Kansas community of Mount St. Scholastica offers the reader valuable information about the struggle of the Benedictine sisters of Atchison in their early years.

Sharum, Elizabeth, O.S.B. *Write the Vision Down: A History of St. Scholastica Convent*. Fort Smith, Ark.: American Printing, 1979.

Sister Louise, a member of the Fort Smith community with a doctorate in history, gives a very revealing account of the difficulties and demands undergone by this Arkansas foundation. In this respect, it is an accurate depiction of the development of many other convents of Benedictine women in the United States.

Skudlarek, William, O.S.B., ed. *The Continuing Quest for God*. Collegeville, Minn.: The Liturgical Press, 1982.

This volume consists of the proceedings of a symposium held at Collegeville in the summer of 1980 and incorporates articles in the areas of history, spirituality, and liturgy by a variety of American Benedictine men and women. It testifies to the pluralism of style and interpretation given to the monastic vocation after Vatican Council II.

Sutera, Judith, O.S.B. *True Daughters: Monastic Identity and American Benedictine Women's History*. Atchison, Kans.: Benedictine College Press, 1987.

The author made judicious use of the archives of the four major congregations of religious women in telling the involved story of American Benedictine sisters' efforts to achieve canonical status as monastics and unification as a congregation.

Voth, Agnes, O.S.B. *Green Olive Branch*. Chicago: Franciscan Herald Press, 1973.

This history of the Olivetan Benedictine Sisters of Arkansas paints a portrait of their roots as sisters of Perpetual Adoration. It also provides a thoroughly researched treatment of a congregation of Benedictine women who maintained an active apostolate from the start.

Index

Abbelen, Peter, 121, 122
Alemany, Archbishop Joseph, O.P., 62
Allegheny, Pa., 101
Altötting, Germany, 16
American Benedictine Academy, 129, 208, 251
American Benedictine Review, 129, 208, 251
American Cassinese Congregation, 35, 43, 70, 79, 81, 103, 139, 165, 167, 195, 196, 216, 227, 228, 240, 246, 248, 250, 252
American Indians, 17, 35, 53, 66, 89, 93, 130–141, 146, 147
American Protective Association, 112
Americanizers, 94, 108, 122
Amrhein, Abbot Andreas, O.S.B., 14
Annalen of the Ludwig-Missionsverein, 44
Armen Seelen Freund, 99
Assumption Abbey, Richardton, N. Dak., 240 (*also see* St. Mary's Abbey, Richardton)
Atchison, Kans., 36, 125, 175, 237
Augsburger Postzeitung, 22
Aurora, Ill., 7, 128
Awful Disclosures of Maria Monk, The, 112

Bachmann, Jerome, O.S.B., 45, 46
Badin, Stephen, 16, 211
Bahama Islands, 43, 224
Baker, Imogene, O.S.B., 251
Balleis, Nicholas, O.S.B., 109
Baraga, Frederic, 130
Barnabo, Cardinal Alessandro, 78, 79
Barry, Colman, O.S.B., 7, 251
Bath, Aloysia, O.S.B., 84
Baumstein, Paschal, O.S.B., 7
Bavaria, 17, 21, 23, 24, 72, 74

Bayley, Bishop James, 35
Beauduin, Lambert, O.S.B., 186, 189
Beech Grove, Ind., 237
Belleville Diocese, 215
Bellinzona, Switzerland, 44
Belmont Abbey, Belmont, N.C., 41, 134, 154, 165, 197, 246
Benedict XV, 81
Benedictine Bohemian Press, 102
Benedictine Institute of Sacred Theology, 205
Benedictine Liturgical Conferences, 188
Benedictine Sisters of Perpetual Adoration, 81, 185
Benedictus Verein, 99
Benet Lake, Wis., 176, 218, 234
Benetz, Hilarin, O.S.B., 67
Berwyn, Ill., 102
Beste, Ulric, O.S.B., 246
Beuron Abbey, 12, 15, 16, 30, 52, 56, 58–60, 184, 195, 198, 211, 212
Big Horn, Wyo., 222
Big Sur, Calif., 218
Binzegger, Bonaventure, O.S.B., 68
Bismarck, N.Dak., 125, 175
Black Americans, 141–146
Black Forest, 12, 132
Blessed Virgin, 79, 88, 150, 201, 202
Bliemel, Emmeran, O.S.B., 111
Blue Cloud Abbey, Marvin, S.Dak., 140, 241
Bohemians, 100
Böllingen (Black Forest), 132
Bonifatius Verein, 99
Botz, Paschal, O.S.B., 188, 206
Boulder, Colo., 218, 222
Boulder County, Colo., 103

291